STUDY GUIDE

to Accompany

BUSINESS COMMUNICATION TODAY

# STUDY GUIDE

## to Accompany

# BUSINESS COMMUNICATION TODAY

**Courtland L. Bovée**

**John V. Thill**

**with the assistance of
Rebecca Smith**

**New York**

**Random House**

## PERMISSIONS ACKNOWLEDGMENTS

**Text**

**5:** Adapted from *Jobs and Opportunities for Writers*, by the editors of *Writer's Digest*, pp. 1-16. Copyright © 1972 by *Writer's Digest*. Reprinted by permission of *Writer's Digest Books*, a division of F & W Publications, Inc., Cincinnati, Ohio 45242.

**23:** Adapted from "Mail Call at the Oval Office," *New York Times*, November 23, 1981, p. 20. Copyright © 1981 by The New York Times Company. Reprinted by permission.

**30:** Adapted from *The Art of Readable Writing*, by Rudolph Flesch, pp. 20-21, 151, 213-216. Copyright © 1949 by Rudolph Flesch. Reprinted by permission of Harper & Row, Publishers, Inc.

**54:** Adapted from *Assert Yourself*, by Merna Dee Galassi and John P. Galassi, pp. 97-98. Copyright © 1977 by Merna Dee Galassi and John P. Galassi. Reprinted by permission of Human Sciences Press.

**77:** Adapted, by permission of the publishers, from "Increasing Your Credibility," by Judi Brownell, *Supervisory Management*, December 1982, pp. 32, 34. © 1982 AMACOM Periodicals Division, American Management Associations, New York. All rights reserved.

**Photo Credits**

**14:** AP/Wide World Photos
**15:** Top, AP/Wide World Photos; bottom, Union-Tribune Publishing Company.

## EXPERIENCE IS THE BEST TEACHER . . .

A college course in business communication can teach you quite a bit about how people in business write and speak, read and listen. The textbook, the teacher, and the interaction of students eager to learn all contribute to the educational process. But if you really want to learn how to communicate in business, you must practice and get feedback on your work. You must actually write letters, memos, and reports and speak in small meetings and before large groups. Although your first efforts may be amateurish, they are the necessary forerunners to more polished products.

"Great," you say. "I know I need practice, but how am I going to get it? Many employers hire only people who already have on-the-job experience." We'd like to propose a solution to this dilemma. First, realize that communication skills are very obvious to employers as you go through the application and interview process. Your writing skills show in your resume and application letters; your speaking skills, in conversations with potential employers. Thus you get a chance to demonstrate your skills without having previous job experience, a privilege not available in many other fields. Our second point is this: if you take advantage of every opportunity to practice the types of communication common in business while you are still a student, you will enter the job market with an advantage.

This *Study Guide* has been designed to guide your practice. Used in conjunction with its companion textbook, *Business Communication Today,* it can help you

- Understand the content of the textbook chapters
- Prepare for quizzes and tests
- Apply what you have learned to practical problems
- Understand related issues in business communication
- Improve your spelling and expand your vocabulary
- Improve your knowledge of grammar, punctuation, and mechanics

These goals are accomplished through a wide variety of exercises. Simply by reading, you can gain a new perspective on the chapters in the textbook and new insights into peripheral issues. Multiple-choice, fill-in, and essay exercises test your understanding and recall of chapter content and your ability to spell and use words correctly. (Because the answers to these exercises are provided at the end of each chapter, you can check your own work and get immediate feedback on your progress.) Crossword puzzles in the last four chapters further test your ability to spell and use words correctly. Application exercises allow you to take the role of a professional communicator—whether writer, editor, or speaker. A separate section at the end of this book offers a short course in the basics of English, with explanation and exercises interwoven.

We propose the following study program for making the best use of these aids:

1. Read the one-paragraph summary/statement of objectives at the beginning of each chapter in the *Study Guide.*

2. Read the corresponding chapter in *Business Communication Today.*

3. Immediately complete two sections of the *Study Guide*—Master Key Concepts and Quiz Yourself—checking your answers right away and rereading any portion of the textbook that seems to have given you trouble. (The answer section provides textbook page numbers to make this task easier.)

4. When you feel comfortable with the textbook's content, do the application exercise described in Build Your Skills; then read Expand Your Knowledge.

5. Work through Develop Your Word Power. (The answers are at the end of the chapter, but keep a dictionary at hand so you can look up any spelling or vocabulary words you have trouble with.)

6. Do one of the English Essentials lessons at the back of this book; they are numbered to correspond to the chapters but do not reflect any of the chapter content.

If you work at this program consistently and diligently, we can guarantee that it will give you practice in many of the skills that are important to business communicators.[1]

---

[1] The vocabulary and grammar sections of this *Study Guide* have used the University of Chicago *Manual of Style*, the *Harbrace College Handbook*, and the *Random House College Dictionary* as authorities.

# CONTENTS

## Chapter 1

## COMMUNICATING SUCCESSFULLY IN AN ORGANIZATION

The main point of Chapter 1 is that communication is an important part of every job in the wide world of business. As you read the chapter, think about the different ways that people in business communicate; think too about the ways that communication—written, spoken, and nonverbal—serves the functions of organizations. When you finish reading, analyze your own communication skills and preferences and then plan how you can develop your strengths.

### MASTER KEY CONCEPTS

Use the following terms to fill the blanks in the outline. All terms are used, but none is used more than once.

| | | | |
|---|---|---|---|
| communication | information | management | practice |
| distorted | intentional | nonverbal | records |
| feedback | listen | permanence | suppliers |
| "grapevine" | | | |

I. Communication takes many forms and pervades the business world.
   A. Although we typically think of _intentional_ (p. 6) messages when we talk about communication, much communication is actually unintentional, meaning that it reflects attitudes unconsciously.
   B. _feedback_ (p. 6) communication—consisting of tone of voice, facial expression, body position, and grooming—adds an important dimension to oral (spoken) communication.
   C. Every organization has both formal channels for transmitting official messages and informal channels—the _grapevine_ (p. 7)—that transmit both fact and rumor.
   D. People in business communicate both within their organizations and with outsiders.
   E. All the various modes of communicating have special strengths: the major strength of oral communication is _feedback_ (p. 8); the major strength of written communication is _permanence_ (p. 8); the major strength of automated communication is mass production.

II. Almost every conceivable organizational activity depends on _Communication_ (p. 9).
   A. To set goals and objectives, managers discuss their ideas and then commit them to paper.
   B. In making and implementing decisions, managers read, ask questions, and evaluate information provided by lower-level employees; meet to discuss options; and explain their decisions to other employees and/or outsiders, either in writing or face to face.
   C. In measuring the results of decisions, managers seek _information_ (p. 11) from other employees both orally and in writing.
   D. To hire and develop employees, managers and personnel staff recruit, train, motivate, and evaluate employees and potential employees both orally and in writing.

1

E. In dealing with customers and _____Suppliers_____ (p. 12), people in organizations send sales letters, brochures, catalogs, and proposals; make personal and telephone sales calls; check credit; handle bills, complaints, and questions; write specifications, place orders, and negotiate terms; and raise capital by applying for loans or offering stock.

F. To produce products, employees develop designs, prepare written manufacturing plans, explain production tasks orally and in writing, and maintain _____records_____ (pp. 12–13).

G. In interacting with regulatory agencies, employees write reports.

III. Different organizations have different communication needs.

A. The bigger an organization, the more likely it is that messages will become _____distorted_____ (p. 14) as they travel up and down the hierarchy; however, people in smaller organizations have to perform so many different communication functions that they may not perform all of them adequately.

B. Different types of communication are required for selling products and services to different types of markets.

C. Passing events create one-time communication needs.

D. The _____management_____ (p. 16) style in some organizations encourages the open exchange of information; communication in some organizations, however, is relatively restricted.

IV. Different occupations require different communication skills.

V. You can improve your communication skills, including your ability to read, _____listen_____ (p. 19), engage in casual conversation, interview, deal with small groups, deliver speeches and presentations, and write memos, letters, and reports.

A. Evaluate your skills and concentrate on building competence.

B. Set goals for developing skills related to your intended career.

C. Study and _____practice_____ (p. 19) in order to improve your skills.

VI. This book can help you by explaining communication theory, accepted formats, and basic principles of writing and speaking—as well as by exposing you to real-world examples of written and oral communication.

*Check your answers at the end of this chapter.*

## QUIZ YOURSELF

1. List three specific actions an employee can take to communicate his or her desire to do a good job. 1. Arriving on time for work
   2. Taking lunch breaks and coming back in time.
   3. Completing work on time.

2. Briefly describe the differences between oral and written communication.

A. Oral Communication is faster. You can get immediate response on a idea and it much better (more personal) in dealing with bad news or important subject.

B. Written Communication allows permanent, reproducible records of your ideas. Allows writer and reader handle complex messages by letters. Also in writing the same messages to different people in different location makes task much easier.

3. List seven important organizational activities that require communication.

   1. Setting up objectives and goals.
   2. Making and implementing Decisions
   3. Measuring Results
   4. Hiring and developing Staff.
   5. Dealing with customers and Supplies
   6. producing the product.
   7. Interacting with regulatory agencies.

4. List ten ways that companies communicate with customers and suppliers.

   1. Price tags
   2. Sales letters
   3. brochures
   4. Obtaining financing
   5. Advertisement
   6. telephone solicitations
   7. Personal sales calls
   8. formal Proposals
   9. Orders for materials
   10. Credit Checking
   11. handling Complaints & Questions
   12. Sending bills

5. What are some of the ways in which companies can overcome the drawbacks of complex, multi-level communication systems? By developing a system were exchange of information among the all levels and all area of the Company can take place.

6. Give a specific example of how an organization's communication requirements can suddenly change. When an unexpect incident occur in a company New the Company may need to speak to reporters, and public official to explain the incident.

7. What is the most effective communication climate for a company engaged in creative activities? What communication climate is best if the company's success depends on rapid decision making and quick reactions?

8. List some ways that writing skills can help advance your career.

   1. Help you get the job or position you want.
   2. Enable you to get things done.
   3. Buy it your own business
   4. Advance you socially

9. As Jon Slangerup of Federal Express points out, "The important thing to remember in this job is that you're not writing for ___yourself___, you're writing for the ___audience___."

10. List seven specific communication skills required in business.

    1. Reading
    2. Listening
    3. Interviewing
    4. Writing letters, memos and reports.
    5. Delivering Speeches and presentations.
    6. Engaging in Casual Conversations
    7. Dealing with small groups.

*Check your answers at the end of this chapter.*

**BUILD YOUR SKILLS: WHAT ARE YOUR STRENGTHS
AND WEAKNESSES AS A COMMUNICATOR?**

Knowing your strengths and weaknesses as a communicator helps you set priorities for self-improvement. Ask yourself the following questions. Then put a *W* by the items that require the most work, a *P* by those that need polishing, and a *U* by those you can use to the fullest right away.

## Reading

| | |
|---|---|
| _U_ | Do you read fast enough for your work? |
| _P_ | Are you able to pick out and remember key points? |
| _P_ | Can you vary your approach to reading to match different types of reading situations? |

## Listening

| | |
|---|---|
| _U_ | Are you able to focus your attention on what a speaker is saying? |
| _P_ | Can you identify and recall key points of a speech to your satisfaction? |
| _U_ | Are you able to put aside your preconceptions and judge the speaker's message on its merits, regardless of whether you agree or disagree with the ideas or like or dislike the speaker as an individual? |
| _W_ | Are you able to analyze a speaker's message and ask questions to test its logic and accuracy? |
| _P_ | Are you satisfied with your ability to take notes during a lecture? |

## Engaging in Casual Conversation

| | |
|---|---|
| _W_ | Are you confident in conducting casual, social conversations? |
| _W_ | Can you think of interesting things to say to keep up your end of a conversation? |
| _W_ | Do you ask good questions? |
| _P_ | Do you listen empathetically to the other person and draw her or him out? |
| _W_ | Are you comfortable talking with a wide range of people, including those who differ from you in background, age, and interests? |
| _U_ | Do you give the other person a chance to talk too? |
| _U_ | Are you sensitive to the other person's reactions? |

## Interviewing

| | |
|---|---|
| _____ | Do you prepare adequately for interviews by developing a list of questions to cover and by preparing answers to anticipated questions? |
| _W_ | Are you confident in interview situations? |
| _U_ | Are you able to remain objective in difficult interviews? |
| _____ | Can you use different types of questions to obtain the information you want? |
| _____ | Are you able to match your interview style to the situation? |
| _____ | Can you draw out the other person? |
| _____ | Are you able to give and receive criticism effectively? |
| _____ | Are you relaxed in interviews with people who outrank you or have more power than you do? |
| _____ | Are you considerate in interviews with people in a subordinate position? |

## Dealing with Small Groups

| | |
|---|---|
| _____ | If you are in charge, do you lay the proper groundwork for the meeting by preparing an agenda and making necessary arrangements well in advance? |

_____ As the leader, are you able to keep the group focused on the business at hand?

_____ Are you familiar with the rules of parliamentary procedure?

_____ Can you facilitate interaction by balancing the contributions of group members?

_____ Are you able to build consensus among group members?

_____ Are you able to summarize results and assign responsibilities?

_____ As a group participant, do you make useful and constructive comments?

_____ Are you sensitive to the needs and concerns of other group members?

### Delivering Speeches and Presentations

_____ Are you able to plan a speech or presentation that is suitable for various situations and times?

_____ Are you able to control your stage fright?

_____ Can you speak clearly and distinctly so that people understand you?

_____ Do you sound natural and engaging?

_____ Are you able to use visual aids effectively in a speech or presentation?

_____ Can you handle unexpected or hostile comments effectively?

_____ Can you deliver a speech from notes?

### Writing Letters, Memos, and Reports

_____ Do you have an adequate command of basic grammar and punctuation?

_____ Are you able to vary the style and tone of your writing to suit different situations?

_____ Can you write clearly, accurately, and concisely?

_____ Are you able to organize messages logically and persuasively?

_____ Are you familiar with different formats and their uses?

_____ Can you construct tables, charts, and other illustrations to supplement your writing?

_____ Are you careful about editing and proofreading your work?

## EXPAND YOUR KNOWLEDGE: WHERE THE JOBS ARE

It is hard to imagine a career that doesn't require some sort of writing. Thus everyone should acquire the basic skills. Some people, however, develop a better-than-average ability to write. If you're one of them, you may want to consider one of these business-writing careers:

- _Business and industry_: Writers are employed in advertising, public relations, sales promotion, and training departments, and as publication editors and speechwriters.

- _Copywriting_: A flair for writing ads, commercials, booklets, and brochures may land you a job as a copywriter in an advertising agency or with the media. Jobs for copywriters may also be found with manufacturers, retailers, banks, hotels, and public utilities.

- _Public relations_: If writing news releases and articles interests you, consider a career in a public-relations or advertising agency, in the PR department of a large company, in a trade or professional association, or in a government agency.

- *Fundraising*: Staff writers develop grant proposals, ads, features, and promotional material for the media. They also write speeches that administrators deliver to business and civic groups.

- *Publishing*: Book publishers have jobs for manuscript readers, editors, copyeditors, staff writers, and advertising and promotion writers. Business magazines, newspapers, wire services, and syndicates employ editors, staff writers, rewriters, copyeditors, correspondents, and advertising copywriters.

- *Government*: Thousands of jobs exist in federal, state, and local government agencies for writers and editors, as well as for radio, TV, and film script writers. Their assignment: to write about government and agency activities for the media. They also create pamphlets that describe public benefits and services.

Other career opportunities for business writers include radio and TV writing and editing, science writing, and technical writing. Writers are needed by chambers of commerce to write and edit publications, handle publicity for special events, and create materials to promote business and tourism in the area. Some interesting free-lance opportunities also exist: writing articles for business magazines, ghostwriting material for leaders in business and industry, writing new-product releases for small manufacturers, creating audiovisual materials for business, operating a resume-writing service, or even writing manuscripts for business-book publishers. Professional secretaries, too, often are called on to write for their bosses. These and other challenging opportunities can be yours as a business writer.

*Source*:  Adapted from *Jobs and Opportunities for Writers* (Cincinnati, Ohio: Writer's Digest, 1972), pp. 1-16.

1. Do any of these business-writing careers sound interesting to you? If so, do a little research to find out more about the job requirements. Talk to someone who holds such a position. What are some of the person's duties? How did she or he prepare for this career? If you don't know anyone who has a job like this, look in the Yellow Pages for advertising or public-relations agencies, newspapers or magazines, government agencies, and businesses that employ writers; if approached courteously, they may connect you with someone willing to share information.

2. Over the next few weeks, develop a collection of business-writing samples: direct-mail and other letters that you receive, ads from magazines and newspapers, product brochures, news stories about companies, government pamphlets. Keep your eyes open. You may be surprised at how many samples you accumulate. What can you conclude from your collection?

## DEVELOP YOUR WORD POWER

*Spelling Challenge*    Identify the misspelled word in each of the following sentences, and spell it correctly in the space provided. If all the words in a sentence are spelled correctly, write *C* in the space.

|  |  |
|---|---|
| _____ | 1.  Congratulations for your many acheivements over the past year. |
| _____ | 2.  Our building is adjacent to the hospital. |
| _____C_____ | 3.  They plan to aquire a small manufacturing company. |
| _____ | 4.  In Mark's absense, you can assist me. |
| _____ | 5.  Refinancing would be an acceptable alternative. |

_____    6.  How many new workers can that plant accomodate?

_____    7.  His skills are not adaquate for the position.

_____    8.  You are absolutely right!

_____    9.  Jennifer accidently sent those memos to all staff members.

_____   10.  Speed and acuracy are the two qualities most valuable in a typist.


**Vocabulary Challenge**    Match the words in the first column with the definitions in the second column.

_B_   11.  acumen                A.  opponent

_A_   12.  adversary             B.  something outdated

_C_   13.  antecedent            C.  something going before

_E_   14.  affinity              D.  keen insight

_D_   15.  anachronism           E.  natural likeness or agreement


Circle the best definition of the highlighted word in each of the following sentences.

16.  We should make computers **accessible** to all office workers.

  A.  easily modified        B.  extra                    C.  available

17.  Some modest people prefer to work in **anonymity.**

  A.  without recognition    B.  loose-fitting clothing   C.  solitude

18.  George volunteered with **alacrity** to take on the new project.

  A.  willingness           B.  reluctance               C.  ignorance

19.  The customer was **adamant** about getting a refund.

  A.  angry                 B.  unyielding               C.  unsure

20.  An **ambiguous** answer will only postpone resolution of the problem.

  A.  two-sided             B.  small-minded             C.  indefinite


Select one of these words to complete each of the following sentences, and write the word in the space provided.

  **acrimonious**      **acute**      **adroit**      **aloof**      **amicable**

21.  Contrary to her claims that she wants to get involved, Stacey has remained ____aloof____ from all the group's activities.

22.  Thanks to Deborah Sweeney's ____adroit____ handling of the malfunctioning control mechanism, a disastrous accident has been avoided.

23.  After an ____acrimonious____ exchange between Eric and his boss, Eric stormed out.

24.  To maintain goodwill, we train all our customer-service representatives to seek ____amicable____ settlement of complaints.

25.  An ____acute____ shortage of petroleum products would have severe effects on our ability to keep the plant open.

*Follow-up Word Study*   Check your answers at the end of this chapter. In the spaces below, write the words that you spelled or used incorrectly. (Use a separate piece of paper if you missed more than five words.) Then look up each word in your dictionary, and carefully study its spelling, pronunciation, definition, and history (etymology). Finally, to help fix the word in your memory, write it in a sentence.

Word                          Sentence

_____        _____

_____        _____

_____        _____

_____        _____

_____        _____

---

## CHECK YOUR ANSWERS

**Master Key Concepts**

I.  A. intentional
    B. nonverbal
    C. grapevine
    E. feedback, permanence

II. communication
    C. information
    E. suppliers
    F. records

III. A. distorted
     D. management

V. listen
   C. practice

**Quiz Yourself**

1. Actions like the following indicate an employee's commitment to doing a good job:
    a. Arriving for work on time
    b. Taking lunch breaks that are not too long
    c. Completing assignments on schedule
    d. Doing work quickly and willingly
    e. Volunteering to handle extra work
    f. Working overtime to complete important assignments
    g. Double-checking work for accuracy
    h. Helping other people get things done   (p. 6)

2. Oral communication is generally quicker and cheaper than written communication. In addition, oral communication has the advantage of encouraging a two-way exchange of ideas. It is also more personal than written communication.

   Written communication allows efficient communication with many people in different locations. It provides a permanent, verifiable record of the message and gives both the reader and the writer an opportunity to study what is being said. (pp. 7-8)

3. These seven organizational activities require communication:
   a. Setting goals and objectives
   b. Making and implementing decisions
   c. Measuring results
   d. Hiring and developing staff
   e. Dealing with customers and suppliers
   f. Producing the product
   g. Interacting with regulatory agencies   (pp. 9-13)

4. Here are some specific ways that companies use communication in dealing with customers and suppliers:
   a. Putting price tags on products
   b. Writing sales letters and brochures
   c. Running advertisements
   d. Making personal sales calls
   e. Conducting telephone solicitation
   f. Writing formal proposals
   g. Checking credit
   h. Sending bills
   i. Handling complaints and questions
   j. Developing specifications for raw materials and supplies
   k. Placing orders
   l. Obtaining financing   (p. 12)

5. Companies can overcome some of the drawbacks of complex, multilevel communication patterns by encouraging an open exchange of information among people at all levels and in all areas of the company. For example, top managers might walk around the office, talking to people. (p. 14)

6. One example of a sudden change in communication requirements was the problem Johnson & Johnson faced when an unknown person put cyanide in several bottles of Tylenol. Other examples of unusual situations that require comment from company management include fires, crimes, major accidents, pollution problems, financial difficulties, and strikes.   (p. 15)

7. If a company is engaged in complex or creative activities, an open communication climate is probably most effective. But if success depends on rapid decision making and quick reactions, a more centralized communication pattern is faster, more accurate, and more efficient. (p. 16)

8. Writing skills can advance your career in the following ways:
   a. Help you get the job you want
   b. Boost your chances of promotion
   c. Help you advance other people's careers
   d. Enable you to get things done
   e. Benefit your own business
   f. Advance you socially
   g. Ensure your future
   h. Enhance your other skills   (pp. 10-11)

9. As Jon Slangerup points out, "The important thing to remember in this job is that you're not writing for yourself, you're writing for the audience." (p. 18)

10. The seven specific communication skills required in business are
    a. Reading
    b. Listening
    c. Engaging in casual conversation
    d. Interviewing
    e. Dealing with small groups
    f. Delivering speeches and presentations
    g. Writing letters, memos, and reports   (p. 19)

**Develop Your Word Power**

| | | | | |
|---|---|---|---|---|
| 1. achievements | 6. accommodate | 11. D | 16. C | 21. aloof |
| 2. adjacent | 7. adequate | 12. A | 17. A | 22. adroit |
| 3. acquire | 8. C | 13. C | 18. A | 23. acrimonious |
| 4. absence | 9. accidentally | 14. E | 19. B | 24. amicable |
| 5. C | 10. accuracy | 15. B | 20. C | 25. acute |

## Chapter 2

## OVERCOMING BARRIERS TO COMMUNICATION

The main point of Chapter 2 is that the communication process is subject to breakdown—and repair—at any point. As you read the chapter, think about how misunderstandings can arise, especially in business. When you finish reading, mentally review some personal experiences with communication barriers and then try to figure out how those barriers were or could have been overcome.

### MASTER KEY CONCEPTS

Use the following terms to fill the blanks in the outline. All terms are used, but none is used more than once.

| | | | |
|---|---|---|---|
| assumptions | interpretations | receiving | reviewed |
| audience | misunderstandings | repeating | transmitted |
| business | open-minded | respond | understand |
| developing | purpose | | |

I. Someone who writes or speaks to convey a message has three basic goals: to make the audience _____ (p. 25) the message, to get the audience to _____ (p. 25) in the desired way, and to maintain good relations with the audience.

II. Communication takes place in a _____ (p. 26) cycle of five steps.
   A. The sender forms an idea, but this idea is only an imperfect "map" of reality and is based on personal _____ (pp. 26-27), only some of which are correct.
   B. The idea (thought) is translated into a message (words), but the form of the message is influenced by the sender's environment, attitudes, purposes, and ability to express ideas.
   C. The message is _____ (p. 27) via some sort of communication channel, the choice of which depends on the nature of the information, the audience, and the situation; the type of channel used affects the content and reception of the message.
   D. The receiver gets the message, assuming that the receiver can actually see it or hear it and can understand it.
   E. The receiver gives feedback to the sender, which allows the sender to evaluate the effectiveness of the message and perhaps start the five-step process all over again.

III. _____ (p. 30) are common, and they may arise at any point in the communication process.
   A. Problems in _____ (pp. 30-31) the message may result when the sender can't decide what to include in a message, isn't sure about how the information will be used or who will use it, has strong or conflicting emotions about the subject of the message, or finds it difficult to express ideas.
   B. Problems in transmitting the message may arise because of such physical barriers as faulty equipment or execution, because of a conflict between two or more simultaneous messages, or because of an excessive number of links in the communication chain.

C.  Problems in _____ (pp. 33–34) the message are likely to result when the audience cannot effectively hear it or see it or concentrate on it.

D.  Problems in understanding the message may result when the sender and the receiver have different backgrounds, different _____ (p. 35) of words, or different emotional reactions.

IV.  The special nature of _____ (p. 38) communication makes it especially susceptible to breakdown.

A.  Business messages are complex, because the sender is representing the organization's views and not necessarily her or his own, because the material is often difficult to express, and because the work environment is rife with time pressures, interruptions, and the need to work with others.

B.  Transmission and reception conditions are difficult in the business world: a variety of people translate, embellish, and augment the message as it travels between sender and receiver, and the receiver may be overwhelmed by competing messages.

C.  The differences between sender and receiver not only are wide on occasion but may also be unknown.

V.  Steps can be taken to overcome the barriers to communication.

A.  The message should be created carefully: the _____ (p. 40) and _____ (p. 40) should be carefully defined, the audience should be told what to expect right at the beginning of the message, concrete and specific language should be used to reduce misunderstanding, information that is not directly related to the purpose of the message should be eliminated, new information should be connected to existing ideas, and key points should be _____ (p. 42) at the end of the message.

B.  Opportunities for feedback should be carefully planned: the transmission channel that permits the most appropriate type and amount of feedback should be chosen, and the sender should be _____ (pp. 42–43) about feedback that has been solicited, even if it is negative.

*Check your answers at the end of this chapter.*

## QUIZ YOURSELF

1.  What are the three goals of business communication?

2.  Identify the five steps involved in the communication process.

3.  Which step in the communication process makes it truly interactive?

4. List four problems that may arise when a message is being developed.

5. What measures can a person take to overcome problems in transmitting a message?

6. Every message contains both a _____ meaning, which deals with the subject of the message, and a _____ meaning, which suggests the nature of the interaction between the sender and the receiver.

7. Describe three ways in which business messages are particularly complex.

8. What particular problems arise in transmitting and receiving business messages?

9. Briefly summarize the six steps you can take to overcome the barriers to effective communication.

10. Discuss the characteristics of feedback in business communication.

*Check your answers at the end of this chapter.*

**BUILD YOUR SKILLS: CAN YOU READ THE BODY
LANGUAGE IN THESE PHOTOS?**

Take a close look at the photographs below. What can you infer from the pictures? What do you think is happening? Who are the people? What is their probable background? What are their relationships to one another? What are their feelings?

## EXPAND YOUR KNOWLEDGE: TEST YOUR COMMUNICATION "IQ"

How good are you at getting your message across to others?  To find out, mark the most appropriate column for each of the following questions.  Scoring instructions appear at the end.

| | Very Seldom | About 1/4 of Time | About 1/2 of Time | About 3/4 of Time | Almost Always |
|---|---|---|---|---|---|
| 1. I realize that what I see is an incomplete picture of what might be observed. | | | | | |
| 2. I realize that what people say to me about a situation or person is a condensed version of what might be said. | | | | | |
| 3. I realize that my interests and feelings may affect what I see, hear, or say. | | | | | |
| 4. I use language so that the main parts of a message are emphasized. | | | | | |
| 5. When I speak, I take into account the danger that some of my words may be misinterpreted. | | | | | |
| 6. I am alert to nonverbal signs of misunderstanding, and I adjust to such silent feeling by restating and improving. | | | | | |
| 7. I show that I am glad to have listeners ask questions or restate my message. | | | | | |
| 8. I avoid exaggeration by quantifying and qualifying whenever possible. | | | | | |
| 9. I use words showing degrees of difference when possible. | | | | | |
| 10. I use *you* and *we* in place of *I* wherever appropriate. | | | | | |
| 11. Since the world of facts changes, I use words in their up-to-date meanings. | | | | | |
| 12. I try to understand a speaker's frame of reference before I react to his or her statement. | | | | | |
| 13. I am aware of whether I am stating facts or opinions. | | | | | |
| 14. I avoid using words that threaten the self-respect of the listener. | | | | | |

Give yourself 1 point for each "Very Seldom" answer, 2 points for "About 1/4 of Time," 3 points for "About 1/2 of Time," 4 points for "About 3/4 of Time," 5 points for "Almost Always." A score of 70 is perfect. (But do you put this understanding into practice?) A score under 42 indicates that you have a real need to improve your communication ability.

*Source*:   Adapted from Carol Sapin Gold, *Solid Gold Customer Relations* (Englewood Cliffs, N.J.: Prentice-Hall, 1983), pp. 51-52.

1. What did you score on the test?  Were you surprised by your score?  What can you do to improve your communication "IQ"?

2. Describe in general terms how you would characterize the communication problems represented by the items in the text.

## DEVELOP YOUR WORD POWER

*Spelling Challenge*   Identify the misspelled word in each of the following sentences, and spell it correctly in the space provided.  If all the words in a sentence are spelled correctly, write C in the space.

_____   1.   What would it cost to advertize in *Newsweek*?

_____   2.   Bill is anxous because he has not heard from his associate yet.

_____   3.   Ms. Hansen will analyse your income statement.

_____   4.   Standish Corp.'s anual meeting will be held on August 17.

_____   5.   That typewriter is ancient!

_____   6.   We will issue stock when it is advantageous to do so.

_____   7.   What kinds of returns are allowible?

_____   8.   I must apologise, Mike, for being unable to attend your meeting.

_____   9.   What did you think of her analisis?

_____   10.   It is not adviseable to wear your Sport watch while swimming.

*Vocabulary Challenge*   Match the words in the first column with the definitions in the second column.

\_\_\_\_\_   11.   benign          A.   pleasant

\_\_\_\_\_   12.   apathetic          B.   independent

\_\_\_\_\_   13.   bilateral          C.   haughty

\_\_\_\_\_   14.   arrogant          D.   two-sided

\_\_\_\_\_   15.   autonomous          E.   uninterested

Circle the best definition of the highlighted word in each of the following sentences.

16.   Her remarks about market trends were **apropos** because we are considering a major change in our marketing approach.

A.   pertinent          B.   spooky          C.   positive

17. We can **avert** future disaster only by taking precautions against accidents now.

    A. predict          B. lessen          C. prevent

18. I **ascribe** our poor sales last month to consumer uncertainty about the economy.

    A. assume          B. credit          C. report

19. We should not purchase any business until we **audit** its books.

    A. examine          B. read          C. hear

20. All Persian carpets from the House of Nasseri are **authentic**.

    A. original          B. genuine          C. high quality

Select one of these words to complete each of the following sentences, and write the word in the space provided.

**anticlimax          antipathy          antithesis          apathy          attrition**

21. Because of his _____ toward office work, he has decided on a career that will seldom require him to sit behind a desk.

22. Her _____ may infect the other programmers, who might then lose their enthusiasm for the project.

23. The _____ of right is wrong.

24. After all the talk about changing store operations, the minor change in store hours seems an _____.

25. She doesn't like to fire anybody, so she'll whittle her staff through _____.

**Follow-up Word Study**    Check your answers at the end of this chapter. In the spaces below, write the words that you spelled or used incorrectly. (Use a separate piece of paper if you missed more than five words.) Then look up each word in your dictionary, and carefully study its spelling, pronunciation, definition, and history (etymology). Finally, to help fix the word in your memory, write it in a sentence.

Word                    Sentence

_____    _____

_____    _____

_____    _____

_____    _____

_____    _____

## CHECK YOUR ANSWERS

### Master Key Concepts

I. understand, respond

II. repeating
   A. assumptions
   C. transmitted

III. misunderstandings
   A. developing
   C. receiving
   D. interpretations

IV. business

V. A. purpose, audience, reviewed
   B. open-minded

### Quiz Yourself

1. Business communication has these three basic goals:
   a. To let the audience understand exactly what you mean, so that the idea in their minds corresponds to the idea you intended to convey
   b. To get the audience to respond to the message as you intended
   c. To maintain good relations with the audience  (p. 25)

2. The five steps involved in the communication process:
   a. The sender has an idea.
   b. The idea becomes a message.
   c. The message is transmitted.
   d. The receiver gets the message.
   e. The receiver reacts and sends feedback to the sender.  (p. 26)

3. The final step, when the receiver sends feedback to the source, is what makes the communication process truly interactive.  (p. 29)

4. Four common problems that may occur when a message is being developed:
   a. Indecision about message content
   b. Lack of familiarity with the situation or the audience
   c. Emotional conflicts
   d. Difficulty in expressing ideas  (pp. 30–31)

5. To overcome transmission problems, a person should
   a. Attempt to reduce competing distractions
   b. Send one clear message at a time
   c. Reduce the number of links in the communication chain  (p. 32)

6. Every message contains both a *content* meaning, which deals with the subject of the message, and a *relationship* meaning, which suggests the nature of the interaction between the sender and the receiver. (pp. 35–36)

7. Business messages are complex in a number of ways:
   a. The sender of the message may not always completely agree with the ideas that have to be expressed or may be emotionally reluctant to send the message.
   b. The subject is often inherently dry or difficult to explain.
   c. The message may have to be developed under difficult conditions involving uncertainties about the purpose or audience for the message, time or budget pressures, interruptions, or collaboration with people of different opinions.  (pp. 38–39)

8. Interference in the transmission and reception of business messages occurs because
   a. Many people may be involved in filtering the message between the sender and the receiver.
   b. The receiver is frequently interrupted in the process of trying to interpret the message. (p. 39)

9. Here are some of the things you can do to overcome the barriers to effective communication:
   a. Think about the purpose of the message and the needs of the audience.
   b. Tell the audience what to expect so they will understand the relationship among the ideas you hope to convey.
   c. Use concrete, specific language.
   d. Stick to the point; eliminate any information that does not directly contribute to your purpose.
   e. Connect new information to information the audience is already familiar with.
   f. In concluding the message, review the key points. (pp. 40-43)

10. The feedback loop is often particularly complex in business communication for the following reasons:
    a. If your message is in writing, feedback is difficult to obtain and does not occur immediately.
    b. Many messages are directed to several receivers, who may react in different ways. In these circumstances, it is difficult to adjust the message to respond to the feedback.
    c. In some situations, feedback is a distraction. For example, responding to questions and comments throughout a speech may prevent the speaker from completing the message in a logical way.
    d. Because of their relative positions in an organization, people may be reluctant to provide honest feedback. For example, a lower-level employee may hesitate to criticize points made by the boss. (pp. 42-43)

## Develop Your Word Power

| | | | | |
|---|---|---|---|---|
| 1. advertise | 6. C | 11. A | 16. A | 21. antipathy |
| 2. anxious | 7. allowable | 12. E | 17. C | 22. apathy |
| 3. analyze | 8. apologize | 13. D | 18. B | 23. antithesis |
| 4. annual | 9. analysis | 14. C | 19. A | 24. anticlimax |
| 5. C | 10. advisable | 15. B | 20. B | 25. attrition |

**Chapter 3**

## COMMUNICATING IN THE ELECTRONIC OFFICE

The main point of Chapter 3 is that the modern office is an integrated communication machine made up of both people and equipment. As you read the chapter, think about how a memo, letter, or report might be processed in a large organization; then think about how it might be processed in a small one. When you finish reading, assess your familiarity with various types of office equipment and then seek opportunities to work on big projects with other people, especially those that require the use of equipment you are not familiar with.

### MASTER KEY CONCEPTS

Use the following terms to fill the blanks in the outline. All terms are used, but none is used more than once.

| | | | |
|---|---|---|---|
| compose | managing | processing | systems |
| electronic | photocopiers | production | team |
| equipment | physical | storage | |

I. In a sense, a business organization is like a machine for _____ (p. 49) information.
   A. The people in the organization (sometimes with outside help) must work together as a _____ (pp. 49–50) to produce and distribute information: planning and creating the message, editing the message, reproducing and distributing the message, and producing visual aids when necessary.
   B. Someone must take responsibility for _____ (pp. 50–51) the communication process; the process can be improved if the manager tries to reduce the number of messages, make instructions clear, delegate responsibility, and train writers and speakers.

II. Business communication usually takes place with the aid of office _____ (p. 53) that originates, produces, reproduces, distributes, and stores information.
   A. Origination equipment, which is used to _____ (pp. 53–54) messages, includes pens/pencils and paper, dictation machines, adding machines and calculators, and such keyboard devices as typewriters, word processors, and microcomputers.
   B. _____ (p. 54) equipment, which is used to transform the original message into finished form, includes standard and electronic typewriters, word/information processors, computers, and phototypesetting equipment.
   C. Reproduction equipment, which creates multiple copies of a message, includes carbon paper, carbonless copy sets, _____ (p. 55), mimeograph and ditto machines, offset-printing equipment, audio and video recorders, and computer printers.
   D. Distribution/transmission equipment, which is used to deliver messages, may be classified as either _____ (p. 58) (hand delivery, interoffice mail, meetings, U.S. Postal Service, private delivery systems, messenger services) or _____ (p. 60) (telephone, telephone switchboard systems, teletypewriters, telegrams/mailgrams,

electronic mail, dataphones, facsimile equipment, communicating word/information processors, video and film projectors, public address systems, closed-circuit television, teleconferencing).

E. _____ (p. 62) equipment, which is used to maintain information for future use, includes file cabinets, magnetic disks/tapes/cards, video and audio disks/tapes, microfilm, and computer memory.

F. The electronic office—the office of the future—will rely not so much on individual pieces of equipment to perform these functions but mainly on interactive _____ (pp. 62-64) of computers and telephone lines (with some audiovisual equipment) for the origination, production, reproduction, distribution/transmission, and storage of information.

*Check your answers at the end of this chapter.*

## QUIZ YOURSELF

1. Briefly describe the people and organizations that might become involved in producing a major business report.

2. Identify four things that managers can do to improve the communication function.

3. What are the four basic types of form letters?

4. Define the term *origination equipment* and give some examples.

5. A document that is described as being _____ has lines of type that all end at the right-hand margin.

6. What type of production equipment is frequently used by organizations that produce many documents for outside distribution, such as annual reports, brochures, and magazines?

7. The term _____ refers to the process of sorting multiple copies of a multi-page document into the proper order.

8. List at least five examples of physical distribution technology.

9. The parents of "electronic mail" are the _____ and the _____.

10. Briefly describe how a person might send a message to all the employees in an "electronic office."

*Check your answers at the end of this chapter.*

## BUILD YOUR SKILLS: SUPPOSE YOU WERE EQUIPPING AN OFFICE . . .

Let's say that you have decided to go into business for yourself by opening a one-person real estate office in your hometown. You have rented space in a new building. Now you must obtain the furnishings, equipment, and supplies you need to get started. Make a list of all the items you need. Remember, you're on a tight budget.

## EXPAND YOUR KNOWLEDGE: MAIL CALL AT THE OVAL OFFICE

A 10-year-old writes, wanting to join the Army. A woman in Virginia pleads for help in finding the son kidnapped by her estranged husband. Letters like these make up the roughly $5\frac{1}{2}$ million pieces of correspondence that the President of the United States will receive this year. (By contrast, the average American receives about 500 pieces.) Of this total, fewer than 100 a week actually reach the Oval Office.

In the past 25 years, the country's population has increased 25 percent, but the number of people writing to the President has gone up almost 600 percent. A George Washington University study indicates that expanded television news coverage has had a profound impact on the volume of mail.

The Special Assistant to the President and Director of Correspondence has a staff of 58 and about 100 volunteers who deal with as many as 50,000 letters and an average of 1,000 telephone calls each day. From her office, about 20 to 40 percent of all letters are forwarded to the White House liaison offices in Cabinet-level departments, with a large part of that mail headed for the departments of Health and Human Services, State, and Defense.

Most of the responses issued by the White House are produced by a large mainframe computer that uses a software system specially developed for this purpose. This computer, also used by other White House offices, has 22 terminals dedicated to correspondence work. A minicomputer-based software package is used to produce more individualized responses to the President's mail. These two systems share a number of output devices, including laser, ink-jet, and daisy-wheel printers. The White House also uses a number of stand-alone word processors and memory and magnetic-card typewriters for special situations.

Is the bulk of the mail concerned with highly topical or controversial issues, such as arms sales or budget cuts? Hardly. Many people write merely to request a photograph or to extend birthday greetings. Others send pictures of themselves. Most letter writers discuss personal problems that they think the President can help with, and much of the correspondence has a humorous side.

One writer, a retired Army man, enclosed the insoles of his shoes and wondered why, in spite of Presidential directives to save money, he could not get new insoles instead of a whole new pair of shoes. After arriving at 1600 Pennsylvania Avenue, the letter was read and routed across the Potomac to the Pentagon.

After passing through perhaps a dozen hands, at a cost in hours many times that of providing a set of insoles, the man's letter found its way to the Army's Deputy Chief of Staff for Logistics, the division that handles matters of supply. Several weeks later, the writer received a reply thanking him for his letter to the President and informing him that the government could not supply him with a new pair of insoles. So much for all that fancy mail-handling hardware!

*Source*:   Adapted from "Mail Call at the Oval Office," *New York Times*, November 23, 1981, p. 20; letter from Anne Higgins, Special Assistant to the President and Director of Correspondence, The White House, July 11, 1983.

1. Write your own letter to the Oval Office, expressing an opinion about something or asking for information. See what sort of response you get.

2. Do you think that the Oval Office should respond to all 5½ million pieces of mail sent to the President each year? Why or why not? What benefits does the federal government receive in return for the money and effort expended to handle all this mail?

## DEVELOP YOUR WORD POWER

**Spelling Challenge**   Identify the misspelled word in each of the following sentences, and spell it correctly in the space provided. If all the words in a sentence are spelled correctly, write *C* in the space.

| | |
|---|---|
| _C_ | 1. How large is the balance in my account? |
| _athlete_ | 2. The applicant was an outstanding athelete in high school. |
| _arrangements_ | 3. Would you please handle the arangements for the open house. |
| _appreciated_ | 4. Mr. Blevins apreciates loyalty. |
| _C_ | 5. There were no apparent cracks in the housing. |
| _apparel_ | 6. Patrick's carries an extensive line of fine apparrel for men. |
| _applicable_ | 7. All applible equal-opportunity laws will be observed during the hiring process. |
| _arguments_ | 8. Avoid arguements with all customers. |
| _assumption_ | 9. Her decision was based on the assumtion that Louise is retiring. |
| _awkward_ | 10. See how well the applicants handle akward encounters. |

**Vocabulary Challenge**   Match the words in the first column with the definitions in the second column.

| | | |
|---|---|---|
| C | 11. blasé | A. obvious |
| A | 12. blatant | B. inclusive |
| E | 13. cogent | C. unimpressed |
| D | 14. comprehensible | D. understandable |
| B | 15. comprehensive | E. to the point |

Circle the best definition of the highlighted word in each of the following sentences.

16. They will accept any **bona fide** offer for the company.

   A. high            B. from the loyal            C. genuine

17. Take the criticisms of a **chronic** complainer with a grain of salt.

   A. timely            B. grouchy            C. habitual

18. We answer letters in **chronological** order.

   A. customary            B. by time            C. haphazard

19. Only the most **circumspect** middle managers should be given a copy of this report.

   A. discreet            B. overweight            C. around for a long time

20. The expression "What goes up must come down" is a **cliché**.

   A. puzzle            B. trite saying            C. metaphor

Select one of these words to complete each of the following sentences, and write the word in the space provided.

   **capitulate**            **chide**            **circumvent**            **compel**            **compromise**

21. If we insist, they will eventually _____Capitulate_____ to our demands.

22. We cannot _____compel_____ any employee to contribute to this fund drive.

23. Attendance at that meeting will _____compromise_____ your reputation for objectivity.

24. You can _____circumvent_____ health and safety regulations for only so long before a serious accident occurs.

25. Do not _____chide_____ your employees if they fail to read your mind.

**Follow-up Word Study**    Check your answers at the end of this chapter. In the spaces below, write the words that you spelled or used incorrectly. (Use a separate piece of paper if you missed more than five words.) Then look up each word in your dictionary, and carefully study its spelling, pronunciation, definition, and history (etymology). Finally, to help fix the word in your memory, write it in a sentence.

Word                Sentence

_____    _____

_____    _____

_____    _____

_____    _____

_____    _____

---

## CHECK YOUR ANSWERS

---

### Master Key Concepts

I. processing
  A.  team
  B.  managing

II. equipment
  A.  compose
  B.  production
  C.  photocopiers
  D.  physical, electronic
  E.  storage
  F.  systems

### Quiz Yourself

1. A major business **report might be planned** by a committee, written by a team, reviewed and revised by an editor, typed by a crew of secretaries, illustrated and packaged by the art department, and distributed internally by mailroom or other clerical staff and externally by the U.S. Postal Service.  (p. 49)

2. Managers can improve the communication function by
   a. Reducing the number of messages
   b. Making assignments and procedures clearer
   c. Giving more responsibility to others
   d. Training employees to be better writers and speakers  (pp. 50-53)

3. The four basic types of form letters:
   a. Mass mailings that are not individualized in any way except for the address
   b. Guide letters, which are used as models for individually typed letters
   c. Letters composed of optional paragraphs selected to suit the occasion
   d. Fill-in forms, which leave blanks for typed or handwritten information  (p. 52)

4. The term *origination equipment* refers to the tools that are used to compose and record messages coming from a person's mind.  Examples of origination equipment:
   a. Pens/pencils and paper
   b. Shorthand
   c. Dictation equipment
   d. Calculator
   e. Personal computer
   f. Typewriter  (pp. 53-54)

5. A document that is described as being *justified* has lines of type that all end at the right-hand margin.  (p. 54)

6. Organizations that produce many documents for outside distribution frequently use phototypesetting equipment.  (p. 55)

7. The term *collating* refers to the process of sorting multiple copies of a multipage document into the proper order.  (p. 56)

8. Physical distribution technology:
   a. Hand delivery
   b. Interoffice mail
   c. Meetings
   d. U.S. Postal Service
   e. Mail sorters
   f. Optical character readers
   g. Delivery services
   h. Messenger services   (p. 58)

9. The parents of "electronic mail" are the *telephone* and the *computer*.   (p. 60)

10. To send a message to all the employees in an "electronic office," a person might begin by composing the message on a personal computer, using various software to perform calculations, prepare visual aids, and type the text of the message. Before finalizing the document, the person might arrange a teleconference with executives in other locations to discuss certain points, using electronic mail to transmit the draft.

   To produce the final version, the person might use a voice-activated computer or update the draft using a computer and the original disk. The disk would then be edited, using computer software to correct spelling, grammar, and punctuation and to put the text in the approved format. The final version would be transmitted from the central computer to terminals throughout the company, where it could be stored in computer memory or used to generate paper copies on printers.

   The message could then be discussed in a teleconference with employees at various locations. (pp. 62-64)

## Develop Your Word Power

| | | | | |
|---|---|---|---|---|
| 1. C | 6. apparel | 11. C | 16. C | 21. capitulate |
| 2. athlete | 7. applicable | 12. A | 17. C | 22. compel |
| 3. arrangements | 8. arguments | 13. E | 18. B | 23. compromise |
| 4. appreciates | 9. assumption | 14. D | 19. A | 24. circumvent |
| 5. C | 10. awkward | 15. B | 20. B | 25. chide |

## Chapter 4

## WRITING FOR READABILITY

The main point of Chapter 4 is that the best writing style is the one that makes it easiest for the reader to understand exactly what you mean, exactly in the way you meant it. As you read the chapter, think about the ways that word choice, sentence construction, and paragraph development contribute to readability. When you finish reading, analyze the weaknesses in your own writing style and try to undertake a program for improving it.

## MASTER KEY CONCEPTS

Use the following terms to fill the blanks in the outline. All terms are used, but none is used more than once.

| | | | |
|---|---|---|---|
| **classification** | **illustration** | **predicate** | **topic** |
| **compound** | **modifiers** | **pronoun** | **transitional** |
| **content** | **nouns** | **subordinate** | **verbs** |
| **functional** | **obsolete** | | |

I.  The best words to use are those that are both correct and effective.
   A.  _____ (p. 73) words (conjunctions, prepositions, articles, and pronouns) are used to express relationships; _____ (p. 74) words (nouns, verbs, adjectives, and adverbs)—whether connotative or denotative, concrete or abstract—carry meaning.
   B.  In business writing, the best words to use are those that are strong (meaning _____ [pp. 76-77] and _____ [pp. 77-80]), familiar, short, active, and uncamouflaged by unneeded suffixes.

II.  Words do not achieve their full meaning until they are assembled into sentences, which must have at least a subject (noun or pronoun) and a _____ (p. 80) (verb).
   A.  Effective writing mixes the three types of sentences: simple, consisting of one subject-predicate set; _____ (p. 80), consisting of two or more subject-predicate sets joined by such words as *and* and *but*; complex, consisting of one main subject-predicate set and a _____ (p. 80) subject-predicate set, which cannot stand alone.
   B.  The most readable writing has many short sentences, has no unnecessary words or phrases, avoids _____ (p. 83) and pompous language, takes a moderate tone, does not string together sentences that should be separate, makes firm statements whenever possible instead of hedging, minimizes indefinite _____ (p. 71) starters, expresses parallel ideas in parallel form, reduces awkward pointers to a minimum, eliminates dangling _____ (p. 86), and places subjects and verbs close together.

III.  A paragraph is a series of sentences related to a single thought.
   A.  The typical paragraph consists of a _____ (p. 87) sentence, related sentences that develop the topic, and _____ (p. 87) words and phrases.

B.  Of the many ways paragraphs can be developed, these five are most common: by
_____ (p. 88), by comparison or contrast, by discussion of cause and effect, by _____ (p. 89), and by discussion of problem and solution.

C.  Paragraphs are most effective when they stick to one point, are relatively short (about 100
words), and are varied in structure and length.

*Check your answers at the end of this chapter.*


## QUIZ YOURSELF

1.  Conjunctions, prepositions, articles, and pronouns are all _____ words.

2.  An _____ word stands for a concept, quality, or characteristic instead of
a thing you can touch or see.

3.  Explain what an "active" verb is.


4.  A _____ sentence contains two or more independent thoughts of equal importance joined by *and, but,* or *or.*

5.  What is the Fog Index, and how is it calculated?


6.  Relative pronouns such as _____, _____, and _____ are frequently a
source of wordiness.

7.  What is a hedging sentence?


8.  Give an example of a dangling modifier.


9.  What is a paragraph?


10.  Identify five of the most common ways that paragraphs can be developed.


*Check your answers at the end of this chapter.*

## BUILD YOUR SKILLS:  CAN THIS LETTER BE IMPROVED?

This letter from a bank manager is designed to interest checking-account customers in opening an Individual Retirement Account (IRA) with the bank.  Rewrite the letter so that it has stronger words, more effective sentences, and more coherent paragraphs.

Dear Valued Customer:

As a highly esteemed and valued customer of this financial establishment, I know that you appreciate it whenever we are able to offer you an opportunity to earn a higher return on your financial investments.  For this reason, I would like to inform you of the benefits that can be obtained by making an investment in an Individual Retirement Account (IRA) with American Atlantic Bank and Trust.

It is possible to move closer to achieving your financial goals by opening an IRA, which enables you to obtain the protection of your income dollars from taxes, while at the same time giving you earnings growth and a cushion of financial comfort for impending retirement years.

The mechanism that affords you this valuable opportunity is simple.  The full amount of your financial contribution to your IRA in a given tax year can be deducted from your taxable income in that year.  In addition, the interest earned on your investment accumulates on a tax-exempt basis until such time as you withdraw it after your retirement.  At the time of your retirement, most people who rely on earned income for the bulk of their working years are in a lower tax bracket.  Hence, the interest earned on the IRA, as well as the principal withdrawn, are taxed at a lower rate than they would have been had they been declared as income during the wage-earning years.

We at American Atlantic Bank and Trust are able to offer you IRA terms that are attractive.  For example, did you know that you are allowed to invest up to 100 percent of your annual earnings or a maximum of $2,000, whichever is higher, in an IRA?  Furthermore, if your wife doesn't work and if you file jointly, you can contribute up to $2,250.  And if both you and your wife are employed, as much as $4,000 can be invested on your behalf in a jointly held IRA each and every year in which both of you are employed.

Opening an IRA at American Atlantic Bank and Trust is truly easy.  If you must make a withdrawal before you reach age 60, the amount you withdraw will be subject to an Internal Revenue Service tax penalty; however, the penalty does not apply if the withdrawal of funds is necessitated by death or by permanent disability.

Just complete the enclosed document at your earliest convenience and return it to me, the undersigned.  By taking a few moments to complete the enclosure at this time, you will make your retirement appreciably more secure and vastly more comfortable in the long run.  Isn't it worth it?

Do not delay!  Act now!

Very truly yours,

Jocelyn Burkhardt

## EXPAND YOUR KNOWLEDGE:  READABILITY = EASE + INTEREST

It is one thing to make your letters, memos, and reports easy to read—but quite another to make them interesting.  And what makes a written document interesting?  To a large extent, "personal words" and "personal sentences" are the elements that involve readers, according to Dr. Rudolf Flesch.  He has developed a method for measuring human interest:

1. Count the number of words in a writing sample.

2. Count the personal words:
   - All pronouns, except *it, its, itself* and *them, their, theirs, themselves* when referring to things rather than to people.
   - All words, singular and plural, that refer to men or to women, such as *John Jones, Mary, father, sister, actress*—not common-gender words like *teacher, doctor, employee, assistant, spouse*
   - The group words *people* (with the plural verb) and *folks*

3. Divide the total number of personal words by the total number of words in the sample and multiply by 100 to get the number of personal words per 100 words.

4. Count the number of sentences in the sample.

5. Count the personal sentences:
   - Spoken sentences, marked by quotation marks or otherwise, often including speech tags like "he said," set off by colons or commas (such as *We told him: "You can take it or leave it"*)
   - Questions, commands, requests, and other sentences directly addressed to the reader (such as *Does this sound impossible?* or *It means a lot to people like you and me*)—but not sentences that are only indirectly or vaguely addressed to the reader (*This is typical of our national character* or *You can never tell*)
   - Exclamations
   - Grammatically incomplete sentences whose full meaning has to be inferred from the context (such as *Well, he wasn't* or *The minute you walked out*)

6. Divide the total number of personal sentences by the total number of sentences in the sample and multiply by 100 to get the number of personal sentences per 100 sentences.

7. Multiply the number of personal words per 100 words by 3.635.

8. Multiply the number of personal sentences per 100 sentences by 0.314.

9. Add the figures from steps 7 and 8 to get the human-interest score, which indicates the percentage of personal words and sentences in the sample. If the human-interest score is 0, your sample has no human interest; if the score is 100, the sample is full of human interest.

In the following passage from Dr. Flesch's *The Art of Readable Writing*, all personal words are in capital letters and all personal sentences are italicized:

*SCHOPENHAUER said: "The first rule for a good style is to have something to say; in fact, this in itself is almost enough."* The British diplomat HAROLD NICOLSON wrote: *"The first essential is to know what one wishes to say; the second is to decide to whom one wishes to say it."* And the Hungarian mathematician GEORGE POLYA came up with this one: *"The first rule of style is to have something to say. The second rule of style is to control YOURSELF when, by chance, YOU have two things to say; say first one, then the other, not both at the same time."*

*No doubt NICOLSON and POLYA made valuable additions; but, as YOU see, SCHOPENHAUER'S first rule still stands.* It is likely to be put in first place by anybody else who may want to draw up rules of style.

*But, YOU will say, that doesn't help much.* That just passes the buck back to the person who wants to know how to write. *"Have something to say" sounds much like saying "Be smart" or "Have a mind of YOUR own."*

*In the main, that's true.* But having something to say also means having a good stock of facts; and there are ways and means of getting at facts and keeping them handy. Most PEOPLE who do any writing (without being professional writers) are handicapped by simply not knowing how to collect THEIR material.

*Let ME tell YOU a little story: It was a Sunday evening.* I was putting the finishing touches on a research report I was working on. Suddenly I realized that I didn't have certain figures on magazine circulation that I had meant to use. If I couldn't get these figures at once I would miss MY deadline. I was on the spot.

The solution was as simple as can be: I called the Public Library and had MY information within two minutes.

The human-interest score for this passage is about 45. Compare the scores that Dr. Flesch computed for a variety of magazines:

| Description of Style | Percentage of Personal Words | Percentage of Personal Sentences | Human-Interest Score | Typical Magazine |
|---|---|---|---|---|
| dull | 2 or less | 0 | 0 to 10 | scientific |
| mildly interesting | 4 | 5 | 10 to 20 | trade |
| interesting | 7 | 15 | 20 to 40 | digest |
| highly interesting | 10 | 43 | 40 to 60 | *New Yorker* |
| dramatic | 17 or more | 58 or more | 60 to 100 | fiction |

Before you try to boost the human-interest level in everything you write, remember that some business documents must remain impersonal. However, personal words and personal sentences do help readers pay attention to your message.

*Source*:   Adapted from Rudolf Flesch, *The Art of Readable Writing* (New York: Harper & Row, 1949), pp. 20-21, 151, 213-216.

1. Both the Fog Index and the Flesch human-interest score are methods for measuring writing effectiveness. But how do they differ?

2. How useful are such methods of measuring readability as the Fog Index and the human-interest score? What's good about them? What's not so good?

## DEVELOP YOUR WORD POWER

*Spelling Challenge*   Identify the misspelled word in each of the following sentences, and spell it correctly in the space provided. If all the words in a sentence are spelled correctly, write *C* in the space.

| | |
|---|---|
| _____ | 1.   The problem is basicly one of quality. |
| brochure | 2.   Please send a broshure on your kitchen lighting fixtures. |
| busness | 3.   We can make your bisness more profitable. |
| _____ | 4.   Mark  January 15 on your calender. |
| _____ | 5.   When you practice your speech, strive to make it believeable. |
| Camplane | 6.   Schedule a meeting to unveil the new advertising campain. |
| _____ | 7.   He has 12 years' experience as a bookeeper. |
| _____ | 8.   Jason has a strong belief in himself. |
| _____ | 9.   Another course in personnel management would be benefical. |
| _____ | 10.   How have you benefited from the program? |

*Vocabulary Challenge*   Match the words in the first column with the definitions in the second column.

_____ 11. concede          A. to approve

_____ 12. concur           B. to squeeze

_____ 13. condone          C. to discuss

_____ 14. confer           D. to agree

_____ 15. constrict        E. to admit

Circle the best definition of the highlighted word in each of the following sentences.

16. This job requires the ability to **conceptualize.**

    A.   form a mental image       B.   agree with others        C.   convince others

17. Annette has **concocted** another excuse for skipping the meeting.

    A.   conspired                 B.   rejected                  C.   devised

18. Ms. Starr will serve as the **conduit** for all suggestions from the staff.

    A.   recorder                  B.   judge                     C.   channel

19. **Conjecture** about Dr. Crandall's successor is premature.

    A.   gossip                    B.   uninformed guesses        C.   strong feeling

20. He is a **consummate** speaker and much in demand.

    A.   superb                    B.   exciting                  C.   bawdy

Select one of these words to complete each of the following sentences, and write the word in the space provided.

   compulsive          compulsory          concise          conducive          contemporary

21. I will need only five minutes to present a _____ overview of the year's accomplishments.

22. The _____ family consists of two breadwinners and one or two children.

23. Attendance at Monday's staff meeting is _____ for all clerks.

24. Brian has a _____ need to correct everyone's grammar.

25. A supportive atmosphere is _____ to creativity and initiative.


*Follow-up Word Study*   Check your answers at the end of this chapter. In the spaces below, write the words that you spelled or used incorrectly. (Use a separate piece of paper if you missed more than five words.) Then look up each word in your dictionary, and carefully study its spelling, pronunciation, definition, and history (etymology). Finally, to help fix the word in your memory, write it in a sentence.

Word                    Sentence

_____    _____

_____    _____

_____    _____

_____    _____

_____    _____

---

## CHECK YOUR ANSWERS

### Master Key Concepts

I. A. functional, content
B. nouns, verbs

II. predicate
A. compound, subordinate
B. obsolete, pronoun, modifiers

III. A. topic, transitional
B. illustration, classification

### Quiz Yourself

1. Conjunctions, prepositions, articles, and pronouns are all *functional* words.  (pp. 73-74)

2. An *abstract* word stands for a concept, quality, or characteristic instead of a thing you can touch or see.  (p. 75)

3. An "active" verb shows its subject in action.  The subject of a sentence usually comes before an active verb, and the object of the sentence follows it.  Active verbs produce shorter, stronger sentences than passive verbs.  (p. 77)

4. A *compound* sentence contains two or more independent thoughts of equal importance joined by *and, but,* or *or.*  (p. 80)

5. The Fog Index measures the readability of a document.  To calculate the Fog Index, choose several 100-word writing samples.  For each sample, count the number of words in each sentence, the number of sentences, and the number of words with three or more syllables.  Calculate the average number of words per sentence and the percentage of words with three or more syllables. Add these two numbers, and then multiply by 0.4.  The resulting number is the Fog Index.  For a general business audience, a level of 8 to 11 is about right.  (pp. 82-83)

6. Relative pronouns such as *who, that,* and *which* are frequently a source of wordiness.  (p. 81)

7. A hedging sentence is one that tries too hard to avoid stating a judgment as a fact.  Hedging sentences frequently include words like *may* and *seem.*  (p. 84)

8. Here are some examples of dangling modifiers—phrases with no real connection to the subject of the sentence:
   a. Walking to the office, a red sports car passed him.
   b. Going down in the elevator, the office seemed to be in a different world.
   c. Working as fast as possible, the budget soon was ready.  (p. 86)

9. A paragraph is a cluster of sentences all related to the same general topic.  It is a unit of thought, separated from other units of thought by the typographical device of indenting the first line.  (p. 86)

10. Five of the most common ways to develop a paragraph:
    a. Illustration
    b. Comparison or contrast
    c. Cause and effect
    d. Classification
    e. Problem and solution  (pp. 88-89)

**Develop Your Word Power**

| | | | | |
|---|---|---|---|---|
| 1. basically | 6. campaign | 11. E | 16. A | 21. concise |
| 2. brochure | 7. bookkeeper | 12. D | 17. C | 22. contemporary |
| 3. business | 8. C | 13. A | 18. C | 23. compulsory |
| 4. calendar | 9. beneficial | 14. C | 19. B | 24. compulsive |
| 5. believable | 10. C | 15. B | 20. A | 25. conducive |

# Chapter 5

## ESTABLISHING A GOOD RELATIONSHIP WITH THE AUDIENCE

The main point of Chapter 5 is that the "you" attitude—looking at things from the audience's viewpoint—is an important tool in business communication. As you read the chapter, think about how messages can be worded to respond to an audience's needs. When you finish reading, mentally review several interpersonal problems in your own life and rehearse how you could have used the "you" attitude to resolve them.

## MASTER KEY CONCEPTS

Use the following terms to fill the blanks in the outline. All terms are used, but none is used more than once.

| | | | |
|---|---|---|---|
| audience | courtesy | personal | psychological |
| businesslike | credibility | positive | tone |
| company | information | practical | "you" |

I. One secret of effective communication is to try to tell your _____ (p. 98) what they need to know in terms that are meaningful to them.

   A. In preparing any sort of business message, you must first respond to the audience's _____ (p. 98) needs: find out what the audience needs to know, and then anticipate unstated questions, provide all the required information, be sure the information is accurate, and emphasize the ideas of greatest interest to the audience.

   B. Each member of an audience has some _____ (p. 104) needs that must be addressed: _____ (p. 104) needs (such as limited time and unlimited distractions) and _____ (p. 105) needs (which can be met by appealing to reason, emotion, or ethics, as required).

II. The proper _____ (p. 106)—the way your communication sounds to the recipient—can be established in five ways.

   A. Establish a _____ (pp. 107-108) relationship by being sensitive to differences in rank, avoiding undue familiarity, using humor cautiously, avoiding obvious flattery, avoiding a preachy or know-it-all attitude, presenting your own credentials with modesty, and being yourself.

   B. Project the _____ (pp. 108-109) attitude by talking in terms of the audience's interests and referring when possible to the audience instead of to you.

   C. Emphasize the _____ (pp. 109-111) by pointing out what you can do to help, focusing on opportunities for improvement instead of trying to assign blame, pointing out what people can gain by cooperating with you, and using terms with pleasant connotations; however, do not make exaggerated claims or misleading promises in the effort to be positive.

   D. Establish your _____ (pp. 111-112) by showing that you understand the other person's viewpoint and by using language that inspires respect.

E.  Maintain an air of _____ (pp. 112-113) by being sensitive to the circumstances, avoiding accusing or insensitive language, looking for ways to give your audience pleasure, and promptly responding to correspondence.

III. In addition to writing for the reader, you are writing for the _____ (pp. 113-114), so make sure that your words are acceptable to the organization and that your style is compatible with the image it wishes to project.

*Check your answers at the end of this chapter.*

## QUIZ YOURSELF

1. What should you do when you are asked to write a memo but the instructions are vague?

2. One good way to check the thoroughness of your document is to check it for what reporters call the _____ .

3. Explain some of the ways you might check a document for accuracy.

4. Given the fact that most business readers will have very little time to devote to your message, what can you do to make the message as convenient as possible?

5. What are some of the techniques you might use in an "appeal to emotion"?

6. What are five specific things to avoid if you want to establish a businesslike relationship with the reader?

7. When you present your message in terms of the reader's wishes, interests, hopes, and preferences, you are using the _____ attitude.

8. Name five specific things you can do to emphasize the positive aspects of your message.

9. List four ways you can exhibit courtesy in business communications.

10. Discuss what it means to "write for the company."

*Check your answers at the end of this chapter.*

## BUILD YOUR SKILLS: ELIMINATE THE LEGALESE, PLEASE!

The following excerpt from a standard contract issued by a moving and storage company is replete with legal terms. Try your hand at rewriting this passage in plain English:

> No liability shall be provided for the mechanical or electrical derangements of pianos, radios, phonographs, clocks, refrigerators, television sets, automatic washers, or other instruments or appliances unless evidence is provided of external damage to such equipment, or unless said articles or appliances are serviced as provided in subparagraph (1) below. The carrier reserves the right to inspect these articles or appliances to determine whether they are in good working order before accepting them for shipment. Carrier assumes no liability whatsoever for returning, refocusing, or other adjustments of television sets unless such services were made necessary due to carrier's negligence.
>
> 1. Upon request of shipper, owner, or consignee of the goods, carrier will, subject to the provisions of subparagraph (2) below, service and unservice such articles as stoves, automatic washers, and dryers at origin and destination. Such servicing does not include removal or installation of articles secured to the premises or plumbing, electrical, or carpentry services necessary to disconnect, remove, connect, and install such articles and appliances.
> 2. If carrier does not possess the qualified personnel to properly service and unservice such articles or appliances, carrier, upon request of shipper or consignee or as agent for them, shall engage third persons to perform the servicing and unservicing. When third persons are engaged by the carrier to perform any service, the carrier will not assume responsibility for their activities or conduct; amount of their charges; nor the quality or quantity of service furnished.

## EXPAND YOUR KNOWLEDGE: WINNING FRIENDS AND INFLUENCING PEOPLE

Much business communication is meant to win people over. You may want to change their opinions or behavior or just accomplish your goals while maintaining their goodwill. Dale Carnegie, a long-acknowledged master of human relations and communication, recommended 12 rules for winning people to your way of thinking:

1. *The only way to get the best of an argument is to avoid it.* Say that you win a verbal battle. Is the person you've argued with going to like you more for winning? Undoubtedly not! You're better off either avoiding a confrontation or conceding, especially on the smaller, less important points. And remember: you could lose an argument.

2. *Show respect for other people's opinions; never tell them that they are wrong.* Even if a person is actually wrong, saying "You're wrong, and I'm going to tell you why" will never influence her or him to admit the error. Instead, say something like this: "I might be mistaken in my opinions, but I disagree with you. Can we talk about our differences?"

3. *If you are wrong, admit your error quickly and emphatically.* An odd thing happens when you criticize yourself before someone else does. Frequently, the other person forgets all about blaming you and defends you instead.

4. *Begin in a friendly way.* If someone steams toward you and begins yelling, will you listen? Probably not. In fact, you will be either too scared to listen or so offended that you will go out of your way to thwart the person. You will be much more likely to go along with someone who seems to understand you and like you. Other people react the same way.

5. *Get other people saying "yes, yes" immediately.* As much as you can, make statements that the other person can agree with—especially at the beginning. Try to emphasize the similarities in your goals and characterize your differences as relating only to methods. Once people say no, they won't want to back down.

6. *Let other people do a great deal of the talking.* Many a salesperson tells a tale like this: "I had a presentation to make but couldn't talk. So I let my client talk, and he (or she) convinced himself." The reasons? First, people would rather talk about themselves than hear about you. Second, by listening, you learn about needs you may never have guessed.

7. *Let other people feel that the idea is theirs.* Would you rather get credit for a great idea or achieve the results intended by the idea? If you are more interested in results, plant suggestions in people's minds or ask them for advice.

8. *Try honestly to see things from other people's point of view.* People usually have a comprehensive set of reasons for their actions or beliefs. If you take the time to learn their reasons, you will encourage them to try to see your point of view too.

9. *Be sympathetic with other people's ideas and desires.* When blocked by seemingly petty complaints or strivings, try this approach: "I don't blame you for feeling the way you do. If I were you, I would undoubtedly feel the same way."

10. *Appeal to the nobler motives.* Most people want to be—and want to be thought of as—honest, fair, sincere, truthful, and so on. If you act on the assumption that they do embody all these noble ideals, you will usually reap positive results.

11. *Dramatize your ideas.* Unfortunately, plain facts—even the most relevant, important facts—are often not enough. But facts in the from of demonstrations, illustrations, examples, even vivid turns of speech do get people's attention. And once people are paying attention, they are open to the influence of facts.

12. *Throw down a challenge.* People want to excel and feel important. Therefore, they can often be motivated by an opportunity to show that they are winners.

These ideas, first published in 1936 in a book filled with anecdotes proving their value, have stood the test of time. In a nutshell, they represent the "you" attitude.

*Source:* Adapted from Dale Carnegie, *How to Win Friends and Influence People* (New York: Simon and Schuster [Pocket Books], 1972), pp. 111–185.

1. Dale Carnegie's ideas have been popular since their original publication in 1936. Why do you suppose this is so?

2. How might you let someone feel that an idea is his or hers instead of yours?

## DEVELOP YOUR WORD POWER

*Spelling Challenge*    Identify the misspelled word in each of the following sentences, and spell it correctly in the space provided.  If all the words in a sentence are spelled correctly, write *C* in the space.

_____    1.    How many commitee members are from Purchasing?

_____    2.    Add the colum of figures twice to make sure the total is right.

_____    3.    Mr. Nguyen's choise is the brown chair.

_____    4.    All your purchases are chargible when you have King credit.

_____    5.    He is certanly going to ask for a raise.

_____    6.    I would put it in the business category.

_____    7.    Current conditions are very changable.

_____    8.    Quality products are not cheep!

_____    9.    A new office manager has already been choisen.

_____    10.    I turned over all my comercial accounts to Suzanne.

*Vocabulary Challenge*    Match the words in the first column with the definitions in the second column.

_____    11.  conviction          A.  believability

_____    12.  credence            B.  formal introduction

_____    13.  credential          C.  standard of judgment

_____    14.  criterion           D.  evidence of authority

_____    15.  debut               E.  fixed belief

Circle the best definition of the highlighted word in each of the following sentences.

16.  Melissa **contends** that none of the sites is acceptable.

    A.   believes                B.  asserts                C.  suggests

17.  See if you can hold your **contentious** staff together long enough to finish the project.

    A.   quarrelsome            B.  prize-winning         C.  unmotivated

18.  Paul's conclusions were **contradictory**.

    A.   stubborn               B.  inconsistent          C.  unacceptable

19.  The jute pad was installed **contrary** to our wishes.

    A.   in accordance with     B.  beyond                 C.  against

20.  You have bought a **counterfeit** microchip that we did not produce.

    A.   ready-made             B.  fake                   C.  printed

Select one of these words to complete each of the following sentences, and write the word in the space provided.

| continual | continuous | credible | creditable | cursory |
| --- | --- | --- | --- | --- |

21.  The _____ roar of the air conditioners drowns out casual conversation.

22.  The district attorney cannot prosecute unless a _____ witness is found.

23. A _____ reading of the letter yielded no new information, so she reread it.

24. The team's fans formed a _____ line in front of the stadium, forcing delivery crews to detour to a side gate.

25. Considering your lack of experience, you have done a _____ job.

*Follow-up Word Study*    Check your answers at the end of this chapter. In the spaces below, write the words that you spelled or used incorrectly. (Use a separate piece of paper if you missed more than five words.) Then look up each word in your dictionary, and carefully study its spelling, pronunciation, definition, and history (etymology). Finally, to help fix the word in your memory, write it in a sentence.

Word                          Sentence

_____    _____

_____    _____

_____    _____

_____    _____

_____    _____

## CHECK YOUR ANSWERS

**Master Key Concepts**

I. audience
   A. information
   B. personal, practical, psychological

II. tone
   A. businesslike
   B. "you"
   C. positive
   D. credibility
   E. courtesy

III. company

**Quiz Yourself**

1. When you are faced with a vague assignment, try to get more information about the requester's needs by asking a few questions. Another good approach is to restate the request in more specific terms in order to get the other person to define his or her needs more precisely. A third approach is to ask about the assignment's priority. (p. 101)

2. One good way to check the thoroughness of your document is to check it for what reporters call the *five w's and one h*: *who, what, when, where, why, and how.* (p. 102)

3. To ensure the accuracy of a document, double-check to be certain that your organization is willing and able to honor any promises that you make to the reader. In addition, check for errors in fact or logic. Be sure that your sources are reliable; that your calculations are correct; that all times, dates, and places are right; and that your assumptions and conclusions are valid. (pp. 102-103)

4. To make a document as convenient as possible for the reader, keep it brief. Eliminate any ideas that are not directly related to your purpose as well as any unnecessary words or phrases. In

addition, use format devices that emphasize important ideas and make the document easy to scan: begin with a summary of key points, use plenty of headings, put important points in list format, put less-important information in appendixes, use charts and graphs.  (p. 104)

5. To use an "appeal to emotion," you must make your ideas vivid and appealing to the reader.  For example, you might associate your message with an attractive image or use facts that have dramatic impact.  Or you might use exciting visual aids or incorporate material with human interest: quotations, interviews, examples from real life.  (p. 105)

6. To achieve a businesslike tone,
    a. Don't be too familiar.
    b. Don't be excessive in your use of humor.
    c. Don't flatter the reader too much.
    d. Don't preach to the reader.
    e. Don't brag.  (pp. 107-108)

7. When you present your message in terms of the reader's wishes, interests, hopes, and preferences, you are using the "you" attitude.  (p. 108)

8. To emphasize the positive aspects of your message,
    a. Stress what is or will be, not what isn't or won't be.
    b. In offering criticism or advice, emphasize what the other person can do to improve.
    c. Point out how the reader will benefit from your message.
    d. Avoid words with negative connotations.
    e. Avoid superlatives and exaggerations.  (pp. 109-111)

9. You can demonstrate your courtesy in the following ways:
    a. Use tactful language rather than blunt terms.
    b. Adjust your language so that it is appropriate to the relationship between you and the reader.
    c. Do or say something special to demonstrate your personal interest in the reader.
    d. Be prompt in your correspondence.  (pp. 112-113)

10. Writing for the company means that you must handle your correspondence in a way that is compatible with the interests and style of the organization.  Your own personality and views should be adjusted to project an image that is acceptable to the company, and your way of expressing yourself should conform to the company's wishes.  (pp. 113-115)

## Develop Your Word Power

| | | | | |
|---|---|---|---|---|
| 1. committee | 6. C | 11. E | 16. B | 21. continual |
| 2. column | 7. changeable | 12. A | 17. A | 22. credible |
| 3. choice | 8. cheap | 13. D | 18. B | 23. cursory |
| 4. chargeable | 9. chosen | 14. C | 19. C | 24. continuous |
| 5. certainly | 10. commercial | 15. B | 20. B | 25. creditable |

**Chapter 6**

## SELECTING AND ORGANIZING IDEAS

The main point of Chapter 6 is that any message has more impact when it is based on carefully selected facts and has been organized to suit the audience and purpose. As you read the chapter, think about the various purposes of business messages and the organizational patterns that are most effective for each purpose. When you finish reading, see if you can classify the business messages that you receive according to their organizational patterns.

## MASTER KEY CONCEPTS

Use the following terms to fill the blanks in the outline. All terms are used, but none is used more than once.

| | | | |
|---|---|---|---|
| acceptable | central | outlining | reasoning |
| action | direct | purpose | routine |
| audience | disorganized | questions | subtopics |
| buffer | indirect | reaction | understood |

I. Messages may seem _____ (pp. 120-121) because the author takes too long to get to the point or includes irrelevant material, because ideas are presented in illogical or confusing order, or because necessary information is left out.

II. Good organization can be achieved by establishing the subject and _____ (p. 121) early in the message, by making sure that all the information included in the message is related to the subject and purpose, by grouping and sequencing the ideas logically, and by including all necessary information.

III. Good organization is important because it makes a message more effective.
   A. A well-organized message is more likely to be _____ (p. 122) in the intended way.
   B. A message can be organized to make it more _____ (p. 123), psychologically speaking, to the audience.
   C. Organizing a message before writing it makes the task much easier, especially if the task is to be shared with other people.

IV. Good organization can be achieved by taking two steps.
   A. The first step is to decide what to say: What is the purpose of communicating? Who will receive the message? What central idea will help get the message across?
   B. The second step is to decide how to say it: for letters, memos, and other brief messages, the direct approach puts the main idea first, the indirect approach puts the main idea later; for reports and long presentations, the informational approach focuses on _____ (p. 126) of the subject matter, the analytical approach focuses on logical arguments and the conclusions and recommendations derived from them.

V. _____ (p. 128) a message becomes much simpler when three basic steps are taken.

    A.  Define the purpose of communicating; only one purpose—the business goal—should have priority, and nothing should be committed to paper if there is no legitimate reason for it to be.

    B.  Analyze the _____ (p. 129); this task is much easier when the audience is familiar than when it is not.

    C.  Define the _____ (p. 130) idea of the message, which links your purpose with the audience's needs, interests, and attitudes.

VI.  Letters, memos, and other brief messages should be organized to correspond with the audience's probable _____ (p. 131) to the message: interested and willing, neutral or pleased, displeased, or uninterested or unwilling.

    A.  Direct requests, which are sent to audiences who will be interested in the message and willing to comply, take the _____ (pp. 131–132) approach in order to emphasize the main idea.

    B.  _____ (pp. 132–133) and good-news messages, which are sent to audiences who will have a neutral or pleased reaction, take the direct approach in order to emphasize the main idea or the good news.

    C.  Bad-news messages, which are sent to audiences who will be displeased, take the indirect approach in order to _____ (pp. 133–134) the bad news with information that is easier to accept.

    D.  Persuasive messages, which are sent to audiences who will be uninterested or unwilling to comply, take the _____ (pp. 134–135) approach in order to grab attention before addressing the main issue.

VII.  Longer messages, such as reports and presentations, should be organized to overcome two problems with length: more material for the audience to sort through and organize, and more opportunities for the audience to become bored, confused, or antagonistic.

    A.  Answer all the audience's key _____ (p. 136) using a mix of broad concepts and specific details so that both the rationale and the implications of your message come across.

    B.  Arrange the ideas in logical order—meaning the order that responds to the audience's questions: break the subject into subtopics when writing to inform, and focus on your _____ (p. 139) or the required _____ (p. 139) when writing to analyze a situation.

    C.  Prepare an outline to guide you in selecting ideas, choosing an organizational plan, and placing emphasis properly.

*Check your answers at the end of this chapter.*

## QUIZ YOURSELF

1. What are four common sources of disorganization in business writing?

2. What are the three basic advantages of a well-organized document?

3. The _____, or _____, approach puts the main idea first; the _____, or _____, approach puts the main idea later.

4. Briefly discuss the two basic approaches for organizing longer messages.

5. What four questions can you ask yourself to test the validity of your purpose?

6. Describe the four basic types of letters, memos, and other brief messages and explain how the audience is likely to react to each. Which basic organizational approach (direct or indirect) is best for each?

7. List a few typical examples of routine and good-news messages.

8. What is the best way to begin a bad-news letter?

9. What are the three basic rules of categorization?

10. How should you organize a long, analytical message for a receptive audience?

*Check your answers at the end of this chapter.*

## BUILD YOUR SKILLS:  HOW SHOULD THESE MESSAGES BE ORGANIZED?

For each of the messages described below, select one of the following four organizational plans:
  a. Direct approach for direct requests
  b. Direct approach for routine or good-news messages
  c. Indirect approach for bad-news messages
  d. Indirect approach for persuasive messages

Here are the situations that require some sort of communication. How should each message be organized?

1. You are the manager of a restaurant. A disgruntled customer has complained about the slow service at dinner on a recent evening. You are assuring the customer that you are concerned about the complaint and have taken appropriate action.

2. You are a market-research analyst who has been assigned to study the hospital-products industry. You are asking hospital administrators to allow you to interview them.

3. You are a buyer for a large department store. You are complaining to one of your suppliers about the quality of the last shipment of merchandise you received.

4. You, a stock broker, have recently moved from one brokerage firm to another. You are letting your clients know of the change and encouraging them to continue doing business with you at your new firm.

5. You have opened a gift store in a new shopping mall. Because your initial sales have been below expectations, you are unable to pay your rent on time. You are asking the shopping-center owner for an extension.

6. As the shipping clerk for a building-supply company, you are informing a customer that her order has been received and that her merchandise is being shipped according to her instructions.

7. You are making arrangements with a resort hotel for your firm's annual sales convention.

8. You have been asked to speak at a luncheon meeting of a professional association, but you are unable to accept and are declining the invitation.

## EXPAND YOUR KNOWLEDGE:  HOW TO TAP YOUR CREATIVITY

The greatest untapped resource in the world of business is the underused creative energy of the people in it.  Most people use only about one-fifth of their creativity.  Yet creative thinking brings about the changes most beneficial to society and to us all.  Fortunately, you can learn to think more creatively in only minutes—just by understanding how the creative process works.

What is the creative process?  It's just new ideas to solve problems, primarily by recombining the known into something original and different.  Whether the creative breakthrough is a poem, a painting, a business concept, or a scientific discovery, new ideas come about through a typical sequence.  The creative act involves these five steps, or "stages of thought":

1. Exploring the problem and gathering data on it
2. Reading and absorbing this information in your mind
3. Letting your unconscious mind consider the problem, review the data, and synthesize the solution
4. Giving birth to the new idea—"Eureka, I *have* it!"
5. Shaping and developing the idea to practical usefulness

Creative ability is not limited to a chosen few.  We all have it—or *can*, once we learn how to put these five steps to use.

Now that you understand the creative process, the following guidelines will help you put it to work:

- Write down the problem.  Do not rely on memory.
- Translate the problem into clear, simple language.
- If possible, translate the problem into figures, graphs, charts, or mathematical symbols.
- Search published sources for additional related data.
- Take notes and develop files on this data.
- Discuss the problem and possible solutions with others.
- Expand your thinking by using a checklist of things to think about.
- For a new perspective, try turning the problem upside down.
- If you feel frustrated, don't worry.  Relax.  Turn your attention to other matters.  Rest your mind.  Sleep.

- Take time to be by yourself. Shut out interruptions. Free yourself of trivial work and concerns.
- When the new idea is born, write it down.

*Source*: Adapted from Rudolf Flesch, *The Art of Clear Thinking* (New York: Harper & Row, 1951), pp. 138-148; Vincent W. Kafka, "Encourage the Use of Creative Energy," *Supervisory Management*, October 1975, pp. 32-35; Rudolf F. Sirny, "How's Your Managerial Momentum?" *Supervisory Management*, March 1976, pp. 18-26.

1. Here is a test of your creativity. Suppose that you are going into the food business. Your idea is to sell canned oranges preserved in juice, much like canned peaches or pears. Design a system for peeling the oranges, packing them in cans, labeling the cans, and packing the cans in cartons for shipment to grocery stores.

2. Creativity involves recombining the known into something new and different. To expand your creativity, develop a paragraph that logically ties together these apparently unrelated phrases:

   - Animal noises
   - A shoe factory
   - A little boy in fancy clothes
   - The scent of roses in the air

## DEVELOP YOUR WORD POWER

*Spelling Challenge*    Identify the misspelled word in each of the following sentences, and spell it correctly in the space provided. If all the words in a sentence are spelled correctly, write C in the space.

_____    1. A compitent secretary is an asset to any company.

_____    2. I cannot conceive of any product that everyone would buy.

_____    3. Be slow to condem and quick to praise.

_____    4. Is he concious of how poorly educated he sounds?

_____    5. Enthusiasm is contageous.

_____    6. I brought in a sample of their lotion for comparisen.

_____    7. We are compleatly out of that model but can get another one soon.

_____    8. How can you concentrate with all this construction going on?

_____    9. My consciense will not allow me to quit without two weeks' notice.

_____    10. Her work is consistant although not outstanding.

*Vocabulary Challenge*    Match the words in the first column with the definitions in the second column.

____ 11. defer            A. to put off
____ 12. deplete          B. to scatter
____ 13. deride           C. to misrepresent
____ 14. dispel           D. to scoff at
____ 15. distort          E. to decrease

Circle the best definition of the highlighted word in each of the following sentences.

16. Jack is a **deft** typist.

     A.  hard of hearing          B.  daffy                    C.  skillful

17. It is time to edit all the **defunct** policies out of the employee manual.

     A.  awkward                  B.  sanitized                C.  extinct

18. My position on opening a branch office is **diametrically** opposed to yours.

     A.  in some measure          B.  directly                 C.  firmly

19. It is hard to see the point in a report this **diffuse**.

     A.  wordy                    B.  mild                     C.  different

20. Her **disdain** for the junior accountants has created ill feeling in the office.

     A.  admiration               B.  extra work               C.  scorn

Select one of these words to complete each of the following sentences, and write the word in the space provided.

| **demise** | **dexterity** | **diagnosis** | **dilemma** | **dissonance** |
|---|---|---|---|---|

21. She was faced with the _____ of resigning or being fired.

22. The _____ with which you closed the deal was admirable.

23. The report is based on Hawkes & Associates' _____ of the company's ills.

24. A workplace characterized by _____ creates stress.

25. The _____ of our department left 20 people scrambling for jobs.

***Follow-up Word Study***   Check your answers at the end of this chapter.  In the spaces below, write the words that you spelled or used incorrectly.  (Use a separate piece of paper if you missed more than five words.)  Then look up each word in your dictionary, and carefully study its spelling, pronunciation, definition, and history (etymology).  Finally, to help fix the word in your memory, write it in a sentence.

Word                          Sentence

_____     _____

_____     _____

_____     _____

_____     _____

_____     _____

---

## CHECK YOUR ANSWERS

---

### Master Key Concepts

I. disorganized

II. purpose

III. A. understood
     B. acceptable

IV. B. subtopics

V. outlining
   B. audience
   C. central

VI. reaction
   A. direct
   B. routine
   C. buffer
   D. indirect

VII. A. questions
     B. reasoning,
        action

### Quiz Yourself

1. Business writing seems disorganized when the writer
   a. Takes too long to get to the point
   b. Includes irrelevant material
   c. Groups ideas in a confusing way
   d. Leaves out necessary information   (pp. 120-121)

2. A well-organized document has three basic advantages:
   a. The audience is more likely to understand the message if the document is well organized.
   b. Readers are more likely to respond in the intended way to a well-organized message.
   c. The writing job proceeds more efficiently if the writer has organized the message in advance.   (pp. 122-129)

3. The direct, or *deductive*, approach puts the main idea first; the indirect, or *inductive*, approach puts the main idea later.   (p. 127)

4. Longer messages are organized according to the purpose of the document. If the document is primarily informational, it should be organized around natural breakdowns (subtopics) of the subject matter to be described. If the document is primarily analytical, it should be organized around logical arguments designed to lead the audience to certain conclusions or recommended actions. (p. 126)

5. Ask yourself these questions to test the validity of your purpose:
   a. Do I have a clear and practical purpose in writing?
   b. Am I the right person to be sending this document?
   c. Is this the right time to be writing?
   d. Can a written communication meet the need, or would oral communication be better?   (p. 129)

6. Here are the four most common types of brief messages, the reader's most likely reaction to each, and the best organizational approach for each:
   a. A direct request is a simple, routine inquiry. The recipient is likely to be interested and willing. Use the direct approach.
   b. A routine message provides basic, everyday information. The audience is likely to be neutral, interested, or pleased. Use the direct approach.
   c. A bad-news message conveys disappointing information. The audience is likely to be displeased. Use the indirect approach.
   d. A persuasive message asks the audience to do something that will benefit the sender. The audience may be uninterested in complying or unwilling to comply. Use the indirect approach. (p. 131)

7. Typical routine and good-news messages include
    a. Information provided by an organization about itself, its personnel, or its products
    b. Favorable replies to requests
    c. Notice that an order is being filled or an adjustment is being made
    d. Credit approvals
    e. Pleasant announcements   (p. 132)

8. Begin a bad-news letter with a neutral statement (buffer) that provides a transition to the disappointing information.   (p. 133)

9. The three basic rules of categorization are as follows:
    a. Every item in a given category has to be the same kind of thing.
    b. The categories have to be mutually exclusive.
    c. The categories have to be collectively exhaustive.   (p. 138)

10. The best way to organize a long, analytical report for a receptive audience is to use conclusions or recommendations as the main divisions of thought.   (p. 140)

## Develop Your Word Power

| | | | | |
|---|---|---|---|---|
| 1. competent | 6. comparison | 11. A | 16. C | 21. dilemma |
| 2. C | 7. completely | 12. E | 17. C | 22. dexterity |
| 3. condemn | 8. C | 13. D | 18. B | 23. diagnosis |
| 4. conscious | 9. conscience | 14. B | 19. A | 24. dissonance |
| 5. contagious | 10. consistent | 15. C | 20. C | 25. demise |

## WRITING DIRECT REQUESTS

The main point of Chapter 7 is that direct requests are most likely to yield the desired result and to leave the desired impression on the audience when they are organized according to the direct plan. As you read the chapter, observe how a single pattern—main idea, explanation, courteous close—can effectively be applied to many situations. When you finish reading, try to apply the direct plan to some of the direct requests that you make.

### MASTER KEY CONCEPTS

Use the following terms to fill the blanks in the outline. All terms are used, but none is used more than once.

| | | | |
|---|---|---|---|
| adjustment | direct | memo | qualifications |
| advertisements | discrimination | middle | reference |
| credit | goodwill | purchase | routine |
| customers | letter | | |

I. _____ (p. 150) requests are meant to elicit some action or information from an interested and willing audience.
   A. Begin with a clear statement of the most important question or idea, specifying the exact nature and scope of your request.
   B. Use the _____ (p. 151) section to explain why you are making the request, couching your explanation in terms that show how the audience will benefit by complying.
   C. Conclude with a courteous expression of _____ (p. 151) and a specific request for action, complete with any time limits that apply.

II. In essence, a simple inquiry says this is what I want to know, why I want to know, and why it may be in your interest to tell me.
   A. People write inquiries to businesses in response to _____ (p. 152) or to get answers to specific questions.
   B. Businesses often send inquiry letters to _____ (p. 153) as a means of reestablishing a relationship; in addition to trying to find out why a customer hasn't been more active, the purpose of such a letter is to gently remind the customer that the company values his, her, or its business.
   C. Inquiries to employees, generally written in _____ (p. 154) format, streamline the process of communicating with many people but still help employees feel that they are involved in the decision-making process.

III. For placing orders, the direct plan takes on many of the characteristics of a well-designed order form: an offer to _____ (pp. 155-156) the goods, a complete description of the goods being ordered, a delivery and billing address, payment details, and a courteous close that suggests some future reader benefit.

IV. A request for _____ (p. 158) action may have a significant effect on an organization's relationships with customers, clients, suppliers, and shareholders.

    A. People outside the organization are often asked to do something—attend a meeting, return an information card, endorse a document, confirm an address, supplement information on an order; a brief form letter is sometimes adequate for this purpose.

    B. Requests for action from someone within the organization may be written in memo format but should still make the desired action clear, appealing, and easy.

V. A request for a minor, matter-of-course claim or _____ (pp. 160–163) may follow the direct plan as long as the tone is positive and unemotional and sufficient detail is provided.

VI. The direct plan, in standard _____ (pp. 163–165) or memo format, may be used to issue invitations; invitations may also be laid out more imaginatively.

VII. The direct approach is used for routine _____ (pp. 166–167) applications, although a standardized application form is sometimes used by the creditor; in addition, businesses applying for credit should supply a financial statement and perhaps a balance sheet.

VIII. Letters requesting information about a person's _____ (p. 169) for a job, promotion, scholarship, club membership, or credit card may also follow the direct plan.

    A. Before using someone's name as a _____ (pp. 168–169), you should write a direct request seeking permission to do so; remind the reader of the connection between you.

    B. A letter requesting information about an applicant should follow the direct plan; however, because of _____ (p. 169) laws, you should be careful to ask about only those characteristics related to the job or credit being sought and to reassure the reader that the information will be kept confidential.

*Check your answers at the end of this chapter.*

## QUIZ YOURSELF

1. Briefly explain the organizational plan for a direct request.

2. What type of information should be included in the middle section of a direct request?

3. Why might a business send a simple inquiry to its customers?

4. When an inquiry is written in memo format to employees of the company, how should it be organized?

5. In placing an order for goods, what basic facts should you include?

6. What are some of the reasons why a business might request routine action from people outside the company?

7. What type of information could you include to document a claim or request for an adjustment?

8. What details should be included in an invitation?

9. What information do you need to supply in applying for personal credit?

10. How should you organize a letter asking a former professor to serve as a reference for you?

*Check your answers at the end of this chapter.*

## BUILD YOUR SKILLS:  WHAT'S WRONG WITH THIS DIRECT REQUEST?

Someone representing the publisher of a free monthly bulletin for educators has drafted this letter. What could he do to make it more effective as a direct request?

May 7, 1986

Ms. Betty Morrison
17 Meadow Lane
Bridgewater, MA 02324

Dear Ms. Morrison:

As a reader of *Know-It-Now*, you can take advantage of varied articles on current trends and events in education.  Right now we are updating our mailing list; we hope that you'll be able to take time to help us in this important endeavor.  It should not be too time consuming.

If we are to keep sending you our publication each month, we must ask you to fill out the enclosed card.  Please mail it to us relatively soon.

Sincerely,

Jason Bettancourt
Circulation Department

JB/ta

## EXPAND YOUR KNOWLEDGE:  MEEK PERSON'S GUIDE TO ASKING FOR HELP

Nobody is self-sufficient.  In the world of business, checking references, requesting routine action, filing claims and adjustments, and inquiring about people, products, or services all qualify as asking others for help.  But maybe asking others for help is difficult for you.  Do any of the following views sound like yours?  If so, read the internal dialogs that come after them to learn how you can assert yourself —and ask for help without guilt or discomfort.

- *If I ask someone for a favor, I am imposing on him or her.*  Not true.  I am imposing only if I believe that the person doesn't have the right to deny my request for help—or if I do not allow him or her to do so.  I am also imposing if my request represents an undue inconvenience.  As long as I know the other person has the freedom to say no, and as long as my request isn't overly inconveniencing, I have the right to make it.

- *If I ask for help, the other person will not be able to say no even if he or she wants to.*  People are likely to act in their own best interests.  If I am not sure that another person really wants to help me, I can always ask whether he or she prefers that I ask someone else.  If I expect to behave assertively in making requests, I must assume that others can assertively refuse my requests if they want to.

- *If I ask for help, the other person should realize that I really need it—and should help me.*  People are free to grant or to refuse my requests.  They are not obligated to help me.  All I can do is ask for help and indicate why I need it.  If they say no, I may indicate my disappointment, but I should not try to pressure them to comply.

- *If I ask for and receive a favor from another, I will be obligated to do him or her an equal or greater favor in the future.*  A favor is granted or refused freely.  If I feel obligated, it is probably because I think I am not deserving or because I regard favors as social requirements that are not given freely.  I may feel grateful to one who does a favor for me, and I may want to do him or her a favor in return.  But in most cases, obligation is not written into a favor when it is granted.

*Source:*  Adapted from Merna Dee Galassi and John P. Galassi, *Assert Yourself* (New York:  Human Sciences Press, 1977), pp. 97-98.

1.  Like everything else, asking for help is easier if you have a little experience.  Try these role-playing exercises with your classmates to refine your skill in asking for favors:
    a.  You are a market-research representative who is studying consumer preferences in buying frozen waffles.  Your job is to call households to ask an adult resident to answer a series of questions about his or her attitudes toward frozen waffles.  Try to persuade prospective interviewees (members of your class) to give you 15 minutes of their time.
    b.  Your college or university has asked you to participate in a fundraising drive for the school.  You have been given a list of alumni to call and ask for contributions.  Practice your call.
    c.  You have decided to run for political office.  It is six months before the election, and you are trying to build a campaign organization by calling members of your political party and asking for their help.  What do you say?  Practice your appeal.

    After completing these exercises, are you any better at asking for help?  Does it become easier to face the possibility of rejection after you've talked with a few people?  Do you feel more confident in posing your request?  Does the content of your appeal become more effective?

2.  Some people are reluctant to ask for favors because they don't want to appear weak or dependent.  Are they being silly, or does asking for help actually make you more helpless?  Do people gain power over you when they grant you favors?  Discuss.

## DEVELOP YOUR WORD POWER

*Spelling Challenge*   Identify the misspelled word in each of the following sentences, and spell it correctly in the space provided.   If all the words in a sentence are spelled correctly, write *C* in the space.

| | | |
|---|---|---|
| _____ | 1. | How well do your figures corellate with theirs? |
| _____ | 2. | A curteous attitude helps maintain goodwill. |
| _____ | 3. | Their debt may exceed their ability to repay. |
| _____ | 4. | Do not be decieved by their expressions of friendship. |
| _____ | 5. | With prior permission, you can conduct a controled burn. |
| _____ | 6. | When you finish typing today's correspondance, file these. |
| _____ | 7. | He gets angry whenever he hears any critisism. |
| _____ | 8. | All final desicions on marketing are made by Beth Bryant. |
| _____ | 9. | Please make an appointment for a time convenent to you. |
| _____ | 10. | I will take complete responsibility for any dificiency. |

*Vocabulary Challenge*   Match the words in the first column with the definitions in the second column.

| | | |
|---|---|---|
| \_\_\_\_\_ | 11. divert | A. to trespass |
| \_\_\_\_\_ | 12. emit | B. to deflect |
| \_\_\_\_\_ | 13. emulate | C. to try to equal or excel |
| \_\_\_\_\_ | 14. encroach | D. to intensify |
| \_\_\_\_\_ | 15. enhance | E. to send forth |

Circle the best definition of the highlighted word in each of the following sentences.

16. Investors and farmers should **diversify** to minimize risk.

    A.  branch out          B.  insure themselves          C.  plan

17. The **diversity** of the audience made analysis of their needs difficult.

    A.  restlessness          B.  hostility          C.  heterogeneity

18. The "just-in-time" inventory system aims to increase **efficiency**.

    A.  profits          B.  morale          C.  effectiveness

19. Rick's **élan** is an asset to his sales career.

    A.  dash          B.  luxury automobile          C.  good looks

20. The office staff turned out **en masse** to wish her good luck in her new job.

    A.  in a party mood          B.  after work          C.  as a group

Select one of these words to complete each of the following sentences, and write the word in the space provided.

   **divisive**          **dogmatic**          **dynamic**          **efficacious**          **eloquent**

21. Jane's _____, energetic presentation generated enthusiasm for the new selling season.

22. The federation's _____ appeal conveyed powerful images of human suffering.

23. Try to avoid being _____ in meetings; let others share their opinions too.

24. Promoting from within is sometimes _____ but sometimes beneficial.

25. Terry Lee's group is well known for its _____, results-oriented approach.

**Follow-up Word Study**   Check your answers at the end of this chapter. In the spaces below, write the words that you spelled or used incorrectly. (Use a separate piece of paper if you missed more than five words.) Then look up each word in your dictionary, and carefully study its spelling, pronunciation, definition, and history (etymology). Finally, to help fix the word in your memory, write it in a sentence.

Word                          Sentence

_____    _____

_____    _____

_____    _____

_____    _____

_____    _____

_____

## CHECK YOUR ANSWERS

### Master Key Concepts

I. direct
   B.  middle
   C.  goodwill

II. A.  advertisements
    B.  customers
    C.  memo

III. purchase

IV. routine

V. adjustment

VI. letter

VII. credit

VIII.  qualifications
    A.  reference
    B.  discrimination

### Quiz Yourself

1. Direct requests have three basic parts:
   a. An opening that states the request or presents the main idea
   b. A middle section that explains the request or idea in more detail so the reader knows how to respond correctly
   c. A cordial closing that clearly states the desired action   (p. 149)

2. The middle section of a direct request should include any information that suggests a reader benefit. In addition, this section should cover facts about the subject of your request and your reason for making it.   (p. 151)

3. Businesses send simple inquiries to their customers in order to reestablish a relationship with them. For example, a business might write to encourage people to use their credit accounts more often or to comment on the store's products or services. This indication of interest on the business's part builds goodwill and may also yield useful information.   (p. 153)

4. Inquiries in memo format to employees follow the same direct plan as a letter. They begin with a statement of the purpose of the inquiry, followed by an explanation of the request and a final reminder of the desired action. (p. 154)

5. In placing an order for goods, you should include
   a. The date the order is placed
   b. A clear statement that you want to buy the merchandise
   c. A complete description of the items you want, including catalog number, quantity, name or brand, color, size, price, and total amount due
   d. The address where the goods should be shipped
   e. The billing address (if different from the shipping address)
   f. The method of shipment desired
   g. Payment details (pp. 155-157)

6. Businesses might make a routine request to outsiders for any of the following reasons:
   a. To invite them to attend a meeting
   b. To encourage them to return an information card
   c. To ask them to endorse a document
   d. To request that they confirm their address
   e. To ask them to provide additional information about an order (p. 158)

7. To document your claim or request for adjustment, you could send a copy of your sales slip or receipt, a statement of the date of the transaction, a description or photo of the merchandise, and any other relevant document. (p. 161)

8. An invitation should include the following details:
   a. Nature of the event
   b. Date and time
   c. Location (perhaps with directions or a map)
   d. Sponsor or host of the event
   e. Additional facts that might be helpful to the guests, such as cost, attire, schedule, and so on (p. 163)

9. To obtain personal credit, you must supply such information as the name of your company or employer, the length of your employment, the name of your bank, and addresses of businesses where you already have credit. (p. 166)

10. Use the direct approach when you are writing to ask a former professor to serve as a reference for you. Begin by stating the request, refreshing the professor's memory about your association. Explain why you are making the request and provide information about yourself that the professor can use to support a recommendation. Close with an expression of appreciation, as well as details about where the information should be sent. If appropriate, enclose a resume and a stamped, preaddressed envelope. (pp. 168-169)

## Develop Your Word Power

| | | | | |
|---|---|---|---|---|
| 1. correlate | 6. correspondence | 11. B | 16. A | 21. dynamic |
| 2. courteous | 7. criticism | 12. E | 17. C | 22. eloquent |
| 3. C | 8. decisions | 13. C | 18. C | 23. dogmatic |
| 4. deceived | 9. convenient | 14. A | 19. A | 24. divisive |
| 5. controlled | 10. deficiency | 15. D | 20. C | 25. efficacious |

# Chapter 8

## WRITING ROUTINE AND GOOD–NEWS MESSAGES

The main point of Chapter 8 is that the direct plan—often augmented by resale and sales-promotion material—can be used to organize routine and good-news messages. As you read the chapter, think about all the kinds of messages that fall into this category. When you finish reading, practice weaving subtle resale and sales-promotion material into your messages.

## MASTER KEY CONCEPTS

Use the following terms to fill the blanks in the outline. All terms are used, but none is used more than once.

| | | | |
|---|---|---|---|
| apologetic | direct | main | resale |
| benefits | good–news | objective | services |
| complaint | goodwill | positive | summarizes |
| customer | legally | promotion | |

I. The quickest, most effective way to write routine and _____ (p. 181) messages is to use the direct plan.
   A. By opening with a clear statement of the _____ (p. 181) point, you prepare the reader to understand the message.
   B. The middle and longest section of the message explains the details while reinforcing the _____ (p. 182) aspects of the message.
   C. The final section _____ (p. 183) the main point, courteously indicates what should happen next, and highlights reader _____ (p. 183).

II. When responding positively to an inquiry, use the _____ (p. 183) plan.
   A. An acknowledgment of an order, which provides an opportunity to build customer _____ (pp. 183-184), should assure the reader that the order is being filled, clarify all details of the transaction, and do a bit of selling through _____ (pp. 183-184) or sales promotion.
   B. In responding to questions about products or _____ (p. 184) when no sale is involved, the main goal is to answer all the questions fairly and honestly and to create a positive impression of the organization; when a potential sale is involved, an added goal is to emphasize the customer benefits of making a purchase and to close with a specific suggestion that will move the customer one step closer to the sale.
   C. When answering requests for a job or credit reference, be sure that the information you provide is accurate, _____ (p. 188), and relevant and that the recipient has a legitimate right to the information; you must be careful not to sound overly enthusiastic about the outstanding candidate and to either ignore the less attractive candidate's bad points or balance them against the good points.
   D. A routine request for action may be answered using the direct plan, but remember that a written reply represents an opportunity to promote the organization and constitutes a _____ (p. 190) binding promise.

III. When responding favorably to a _____ (p. 193) or claim for adjustment, your goal is to make the customer feel that the matter has been handled fairly.

   A. When the organization is at fault, avoid blaming any particular person or division, making lame excuses, or adopting an _____ (p. 193) tone; instead, emphasize that your organization tries to do a good job and is concerned about its reputation.

   B. When the _____ (p. 196) is at fault, courteously state that you will solve matters to the customer's satisfaction before politely explaining what went wrong so that the customer will not be disappointed again; be objective and avoid blame, so that the customer will feel like doing business with you again.

   C. When a third party is at fault, the best solution is usually to honor the claim but to offer at least a partial explanation of the problem to avoid giving the impression that your negligence caused it.

IV. Letters approving credit mark the beginning of a relationship with a customer, so they should build goodwill and offer resale or sales-_____ (p. 199) information as well as explain the terms of credit.

*Check your answers at the end of this chapter.*

## QUIZ YOURSELF

1. What are some of the occasions that call for routine and good-news messages?


2. What should you include in the middle section of a favorable reply to an order?



3. When customers have requested information about a product or service that they may want to buy and are expecting a reply, you can respond with a _____ sales letter that follows the _____ organizational plan.

4. What information should be included in a letter of recommendation?



5. If you make a false or malicious written statement that injures someone's reputation, you may be sued for _____.

6. In responding to a routine request for action from outside the company, remember that a letter written on letterhead stationery is a _____ document binding the company to fulfill any promises but that it also offers an opportunity to _____ a particular product or service or the organization in general.

7. What is the best organizational plan and format to use in granting employee requests?

8. Why should a company encourage its customers to complain?

9. What general impression should you try to convey in responding to claims when your company is at fault?

10. What details should be included in the middle section of a routine approval of a request for credit?

*Check your answers at the end of this chapter.*

### BUILD YOUR SKILLS:  WHAT'S WRONG WITH THIS GOOD–NEWS LETTER?

Someone representing the publisher of mass-market paperbacks has drafted this letter.  What could she do to make it more effective as a good-news message?

August 16, 1986

Mr. Fernando Hidalgo
The Readers' Nook Bookstore
28900 Alameda Way
Phoenix, AZ 85018

Dear Mr. Hidalgo:

This is in response to your query about advertising expenses and local promotion efforts. Our usual policy is to share advertising expenses on a 40-60 basis.

Our new line of Unicorn Romances debuts this month.  It would be in your best interest to display the entire line in a large rack on the counter by the cash register.  We believe that customers will be attracted to our books by a new display.  This display features a beam of light bouncing against the ceiling on what look like clouds.  It's an expensive display and hard to install, but we believe that it's worth it.

As far as your local promotion efforts go, they should get some assists from our national TV and radio campaign.  That's about the best we can offer, although for a short time we will participate in the local efforts you mentioned.  Making a rare exception, we will share expenses for this local campaign on a 50-50 basis.

Call us soon to set up the details for this campaign.

Sincerely,

Kathy Walker Reaban
Promotion Director

KWR/opp

## EXPAND YOUR KNOWLEDGE: GETTING THE WORD OUT

Large organizations with major news to spread often hire public-relations professionals to get the word out. But for lesser news or in smaller organizations, anyone with the skills and know-how may be asked to prepare a press release. Just in case you are someday asked to do this job, you should learn about the requirements for this special type of announcement.

Businesses issue press releases when they open new branches, change locations, appoint senior officers, publicize financial statements, introduce new products, offer open houses, provide new services, engage in public-spirited events, field athletic teams, and the like. Because advertisements are expensive, a free notice in the news section of a paper, periodical, or broadcast is a great bargain.

A press release is intended to appear or be announced exactly as written. Therefore, it should be written to match the style of the medium it is intended for. Furthermore, because no honest editor will run a press release that sounds like an advertisement, PR professionals often put any "plug" for the company's products in the final section of the release.

Press releases should be typewritten on plain 8½ x 11-inch paper—and double-spaced for print media, triple-spaced for electronic media. Otherwise, all press releases should look like this:

---

Davis & Moody Publicity

77 New Street

Englewood Cliffs, NJ 07632

Contact: Esther Moody

        201/909-3071

The name, affiliation, address, and phone number of the person who wrote the release and can provide more information is typed in the upper-left-hand corner.

        <u>Immediate Release</u>

Most news is released immediately.

Leave two inches here so the editor can insert a headline.

ENGLEWOOD CLIFFS, NEW JERSEY, NOV. 10, 1985--Continental Health Services, Inc., today announced the appointment of Rebecca R. Medich as vice president of marketing to succeed Wilson Snow when he retires on December 28.

        --more--

This release for a newspaper starts with a dateline and a summary (who, what, when, where, why) of the rest of the story.

Put a release on one page if you can, but indicate a second page like this.

---

CHS Apppointment        2-2-2-2

Ms. Medich is currently director of operations for Continental, a position she has held for the past six years. She is a graduate of the University of Florida and author of the best-selling book <u>Your Health First</u>.

Head the second page like this.

Do not split a paragraph; start the new page with a new paragraph.

Continental Health Services is a leading pro-
vider of home-health-care services, operating in
11 states east of the Mississippi River.

### # #

The "plug" is all in the last paragraph.

Proofread carefully.

Indicate the end of the release like this.

Notice that the content of this press release follows the customary pattern for a good-news letter: good news first, followed by details and a positive close.

Clean photocopies of a press release may be sent by first-class mail to radio and television news directors and to editors of magazines and weekly newspapers. But to impress the city editors of big daily newspapers, you might want to hand-deliver individually typed copies.

1. Over the next week or two, scan a daily newspaper and clip out any announcements that might have originated as press releases. What characteristics do these articles share in terms of style and organization?

2. Suppose that your school is having a Halloween carnival to raise money for worthwhile campus activities. The event will feature a haunted house, games, entertainment, food, and several contests, including a pumpkin toss, costume contest, and cake-decorating contest. The event will be held from 10:00 A.M. until 6:30 P.M. on Saturday, October 30, on the school's athletic field. You are in charge of publicity. Using your imagination to fill in any necessary details, prepare a press release for the local newspaper.

## DEVELOP YOUR WORD POWER

*Spelling Challenge*    Identify the misspelled word in each of the following sentences, and spell it correctly in the space provided. If all the words in a sentence are spelled correctly, write *C* in the space.

_____    1.    They are definetly planning to attend the meeting on the 9th.

_____    2.    We are dependant on a small distributor for supplies of that item.

_____    3.    Our deluxe vacation package includes a stay at one of the most desire-able resorts.

_____    4.    You will not be dissappointed with your purchase.

_____    5.    The last quarter was disasterous, but sales are improving.

_____    6.    I have no dout that Hal will do a good job.

_____    7.    After deducting operating expenses, you are left with a defecit.

_____    8.    Read the discription of all available modifications on page 3.

_____    9.    Every office worker should have access to a dictionery.

_____    10.    Our goal is to limit the number of disatisfied customers.

*Vocabulary Challenge*    Match the words in the first column with the definitions in the second column.

_____    11.    enumeration          A.    front

_____    12.    esprit de corps          B.    copy

_____ 13. extrovert      C. sense of union

_____ 14. facade      D. list

_____ 15. facsimile      E. outgoing person

Circle the best definition of the highlighted word in each of the following sentences.

16. The most **expedient** course is simply to repackage the unsold items.

     A. speediest      B. least expensive      C. advantageous

17. Gretchen **expended** a lot of energy putting out the first issue of the company newsletter.

     A. spent      B. wasted      C. invested

18. Can we somehow **exploit** our reputation for social responsibility?

     A. publicize      B. take advantage of      C. abuse

19. Her delivery of **extemporaneous** speeches is excellent.

     A. about current events      B. long and complicated      C. with few or no notes

20. His behavior can partially be excused on the basis of **extenuating** circumstances.

     A. a long list of      B. mitigating      C. embarrassing

Select one of these words to complete each of the following sentences, and write the word in the space provided.

**equable**      **equitable**      **esoteric**      **facetious**      **fallacious**

21. Peter's _____ disposition makes him a pleasure to work with.

22. The state will prosecute because Royal's solicitors made _____ statements.

23. Leave the more _____ references out of the bibliography for general readers.

24. The attorneys will negotiate _____ solutions to these disputes.

25. A serious meeting is no place for _____ remarks!

**Follow-up Word Study**    Check your answers at the end of this chapter. In the spaces below, write the words that you spelled or used incorrectly. (Use a separate piece of paper if you missed more than five words.) Then look up each word in your dictionary, and carefully study its spelling, pronunciation, definition, and history (etymology). Finally, to help fix the word in your memory, write it in a sentence.

Word             Sentence

_____    _____

_____    _____

_____    _____

_____    _____

_____    _____

---

## CHECK YOUR ANSWERS

---

### Master Key Concepts

I. good-news
   A. main
   B. positive
   C. summarizes, benefits

II. direct
   A. goodwill, resale
   B. services
   C. objective
   D. legally

III. complaint
   A. apologetic
   B. customer

IV. promotion

### Quiz Yourself

1. Routine and good-news messages are appropriate on such occasions as these:
   a. To respond to customers' questions about products, services, or orders
   b. To respond to credit requests
   c. To provide letters of recommendation for friends and employees
   d. To handle customer complaints
   e. To grant and acknowledge favors
   f. To accept invitations
   g. To offer congratulations
   h. To announce a new policy, condition, or event   (p. 181)

2. The middle section of a favorable reply to an order should provide a clear, accurate summary of the transaction: when the delivery may be expected; the cost of the merchandise, shipping, and taxes; and an explanation of problems that might have arisen. This section might also include a summary of your credit terms, as well as some resale or sales-promotion information. (p. 183)

3. When customers have requested information about a product or service that they may want to buy and are expecting a reply, you can respond with a *solicited* sales letter that follows the *direct* organizational plan.   (p. 186)

4. A letter of recommendation should include
   a. The name of the applicant
   b. The job or benefit that the applicant is seeking
   c. Whether the writer is answering a request or taking the initiative
   d. The nature of the relationship between the writer and the applicant
   e. Facts relevant to the position or benefit being sought
   f. The writer's overall evaluation of the applicant's suitability for the job or benefit being sought   (p. 188)

5. If you make a false or malicious written statement that injures someone's reputation, you may be sued for *libel.*   (p. 189)

6. In responding to a routine request for action from outside the company, remember that a letter written on letterhead stationery is a *legal* document binding the company to fulfill any promises but that it also offers an opportunity to *promote* a particular product or service or the organization in general.   (p. 190)

7. In granting an employee request, the company should write a memo that follows the standard good-news formula:
   a. State the good news.
   b. Provide necessary details.
   c. Close on a warm, courteous note. (p. 192)

8. Research indicates that most businesses have many more dissatisfied customers than they realize. A large percentage of the unhappy customers who do not bother to complain will never buy from the company again; furthermore, they will encourage their friends not to buy from the company either. However, the company can win back most of its dissatisfied customers by handling their problems quickly and well. The key is to encourage customers to complain and then respond to their complaints promptly and courteously. (p. 194)

9. In replying to claims when your company is at fault, try to restore the customer's faith in the firm. Instead of shifting the blame or offering lame excuses, emphasize your company's efforts to do a good job and imply that the error was unusual. (p. 193)

10. The middle section of a letter approving credit should include a full statement of the credit arrangements: the upper limit of the account, dates that bills are sent, possible arrangements for partial monthly payments, discounts for prompt payments, interest charges for unpaid balances, and due dates. (p. 199)

**Develop Your Word Power**

| | | | | |
|---|---|---|---|---|
| 1. definitely | 6. doubt | 11. D | 16. C | 21. equable |
| 2. dependent | 7. deficit | 12. C | 17. A | 22. fallacious |
| 3. desirable | 8. description | 13. E | 18. B | 23. esoteric |
| 4. disappointed | 9. dictionary | 14. A | 19. C | 24. equitable |
| 5. disastrous | 10. dissatisfied | 15. B | 20. B | 25. facetious |

# Chapter 9

## WRITING BAD-NEWS MESSAGES

The main point of Chapter 9 is that bad-news messages are most likely to be accepted when they follow the indirect plan. As you read the chapter, think about how embedding the bad news within positive buffers helps make it more acceptable. When you finish reading, think about bad news you have had to convey and how using the indirect approach might have helped ease the pain.

## MASTER KEY CONCEPTS

Use the following terms to fill the blanks in the outline. All terms are used, but none is used more than once.

| | | | |
|---|---|---|---|
| action | compromise | impersonal | rationale |
| alternatives | fair | indirect | routine |
| buffer | goodwill | positive | substitute |

I.  In presenting bad news, you have three objectives: to make the reader aware that the bad news is a firm decision, to convince the reader that your decision is _____ (p. 211) and reasonable, and to leave the reader with a _____ (p. 211) attitude toward you and your organization.

   A.  The indirect plan is a roundabout approach consisting of a _____ (pp. 211-215) that introduces the subject of the letter, establishes rapport with the reader, and provides a transition to the next section; a statement of the reasons supporting the negative decision; a statement of the bad news itself, couched in positive and _____ (pp. 211-215) language; and a positive close that is neither apologetic nor insincere.

   B.  The direct plan, which emphasizes the bad news itself, may be used when the bad news is _____ (p. 216), when you want to convey a forceful message, or when you know that the audience prefers candor.

II. In conveying bad news about an order, you should try to promote an eventual sale along the lines of the original order, make instructions and additional information as clear as possible, and keep the customer from losing interest by maintaining a positive tone.

   A.  When replying to an unclear order, either in writing or over the phone, the _____ (p. 216) approach allows you to confirm the original order and bolster the sale before explaining the problem.

   B.  When an ordered item is temporarily out of stock, you can either begin with the good news that part of the order is en route or begin by confirming the sale and commenting enthusiastically on the product before explaining why you are unable to ship the order; in either case, close on an upbeat note that reinforces the sale.

   C.  When you must _____ (p. 218) another product for the one ordered, you must write a letter that "sells" the alternative and gives the customer simple directions for ordering; if the substitute is more expensive, you must also convince the customer that it is better than the original item.

D. When you cannot fill the order at all, your goal is to say no but to be as helpful as possible.

E. When explaining that the customer must comply with your requirements before you can fill an order, you must present the reasons for the policy before stating the bad news; you should also make the required _____ (p. 220) as easy as possible, perhaps by enclosing a stamped, preaddressed envelope or supplying a toll-free phone number.

III. When conveying negative answers and information, your goal is to say no without losing the reader's _____ (p. 222); for this, the indirect plan is usually most effective, although the direct plan may also be used.

A. If bad news about products or services is routine and will not have an emotional impact on the reader, the direct approach is more efficient; but if the news will seriously affect the reader, it is better to state the _____ (p. 222) before the bad news.

B. When declining to cooperate with routine requests, you may either use the direct plan or use the indirect plan—with reasons before the bad news.

C. In declining invitations and requests for favors, the indirect plan is better for communicating with acquaintances and strangers; the direct plan, for communicating with friends.

IV. Refusing to extend credit is always a sensitive matter, so the best approach is to use the indirect plan to soften the bad news; be careful, however, to use as positive a tone as possible, to avoid writing anything that may be construed as a personal attack, and to emphasize the positive _____ (p. 226) that remain—such as the possibility that credit can be granted at some time in the future, the benefits of paying cash, and the attractive goods and services that your organization offers to all customers.

V. The indirect plan is most suitable for refusing adjustment of claims and complaints; emphasize how the problem could have been avoided, propose a _____ (p. 229), or state the refusal by implication instead of directly.

VI. Use the indirect plan for conveying unfavorable news about employment—such as negative performance reviews, refusals to job applicants, and termination notices—because the reader will almost certainly be emotionally involved.

VII. When you must release bad news about company operations or performance, it is best to briefly explain the bad news in the context of a positive thought—whether using the direct or indirect plan.

*Check your answers at the end of this chapter.*

## QUIZ YOURSELF

1. What are the four parts of a bad-news letter organized according to the indirect plan?

2. What are the characteristics of an effective buffer?

3. In presenting reasons for your negative decision, what two common evasive tactics should you avoid?

4. What are some of the techniques you might use to end a bad-news letter on a positive note?

5. When you are trying to convince a potential customer to buy a substitute product that is more expensive than the original item, what approach should you use?

6. Discuss when you should use the direct versus the indirect plan in turning down a routine request.

7. How would you vary a letter refusing to extend credit to two candidates—one with a long record of delinquent payment and one who is just starting out professionally and lacks a sufficient credit history to meet your requirements?

8. Briefly explain what your goal should be in writing a refusal to make an adjustment or respond to a complaint.

9. What three goals should you attempt to achieve in writing a termination letter?

10. What three types of situations require bad-news letters about company operations or performance?

*Check your answers at the end of this chapter.*

### BUILD YOUR SKILLS: WHAT'S WRONG WITH THIS BAD-NEWS LETTER?

Someone representing the distributor of lawn-care equipment has drafted this letter. What could he do to make it more effective as a bad-news message?

April 28, 1986

Mr. Luther Dodge
814 South Pinewood Drive
Kansas City, MO 64108

Dear Mr. Dodge:

We regret to inform you that the 22-inch Kleen-Kut mower and grass catcher is unavailable at this time.

However, we do expect to receive a shipment of mowers in a short time.  When they arrive, we'll send one off to you.

These mowers are excellent products, and we are sorry that you are unable to buy one right away.  Please accept our countless apologies for this delay.

While you're waiting for your lawn mower, you might want to flip through our catalog, available at any local hardware store.  Or ask us to send you one.  At any rate, nearly all of our catalog items are in stock and can usually be ordered easily.

Sincerely,

Michael Flynn
Customer Relations

MF/eg

## EXPAND YOUR KNOWLEDGE:  HOW TO SAY "OOPS" GRACEFULLY

Alas, even the best-intentioned companies sometimes make obvious mistakes.  If so, their best course is to try to maintain the trust of customers—by being honest.  Common sense should tell you, however, that it is possible to minimize the bad news by presenting it in as favorable a light as possible.

For example, through an error in its computer programming, the Moody State Bank has not kept separate records of tax-free and taxable interest in IRA and Keogh accounts.  On January 31, forms with the wrong information were sent to customers.  Some customers have called, so the bank's officers have decided to send out a letter explaining the error:

The interest income that you earn from your Individual Retirement Account (IRA) or from your Keogh account is not taxable until you begin drawing from these accounts.  Many of our customers have called in to ask why their IRA and Keogh interest income was included along with regular taxable interest on the 1099 forms sent to them.  They are posing a good question.

The buffer is informative and cooperative.

In an effort to process your accounts as efficiently as possible, Moody State Bank recently purchased a Compuplex-199 computer. It should enable us to give you even faster, more accurate service than before.

The source of the error is introduced in terms of how the change will benefit customers.

But we goofed! In our effort to get your 1099 form to you in January, we rushed the programming of the new computer. The result is that taxable and nontaxable interest income were erroneously combined and listed as a single figure.

The error is admitted in a positive context.

We (and the Compuplex-199) are working full speed to get your corrected 1099 form to you within a week.

The three-paragraph close details the action that is being taken to correct the error and offers help.

Meanwhile, if you have an IRA or a Keogh account, DO NOT declare as taxable interest the amount listed on the 1099s that you received from us last week. You will have your corrected figures in ample time to prepare your tax returns.

If you have any questions about this matter, you're welcome to call us at 675-2028. We will be glad to provide any further information you need.

The final paragraph assures the reader of direct, personal attention.

Although this letter contains negative news, the general tone is objective and supportive. The writer admits the bank's error but does not dwell on an apology. Most readers are likely to place as much confidence in the bank as ever.

1. Although saying "oops!" may occasionally be necessary, the cost of doing so is often considerable. To get an idea of the magnitude of how much it can cost to make and correct a simple mistake, consider the case of the Moody State Bank. Suppose that the bank has 750 customers with IRA and Keogh accounts. Roughly how much do you suppose it cost to send these customers the correct information on tax-free and taxable interest, assuming that three letters were eventually mailed to each account holder?

2. Try your hand at writing an "oops" letter, using the following situation as a point of departure. You are the marketing manager for a line of tricycles designed for three to five-year-old children. After shipping a new lot of the trikes to 1,500 retail outlets around the country, you have discovered that the entire lot was packaged without pedals. Write a letter to the retail store managers explaining the situation and outlining your solution.

## DEVELOP YOUR WORD POWER

*Spelling Challenge*    Identify the misspelled word in each of the following sentences, and spell it correctly in the space provided. If all the words in a sentence are spelled correctly, write C in the space.

_____    1.    Please send either a chrome or a brass easel.

_____    2.    Dr. Mueller empasized the importance of good employee relations.

_____    3.  We are equipt to serve all your ecological needs.

_____    4.  Yours is the eigth request for a commercial energy audit.

_____    5.  BASIC is one of the elementery programming languages.

_____    6.  How can we enhance the engineers' envirement?

_____    7.  Please elimenate all references to egg salad from the new menu.

_____    8.  We have just spent $1 million on new hospital equipment.

_____    9.  Their goal is apparently to embarass us at the annual meeting.

_____   10.  The emphisis in the brochure should be on elegance and style.

*Vocabulary Challenge*    Match the words in the first column with the definitions in the second column.

_____  11. fastidious          A. unprovoked

_____  12. formidable          B. demanding

_____  13. fortuitous          C. supposed

_____  14. gratuitous          D. fortunate

_____  15. hypothetical        E. intimidating

Circle the best definition of the highlighted word in each of the following sentences.

16. The other employees resented her tendency to **flaunt** her promotion.

   A.  mock              B.  brag about              C.  be dissatisfied with

17. So far, Ken has **floundered** in his new position.

   A.  prospered         B.  struggled              C.  failed

18. If she continues to **flout** the new rules, she will be fired.

   A.  scoff at          B.  enforce                C.  complain about

19. Our efforts to market the new product were **hampered** by a lack of funds.

   A.  aided             B.  harmed                 C.  impeded

20. I will not **hinder** your efforts to reorganize the department.

   A.  make fun of       B.  second-guess           C.  obstruct

Select one of these words to complete each of the following sentences, and write the word in the space provided.

| gaffe | gamut | harangue | hyperbole | hypertension |

21. The flower seeds we offer run the _____, from alyssum to zinnia.

22. We cannot afford another _____ like the one Barbara committed during the negotiations yesterday.

23. He suffers from _____ and should not work so hard.

24. Your sales letter will be much more convincing if you eliminate some of the _____.

25. The staff is demoralized and should not be subjected to another _____.

*Follow-up Word Study*    Check your answers at the end of this chapter.  In the spaces below, write the words that you spelled or used incorrectly.  (Use a separate piece of paper if you missed more than five words.)  Then look up each word in your dictionary, and carefully study its spelling, pronunciation, definition, and history (etymology).  Finally, to help fix the word in your memory, write it in a sentence.

Word                    Sentence

_____    _____

_____    _____

_____    _____

_____    _____

_____    _____

## CHECK YOUR ANSWERS

### Master Key Concepts

I. fair, positive
   A. buffer, impersonal
   B. routine

II. A. indirect
    C. substitute
    E. action

III. goodwill
     A. rationale
IV. alternatives
V. compromise

### Quiz Yourself

1. The four parts of a bad-news letter organized according to the indirect plan are
   a. A buffer
   b. Reasons supporting the negative decision
   c. A clear, diplomatic statement of the negative decision
   d. A helpful, friendly, positive close   (p. 211)

2. An effective buffer accomplishes several things:
   a. It starts the message pleasantly with a point agreeable to the reader.
   b. It introduces the subject of the letter.
   c. It expresses neither a yes nor a no.
   d. It provides a smooth transition to the second paragraph.   (p. 212)

3. In presenting reasons for your negative decision, try to avoid these evasive tactics:
   a. Hiding behind company policy
   b. Apologizing needlessly   (p. 213)

4. To end a bad-news letter on a positive note, you might conclude with
   a. A goodwill gesture
   b. A suggestion for action
   c. A look toward the future   (p. 215)

5. Send a letter "selling" the substitute product (but avoid the term *substitute*), and organize it to follow the indirect plan. Give simple directions for ordering. The section containing reasons should show that the more expensive substitute can do much more than the originally ordered item and is therefore worth a higher price. (p. 218)

6. In turning down a routine request, you should use the direct plan if the reader will not be emotionally involved with your response. But you should follow the indirect plan if you believe the reader may react emotionally to your refusal to grant the request. (p. 223)

7. The letter refusing credit to the chronically delinquent candidate should not offer any hope for future credit approval, whereas the letter to the young professional should point to the possibility of future credit business. (p. 226)

8. In refusing to make an adjustment or honor a complaint, your objective as a writer is to avoid accepting responsibility for the unfortunate situation and yet avoid blaming or accusing the customer. In the long run, your objective is to retain the customer's goodwill. (p. 228)

9. In writing a termination letter, you have three goals:
   a. To present the reasons for the termination
   b. To avoid statements that might involve the company in legal action
   c. To leave the relationship between your company and the terminated employee as favorable as possible (pp. 230-231)

10. These three situations might require bad-news letters about company operations or performance:
    a. A change in company policy that has a negative effect on the reader
    b. Performance problems in the company
    c. Controversial or unpopular company operations (p. 232)

## Develop Your Word Power

| | | | | |
|---|---|---|---|---|
| 1. C | 6. environment | 11. B | 16. B | 21. gamut |
| 2. emphasized | 7. eliminate | 12. E | 17. B | 22. gaffe |
| 3. equipped | 8. C | 13. D | 18. A | 23. hypertension |
| 4. eighth | 9. embarrass | 14. A | 19. C | 24. hyperbole |
| 5. elementary | 10. emphasis | 15. C | 20. C | 25. harangue |

# Chapter 10

## WRITING PERSUASIVE MESSAGES

The main point of Chapter 10 is that persuasive messages require a special form of the indirect plan—attention, interest, desire, action (AIDA)—and particular attention to the needs of the audience. As you read the chapter, think about how reader needs, benefits, and appeals are linked in persuasive messages. When you finish reading, analyze the strengths and weaknesses of some of the persuasive messages you have received and then try improving those that are weak.

## MASTER KEY CONCEPTS

Use the following terms to fill the blanks in the outline. All terms are used, but none is used more than once.

| | | | |
|---|---|---|---|
| **AIDA** | credibility | needs | routine |
| **beginning** | defensive | process | selling |
| **collection** | fair | reminder | ultimatum |
| **consumer** | funds | | |

I. Persuasion, an ongoing _____ (p. 243) of changing people's attitudes or influencing their actions, requires a strategy that will overcome the audience's lack of interest, unwillingness, skepticism, or hostility.
   A. Before you can write a persuasive message, you have to know the essential facts behind the message, you have to know about the audience's _____ (p. 243), and you have to know what you want to happen as a result of your letter.
   B. The _____ (pp. 245-247) plan, a form of indirect plan used specifically for persuasive messages, begins with a statement that grabs the audience's attention, develops interest by stressing how your information benefits the audience, builds desire by providing evidence directly related to your point, and ends by urging some easy, beneficial action.
   C. The task of appealing to the audience requires you to understand people's needs, to be able to enlist their emotions and logic, to convey _____ (pp. 247-250), and to choose words that convey what you mean without arousing any undesirable emotions.

II. A systematic approach is most useful in writing sales letters.
   A. The three steps involved in planning a sales letter are to determine the _____ (pp. 250-252) points (most attractive features) and _____ (pp. 251-254) benefits of your product, to define the demographic (socioeconomic) and psychographic (psychological) characteristics of the audience, and to plan the format and approach you should take.
   B. Several special techniques are used in preparing the copy for sales letters: getting attention by making the audience think about needs you might be able to fulfill; emphasizing the central selling point (the point that most distinguishes your product from that of the competition while still meeting the needs of potential buyers); highlighting the consumer benefits of buying your product by referring to them at the _____ (p. 255) and close of the letter; using action words; emphasizing price if it's one of your strong selling

points or deemphasizing a relatively high price; supporting your claims with sufficient evidence; and motivating action by being specific about the action you desire and making action easy.

    C. To enhance their effect, most sales letters are part of a carefully coordinated package of materials, and they are sent to a carefully selected list of potential customers.

III. Because the recipient of a persuasive request for a favor, _____ (p. 263), or information will receive nothing tangible in return, these letters are perhaps even more difficult to write than sales letters are; you should therefore take special care to highlight the direct and indirect benefits of complying with your request.

IV. In making a claim or request for adjustment to someone who you suspect will be hostile or skeptical, use the AIDA plan; take special care to be calm, logical, and cordial, and assume that the recipient will want to do the _____ (p. 266) thing.

V. Most people are interested in settling their debts as quickly as possible, but because credit is such an emotional area, _____ (p. 269) messages must be prepared with all the care lavished on other persuasive messages.

    A. People who cannot pay their bills generally feel _____ (p. 269); therefore, you must first try to neutralize their defensiveness by appealing to their better nature and then, if that approach doesn't bring results, turn to a negative appeal that points up the consequences of not acting.

    B. Collection letters are sent in an escalating sequence of messages, typically beginning with a _____ (p. 270) notification, proceeding to a routine _____ (p. 270), then a more personal inquiry, then a more demanding "urgent notice," and finally a businesslike _____ (pp. 272-273) that avoids malicious or defamatory statements.

*Check your answers at the end of this chapter.*

## QUIZ YOURSELF

1. Persuasive writers use many different plans to organize their messages, but the best known is the _____ plan: _____, _____, _____, and _____.

2. Briefly discuss the contents of the final section of a persuasive message.

3. What is the "hierarchy of needs," and how does it pertain to the creation of persuasive messages?

4. _____ are the most attractive features of a product or service; _____ are the particular advantages that buyers realize from those features.

5. What are some techniques for motivating action in a sales letter?

6. One type of direct-mail list is the _____, which is compiled by the company from the rolls of previous customers and even those who have inquired about the company's products or services.

7. When writing a persuasive request, you must take special care to highlight _____ and _____ benefits. _____ benefits might include a premium for someone who responds to a survey or a free membership to someone who makes a donation to an organization. _____ benefits might include the prestige of, say, giving free workshops to small businesses.

8. In writing a persuasive claim or request for adjustment, what tone should you take?


9. What are five legal actions you might take against someone who fails to respond to a series of collection letters?


10. The final step in the collection series is the _____.

*Check your answers at the end of this chapter.*


**BUILD YOUR SKILLS:  WHAT'S WRONG WITH THIS PERSUASIVE LETTER?**

A business student has drafted this letter.  What could she do to make it more effective as a persuasive message?

544 Collins Avenue
Apartment 6-G
Houston, TX 77077

January 10, 1986

Ms. Michelle Jacobs
Jacobs Consulting Agency
2366 Bakerfield Boulevard, Suite 608
Houston, TX 77079

Dear Ms. Jacobs:

Could you please tell me how I might obtain a copy of the results of the study of male executives' attitudes toward female executives?  In a recent talk you gave, as you'll probably remember, that study was mentioned.

I need this study for a term paper I'm writing.  Please send the information to the above address fairly soon.  If you know of any other such pertinent data, perhaps you could enclose that as well.

By the way, I really enjoyed your talk.  Thanks for all your help.

Sincerely,

Liz Raphael

**EXPAND YOUR KNOWLEDGE:  HOW TO INCREASE YOUR CREDIBILITY**

Business writing is effective only if the audience believes what you say.  How credible are you now?  To find out, answer the following questions.  Give yourself 1 point if your answer is *never*, 2 points for *seldom*, 3 points for *sometimes*, 4 points for *usually*, and 5 points for *always*.

- Do you promise to do something, and then let it slide by?
- Do you find yourself complaining a lot to others?
- Do you have difficulty getting others to pay attention to you?
- Do you focus on your own interests and point of view when presenting information to others?
- Do you make statements and later find out that some of your information is incorrect or write something before you are sure of all the facts?
- When something goes wrong, is your main response to apologize?

If your score is between 6 and 17, you are exceptionally credible.  Keep up the good work.  But if your score is between 18 and 30, you probably will find that you can improve with a little effort.

 To increase your credibility, observe these nine basic rules:

1. Organize and word your message so that it flows smoothly from point to point, projecting an image of strength and composure.

2. Inspire trust from the start by citing personal experiences and illustrations that underscore your character and competence.

3. Avoid not only outright falsehoods but also clever deceptions—statements that are literally true but misleading.

4. Convey a message that not only is true but also sounds true, as if you really believe in and care about what you are saying.  One way to achieve this goal is to understate rather than overstate your case.

5. Support your arguments with facts, which carry more weight than opinions.  Then audience members can make up their own minds.

6. Admit your mistakes.  Nothing enhances your credibility more than a reputation for owning up when you are wrong.

7. Target your message to the audience's needs, emotions, values, and goals.  Write to their point of view.

8. Use crisp, direct words and phrases that impart power and persuasiveness to your writing.

9. Avoid scare tactics and negativity.  Instead, when presenting a problem, offer one or more possible solutions.

*Source*:  Adapted from Judi Brownell, "Increasing Your Credibility," *Supervisory Management*, December 1982, pp. 31-36.

1. Name five public figures who have credibility and inspire confidence.  Why have you selected these people?

2. Is credibility a constant factor, or does an individual's credibility depend on the occasion and the audience?

## DEVELOP YOUR WORD POWER

***Spelling Challenge***    Identify the misspelled word in each of the following sentences, and spell it correctly in the space provided.  If all the words in a sentence are spelled correctly, write *C* in the space.

_____    1.    Amy excells at writing collection letters.

_____    2.    We are extremally grateful for all your help.

_____    3.    A fascinating program has been scheduled for Febuary.

_____    4.    Ye Olde Pet Shoppe is no longer in existance.

_____    5.    Before you incur any additional expence, talk to us.

_____    6.    Yes, I am familar with your financial services.

_____    7.    A full-fledged investigation is feasable but unnecessary.

_____    8.    I am especialy pleased with your latest recruiting trip.

_____    9.    The cost of supplies for the Boise office should not exceed $900.

_____    10.    With your expiriense, you should do well here.

***Vocabulary Challenge***    Match the words in the first column with the definitions in the second column.

_____  11.  incessant

_____  12.  incipient

_____  13.  incoherent

_____  14.  incongruous

_____  15.  inconspicuous

A.  rambling

B.  beginning

C.  not noticeable

D.  not harmonious

E.  without interruption

Circle the best definition of the highlighted word in each of the following sentences.

16.  Even after a day of work, his desk was **immaculate.**

A.  spotless          B.  buried          C.  polished

17.  His talent as a supervisor is to **impel** people to do their best.

A.  allow          B.  urge          C.  shame

18.  In a crowded office, it is all too easy to **impinge** on another's right to privacy.

A.  encroach          B.  presume upon          C.  take advantage of

19.  From the **inception** of this program, Pat has taken an active role.

A.  formulation          B.  outcome          C.  beginning

20.  You will **incur** Mr. Crane's displeasure if you lobby too hard for your own ideas.

A.  bring about          B.  increase          C.  face

Select one of these words to complete each of the following sentences, and write the word in the space provided.

**impending          impenetrable          impertinent          impervious          impulsive**

21.  She has a strong ego that is _____ to their insults.

## Chapter 11

## WRITING GOODWILL MESSAGES

The main point of Chapter 11 is that messages sent purely to reflect goodwill pay off in the long run. As you read the chapter, think about all the different types of goodwill messages that could be sent by a business. When you finish reading, see if you can find a reason for sending a goodwill message of your own, and then write one using the direct plan.

## MASTER KEY CONCEPTS

Use the following terms to fill the blanks in the outline. All terms are used, but none is used more than once.

| | | | |
|---|---|---|---|
| civic | direct | long-term | seasonal |
| condolence | goodwill | promotion | supplier |
| congratulation | greeting | sales | tone |

I.  A _____ (p. 285) message, a pleasant note intended to make the recipient feel good, may enhance a business relationship by building a bond of friendship.
    A.  To write a goodwill message with the proper _____ (pp. 286-288), focus on the recipient instead of yourself, make your compliments honest and sincere, and offer help or sales information with restraint.
    B.  An attractive and appropriate goodwill message would be organized according to the _____ (pp. 288-289) plan, would use a form of address appropriate to your relationship with the recipient, would be handwritten only if a letter of condolence, and would be sent on either special stationery, business letterhead, or plain paper.

II.  Letters of _____ (p. 290), which tell readers that you have noted their accomplishments and are happy about their success, are generally short and informal.
    A.  Sending a goodwill message to someone who has received a _____ (p. 290) or appointment will increase the recipient's pleasure and also call attention to your organization.
    B.  Noting business and _____ (pp. 290-291) accomplishments will also enhance your relationship with the recipient, especially if you mention specific facts.
    C.  Weddings, births, graduations, and competitive successes are all occasions that call for goodwill messages.

III.  A note of thanks or praise for a job well done is a great morale builder; a related message is the letter of _____ (p. 295), which expresses your appreciation for the unfortunate or the deceased.
    A.  A letter praising an employee by name and describing a specific accomplishment may become a part of the employee's personnel file and thereby provide support for promotions or raises.
    B.  Writing a note of thanks to a _____ (p. 292) who has provided a special product or service encourages further excellence.

C.   A grateful note of thanks to someone who has done you a special favor encourages further generosity and lets the person know how much you appreciated the help.

D.   A note of thanks for _____ (p. 294) support is also good for the business relationship.

E.   An expression of sympathy is difficult to write, but if prompt and positive, it helps ease the distress of someone who is suffering from health or business problems or from the death of a loved one.

IV.  Newcomers and long-time customers or suppliers all appreciate letters of _____ (p. 297).

A.   Letters of welcome to new employees and prospective customers get a new relationship off to a friendly start.

B.   _____ (p. 298) greetings are most often sent at holidays, but any reminder that you value a customer or supplier is appreciated, as long as it does not bear a direct _____ (p. 299) message.

*Check your answers at the end of this chapter.*

## QUIZ YOURSELF

1. What is the appropriate tone for a goodwill message, and what are some of the ways of achieving this tone?

2. Discuss the use of sales material in goodwill messages.

3. Both _____ and _____ formats can be used in writing goodwill messages, depending on the kind of message you are sending and the intended recipient. Condolences are always in _____ format, as are messages sent anywhere outside your firm. If you are sending mail to a fellow employee's home, put it in _____ format, but interoffice communications may be put into _____ format.

4. What form of address should you use in a goodwill message?

5. On what three occasions might you send a letter of congratulation to a customer or business associate?

6. In what circumstances might it be appropriate to send a form letter congratulating a person on her or his personal achievements?

7. In writing a thank-you note, should you show your gratitude by offering to do something for the reader in return?  Why or why not?

8. Discuss some of the "dos" and "don'ts" in writing letters of condolence.

9. What type of information might be included in a letter welcoming a new employee to the company?

10. What approach should a company with a limited budget take toward seasonal greetings to customers?

*Check your answers at the end of this chapter.*

### BUILD YOUR SKILLS:  WHAT'S WRONG WITH THIS GOODWILL LETTER?

A representative of a computer company has drafted this letter.  What could he do to make it more effective as a goodwill message?

February 18, 1986

Mr. Ralph Teagarden
Chief of Program Design
Interdata Software
100 Ives Dairy Road
Chapel Hill, NC 27514

Dear Mr. Teagarden:

This letter is to inform you that the recent reception given by you for our programmers was well received.  They liked Interdata Software and the Speedit Editor, which was developed by you.

You will, I trust, accept our appreciation for this assistance.

Cordially yours,

Gerald MacKenzie
Vice-President, Systems

GMK/bn

## EXPAND YOUR KNOWLEDGE:  A "MAGIC" FORMULA FOR BUSINESS SUCCESS

Joe Girard has sold more new cars and trucks, for 11 years running, than any other human being.  In fact, in a typical year Joe sells more than twice as many vehicles as anybody else.  In explaining his secret of success, Joe says, "I send out over 13,000 cards every month."

Joe's magic is the same magic employed by many successful companies.  It is simply service, overpowering service, especially after-sales service.  Joe notes, "I do something that a lot of salespeople don't and that's believe that the sale really begins *after* the sale—not before.  The customer isn't even out the door, and my son has already made up a thank-you note."  A year later, Joe might intercede personally with the service manager on behalf of his customer.  Meanwhile, he keeps the communications flowing.

Joe's customers won't forget him once they buy a car from him; he won't let them!  Every month throughout the year, they get a letter from him.  It arrives in a plain envelope, always a different size or color.  "It doesn't look like direct mail.  And they open it up and the front of it reads, 'I like you.' Inside it says 'Happy New Year from Joe Girard.' "  He sends a card in February to wish customers a "Happy George Washington's Birthday."  In March it's "Happy St. Patrick's Day."  They love the cards, Joe boasts:  "You should hear the comments I get on them."

Out of context, Joe's 13,000 cards sound like just another sales gimmick.  But like the top companies, Joe seems genuinely to care.  Says Joe:  "The great restaurants in the country have love and care coming out of their kitchens, and when I sell cars, my customers are going to leave with the same feeling they'll get when they walk out of a great restaurant.  My customers are not," he says, "an interruption or pain in the neck.  They are my bread and butter."

*Source*:  Adapted from Thomas J. Peters and Robert H. Waterman, Jr., *In Search of Excellence* (New York:  Harper & Row, 1982), pp. 157-159.

1.  How could you use Joe Girard's technique in your intended career?

2.  Sending 13,000 cards every month is an expensive proposition, even though the cost is deductible as a business expense.  Do you think that Joe could achieve the same effect by sending the cards less frequently?

## DEVELOP YOUR WORD POWER

*Spelling Challenge*    Identify the misspelled word in each of the following sentences, and spell it correctly in the space provided.  If all the words in a sentence are spelled correctly, write *C* in the space.

| | |
|---|---|
| _____ | 1.   We communicate with our foren offices via Telex. |
| _____ | 2.   Sandra Hayes is the fourth factory representative we have had. |
| _____ | 3.   Take a vacation that fulfils all your dreams! |
| _____ | 4.   In the annual report, you can generalise about our problems. |
| _____ | 5.   Can you garantee delivery by May 1? |
| _____ | 6.   This photograph was taken from a heighth of 200 feet. |
| _____ | 7.   Over fourty people have applied for the clerical position. |
| _____ | 8.   Your new camera is frajel, so treat it gently. |
| _____ | 9.   The federal goverment requires us to submit several reports. |
| _____ | 10.   Guard against auto theft with a Lookout alarm. |

*Vocabulary Challenge*    Match the words in the first column with the definitions in the second column.

| | |
|---|---|
| _____ 11. induce | A. to provoke |
| _____ 12. infuse | B. to mediate |
| _____ 13. instigate | C. to insert |
| _____ 14. intercede | D. to cause |
| _____ 15. interject | E. to instill |

Circle the best definition of the highlighted word in each of the following sentences.

16. When I think of summer, I have an **indelible** image of blue and white.

    A. strong            B. inappropriate            C. unerasable

17. We might be able to stop the **innuendo** by making a public statement.

    A. indirect criticism            B. competition            C. investigation process

18. Mr. Billings spends an **inordinate** amount of time on the telephone.

    A. excessive            B. unmeasurable            C. unauthorized

19. Can **insipid** conclusions support strong recommendations?

    A. faulty            B. bland            C. brilliant

20. We are **insolvent** and cannot meet our obligations.

    A. inebriated            B. puzzled            C. bankrupt

Select one of these words to complete each of the following sentences, and write the word in the space provided.

**ingenious**        **ingenuous**        **insatiable**        **interminable**        **intermittent**

21. Because she is so sincere and _____, she is able to calm angry people.

22. An _____ beep is probably more effective than a steady tone.

23. New DinnerTime frozen entrees are big enough for even _____ appetites.

24. She came up with an _____ solution to the problem that I had never thought of.

25. His _____ quest for a "hot deal" is finally beginning to irritate me.

*Follow-up Word Study*    Check your answers at the end of this chapter. In the spaces below, write the words that you spelled or used incorrectly. (Use a separate piece of paper if you missed more than five words.) Then look up each word in your dictionary, and carefully study its spelling, pronunciation, definition, and history (etymology). Finally, to help fix the word in your memory, write it in a sentence.

Word                    Sentence

_____    _____

_____    _____

_____    _____

_____    _____

# CHECK YOUR ANSWERS

## Master Key Concepts

I. goodwill
   A. tone
   B. direct

II. congratulation
   A. promotion
   B. civic

III. condolence
   B. supplier
   D. long-term

IV. greeting
   B. seasonal, sales

## Quiz Yourself

1. Goodwill messages should have a warm, sincere, and friendly tone. To achieve this tone, adopt the "you" attitude, focusing on the audience's feelings and interests rather than on your own. Generally, you should keep the message short and relatively casual. Avoid exaggeration, and back up any compliments with specific points that demonstrate your sincerity. (p. 286)

2. For the most part, you should avoid sales material in goodwill messages, because your basic purpose is to make the recipient feel good, not to sell products. If you include overt sales material, the recipient may feel that you are manipulating her or him. The only time to use sales material in a goodwill message is if you can be of particular service or want to resell the recipient on your company's product or service. If you do add a sales pitch, be sure that it takes a back seat to the goodwill message. (p. 288)

3. Both *memo* and *letter* formats can be used in writing goodwill messages, depending on the kind of message you are sending and the intended recipient. Condolences are always in *letter* format, as are messages sent anywhere outside your firm. If you are sending mail to a fellow employee's home, put it in *letter* format, but interoffice communications may be put into *memo* format. (p. 288)

4. The best salutation for a goodwill message uses the form of address you would ordinarily use in conversation with the person. If you are friends or close associates, use the individual's first name—"Dear Mary." However, if you are not acquainted with the reader or know him or her only slightly, say "Dear Mr./Ms./Miss/Mrs. ———." (p. 289)

5. You might want to send a letter of congratulation to a customer or business associate to recognize
   a. A promotion or an appointment
   b. A business or civic accomplishment
   c. A personal achievement or event (pp. 290-291)

6. Some companies develop a mailing list of potential customers by assigning an employee to clip newspaper announcements of births, engagements, weddings, and graduations. The company then sends a copy of the announcement with a brief form letter of congratulation to the person. This simple technique builds goodwill, even though the sender and the reader have never met. (p. 291)

7. Generally, you should avoid offering to do something to prove your gratitude to a person you are thanking. Instead of trying to "even the score," focus on the individual's good deed and keep yourself in the background. (p. 293)

8. In writing letters of condolence, remember these pointers:
   a. Start with a statement of sympathy.
   b. Emphasize the positive.
   c. Convey your concern.
   d. Be supportive.
   e. Add a reassuring note.
   f. Close considerately.
   g. Be warm and genuine.
   h. Write with restraint.
   i. Don't reminisce at length.
   j. Don't quote poetic passages.
   k. Be tactful.
   l. Don't strive for eloquence.
   m. Accept the inevitable.
   n. Don't put it off.
   o. Offer help, if appropriate. (p. 296)

9. A letter of welcome to a new employee might include reassurances about first-day details or a description of what the employee might expect to find on starting work. Such a letter might also include a few words to show that the company is looking forward to having the new employee join the firm. (p. 297)

10. A company on a limited budget should send its seasonal greetings when they will have the greatest impact. In general, the company might want to avoid sending messages during the winter holidays, when people receive many other cards. A note at Easter or the Fourth of July might have more impact. If possible, the greeting should be tied in with a holiday that relates to the company's products or services. For example, a florist might send greetings around Valentine's Day, and a stationery store might send messages in April to coincide with National Secretary's Week. (p. 298)

## Develop Your Word Power

| | | | | |
|---|---|---|---|---|
| 1. foreign | 6. height | 11. D | 16. C | 21. ingenuous |
| 2. C | 7. forty | 12. E | 17. A | 22. intermittent |
| 3. fulfills | 8. fragile | 13. A | 18. A | 23. insatiable |
| 4. generalize | 9. government | 14. B | 19. B | 24. ingenious |
| 5. guarantee | 10. C | 15. C | 20. C | 25. interminable |

# Chapter 12

## WRITING RESUMES AND APPLICATION LETTERS

The main point of Chapter 12 is that a properly prepared resume and application letter are essential to your search for a job. As you read the chapter, think about how both the resume and the application letter are constructed to "sell" you to potential employers. When you finish reading, analyze your own career preferences and then write a resume and a model application letter that can help you get the job you want.

## MASTER KEY CONCEPTS

Use the following terms to fill the blanks in the outline. All terms are used, but none is used more than once.

| | | | |
|---|---|---|---|
| accurate | functional | performance | selling |
| application | job–inquiry | qualifications | solicited |
| attention getter | midsection | references | updates |
| education | objective | resume | |

I. Before you apply for a job, you should think about the career you want.
   A. Begin by analyzing the unique combination of skills, _____ (p. 309), characteristics, values, and interests that differentiates you from other job applicants.
   B. The second step is to determine what you want—your _____ (pp. 310-311) goals (the skills you want to use in your work), your personal _____ (pp. 311-312) goals (the level of financial success and career progress you seek), and your work environment preferences (the kind of company, industry, and geographical area you want to work in).
   C. The next step is to make a list of companies that might be interested in your qualifications and that would enable you to accomplish your goals.

II. A _____ (pp. 314-322) is a brief account of your qualifications in a special format; its purpose is to interest employers in giving you a personal interview.
   A. The opening section summarizes your identity, your job or career _____ (pp. 316-317), and your key qualifications and date of availability.
   B. The body of the resume describes your _____ (pp. 317-318), work experience, activities and achievements, other relevant facts (such as special skills or achievements), personal data, _____ (p. 321), and supporting data that are available (such as transcripts and work samples); in selecting and organizing this information, your goal should be to emphasize your strongest qualifications.
   C. The "perfect" resume is the one that convinces the employer to grant you a personal interview.

III. Your _____ (p. 329) letter tells what you can do for the company and why you believe you are qualified for the job.
   A. If your application letter has been _____ (p. 329) (if you are sending it in response to an announced job opening), you should begin with a simple statement of how

you know about the job and why you qualify for the position; if you are sending an unsolicited letter (one to a company that has not announced an opening), you should open with an _____ (pp. 330-331) of some sort, as in a sales letter, and a statement of your reason for writing.

B. The _____ (pp. 331-333) of your application letter should highlight your key qualifications and indicate how they can benefit the potential employer.

C. In the final paragraph, request an interview and make it easy to arrange; close by referring to your strongest _____ (pp. 333-334) point.

D. The "perfect" application letter achieves the simple purpose of getting you a personal interview.

IV. A job search may require three other types of written messages.

A. A _____ (p. 337) letter—a direct request for an application form—should include enough information to show that you are a reasonable candidate.

B. If you are asked to fill out a standard application form, be complete, _____ (p. 338), and neat.

C. If you have not received a response to your application letter within a month or so, follow up with another letter that _____ (p. 338) your application with any recent job-related information and asks the organization to keep your name in its active file.

*Check your answers at the end of this chapter.*

## QUIZ YOURSELF

1. What is the difference between a "functional goal" and a "performance goal"?

2. Where might you find employment opportunities?

3. What are some of the most common criticisms expressed by people who read resumes?

4. What seven general types of information should you present in the qualifications section of your resume?

5. In writing your resume, should you present your educational qualifications or your work experience first? Discuss.

6. What organizational plan should you use in writing an application letter?

7. The contents of the opening paragraph of your application letter depend on whether it is _____ or _____ . A _____ application letter is one sent in regard to an announced job opening. An _____ , or "prospecting," letter is one sent to a company that has not announced an opening.

8. What should the midsection of an application letter accomplish?

9. What should you try to accomplish in the closing paragraph of an application letter?

10. What is the purpose of a job-inquiry letter?

*Check your answers at the end of this chapter.*

### BUILD YOUR SKILLS: WHAT'S WRONG WITH THIS RESUME?

A college student has drafted this resume. What could she do to make it more effective?

### RESUME

Alicia Suarez
2348 Tigertail
Miami, Florida 33133
Telephone (305) 376-3636

<u>Career Objective:</u> I have always aspired to aman-agement position in a growing firm because I'm good with numbers and love to sell just about any product.

SALARY RANGE: $25,000 plus with good benefits, preferably a company car.

Education

Right now I'm working on a bachelor's degree in business administration. My courses are wide-ranging and include Western Civ., Speech, and various courses in finance and market-ing. I expect to graduate next spring, from the University of Miami at Coral Gables. I also attended Miami-Dade Junior College for one year.

Experience

JUNIOR ACCOUNTANT.  In this position I prepared and processed important financial documents for Pan American Importers, Inc.  In addition, my job included running the computers.  (No secretarial work was involved, although I can type 40 wpm.)  Part-time, while in school.

Sales Rep.  For MCI, Inc.  I handled a large territory and scored meny successses with a range of clients.  The dollor volume of my territory climbed considerably while I was there.  1983.

Volunteer Work at South Miami Hospital.

Activities

Treasurer for Delta Gamma Sorority at Uof M.

Volleyball Team

Involved in Campus Entrepreneurs Socity.

Workshops—This fall I attended a workshop on "Honing Your Persuasive Speaking Skills."  It was sponsored by the Miami Chapter of IABC.

Achievements

Bilingual
Rotary Club Scholarship

Personal Data:  5'2", 140 lbs., recently married

Hobbies—Water Skiing

## BUILD YOUR SKILLS:  WHAT'S WRONG WITH  THIS APPLICATION LETTER?

A young career woman has drafted this application letter.  What could she do to make it more effective?

208 East 83 St.
New York, NY 10028
March 20, 1986

Mr. Alan Frankel, President
Frankel Merchandising, Inc.
11 East 53 St.
New York, NY 10022

Dear Mr. Frankel:

Please consider me for the position in your accounting department that was recently advertised in a trade journal.

I am hardworking, enthusiastic, and have a lot of experience in this field.  My co-workers have always said that I was a star-quality team player.  Just take a look at my resume and you'll see exactly what I mean.  My education also provides valuable preparation for employment in your company.

I hope that we can have an interview soon, although you should keep in mind that Thursday afternoon is the only time I'm available to discuss future employment at this point. Nevertheless, after we speak, I think you'll be convinced that I'm the best applicant for the job!!

Sincerely,

Vanessa Rossetti

## EXPAND YOUR KNOWLEDGE: PUTTING YOUR BEST FOOT FORWARD

The job market is very competitive, and so naturally you want every advantage available to you. Linda Wells, president of Darland-Wells Associates, a Connecticut firm specializing in management recruiting, describes what she does to give her applicants the edge: "In order to maintain my own reputation, I have to send out only the best candidates. It sounds superficial to say so, but appearances are very important. A person who doesn't look right for a job won't get past the front door in a lot of companies. So I always talk with my applicants face to face. I give them little bits of advice on what to wear, what questions to ask, what points in their backgrounds to emphasize."

Charlotte Stier also heads her own placement firm, Char & Associates, in Kent, Washington (near Seattle). Charlotte estimates that she has seen thousands of resumes since she entered the field in 1970. "The more work experience an applicant has," she laughs, "the shorter the resume seems to be. People who don't have much to say generally end up saying too much." Charlotte recommends that you "don't try to be all things to all people. You're better off zeroing in on one or two performance areas where you're really good. That way you can write a brief resume—preferably one page but no more than two—and still provide lots of details, which employers want to see."

Another way to focus your resume is to spell out your goals. Charlotte recommends that job seekers state at the top of their resumes both the immediate position they want and their long-range goals. "An employer should know where you've set your sights."

Once you've stated these goals, you can begin to list your qualifications. "If you've held jobs," Charlotte suggests, "try to present yourself in terms of the skills they involved rather than detailing your job responsibilities. Organizational skills, analytical skills, creative skills, managerial skills—these are what employers understand and look for.

"Be totally honest," she adds. "And be specific. For example, in listing past jobs, say how long you worked at each one, from month/year to month/year."

But what if you're just getting out of school? "Mention the skills you've developed there, such as business writing or accounting. And list your most relevant courses and how you've done in each one, assuming you've done well." Charlotte also recommends emphasizing the work experience that recent graduates may have had while in school. "Even if it was selling shoes or working in a fast-food restaurant, part-time job experience says that you have discipline. It says that you want to make something of yourself."

Another problem many resumes have is their style—or lack of it. Charlotte has seen too many resumes filled with "I did this" and "I did that." She shakes her head. "That's amateurish. And it adds unnecessary words. Be brief," she cautions. "And go with action verbs—not pronouns like *I, me,* and *my.*"

Even more important: "Don't build yourself up beyond believability. I've seen resumes for people who answered the phones for a week while the boss was away and then listed themselves as assistant manager. And the honors you list must relate to the career field you want to enter. Scholastic honors are important—but not the fact that you won a campus pie-eating contest."

When it comes time to type your resume, be very careful about spelling. "When I see a resume with misspellings and an awkward style, I assume that the applicant's verbal skills are equally weak, and so will an employer. Before sending out a resume, check every word for spelling errors. Check punctuation, too."

What types of skills does Charlotte feel will give you an edge in job hunting? "The work picture is changing," she says. "It's hard to know what abilities will be in demand several years down the road. But communication skills are essential now—and always will be. Being able to communicate effectively can be your single most marketable asset."

Suppose that you are Charlotte Stier and that Caleb Green is your client. How would you advise him to modify his resume?

## CALEB M. GREEN

2632 Hesby Avenue
North Hollywood, CA 91434
Phone: (213) 990-6110

Age: 30
Married
2 children

EXPERIENCE

Product Manager, Health Systems, Inc., Burbank, Calif., 1982-1985
I am in charge of a line of respiratory-care products that are sold to hospitals. My job is to plan the production, pricing, and marketing stratey for this line, which is sold by our sales force.

Design Engineer, Helth Systems, Inc., Burbank, Calif., 1979-1982
As an engineeer, I was involved in designing respiratory-care products, such as inhalation machines and nebulizers.

Associate Engineer, Vortex, Encino, Calif., 1977-1979
At Vortex, I worked on designing all sorts of plastic devices for use with hospital products. Most of these items used tubing, valves, and connectors that had to meet high heat tolerances, since they were usually sterilized repeatedly by hospitals.

EDUCATION

Pepperdine University, Malibu, Calif., 1979-1982
I got an M.B.A. at night school at Pepperdine while I was working full time for Health Systems. I graduated with a B average and a major in marketing.

California Institute of Technology, Pasadena, Calif., 1975-1979
I have a B.S. degree in mechanical engineering. My grades were excellent. I was on the dean's list six semesters, and Cal Tech is a tough school, as perhaps you know. I lived in the dorm and worked part time in the school cafeteria. I was also on the swim team.

PERSONAL BACKGROUND

I was born and raised in Kentucky, but my parents moved to California when I was in high school, and I've been hear ever since. I don't ever want to leave, because my hobby is surfing.

## DEVELOP YOUR WORD POWER

*Spelling Challenge*    Identify the misspelled word in each of the following sentences, and spell it correctly in the space provided.  If all the words in a sentence are spelled correctly, write *C* in the space.

_____  1.  Her poor vocabulary is a hinderance to her career.

_____  2.  Those figures are not immedeately available.

_____  3.  We could look for someone who is inexperienced but intelegent.

_____  4.  Your service will be interrupted on September 7.

_____  5.  Can you judge how well we are doing?

_____  6.  He is quite knowledgible about data communications.

_____  7.  We like to educate ignorant consumers.

_____  8.  Since we can choose only two, some disappointment is inevitible.

_____  9.  I will try not to interfear with your decisions.

_____ 10.  At this point, 1980's sales figures are irrevelant.

*Vocabulary Challenge*    Match the words in the first column with the definitions in the second column.

_____  11.  inveterate                   A.  praising

_____  12.  judicious                    B.  chronic

_____  13.  laudable                     C.  clear

_____  14.  laudatory                    D.  praiseworthy

_____  15.  lucid                        E.  prudent

Circle the best definition of the highlighted word in each of the following sentences.

16.  Ms. Jaskowitz refused to **intervene** in the dispute between the two employees.

    A.   keep score              B.  ignore                  C.  interfere

17.  The television station was **inundated** with letters protesting one of its documentaries.

    A.   flooded                 B.  sued                    C.  perversely pleased

18.  The temporary loss of a liquor license **jeopardizes** the financial health of restaurants.

    A.   increases               B.  explains                 C.  imperils

19.  Robin's attitude about the ideal relationship between government and business could best be described as **laissez faire.**

    A.   noninterference         B.  all's fair               C.  let the buyer beware

20.  You will receive a refund in **lieu** of tickets for Saturday's performance.

    A.   payment                 B.  view                     C.  place

Select one of these words to complete each of the following sentences, and write the word in the space provided.

    **interval**        **intrigue**        **introvert**        **inverse**        **liaison**

21.  The tone will sound after a ten-second _____ .

22. The _____ of on is off.

23. No _____ would eagerly volunteer to host a hospitality suite.

24. Their efforts to take over the company were characterized by much _____.

25. Phil will be the _____ between Marketing and Production.

*Follow-up Word Study*    Check your answers at the end of this chapter. In the spaces below, write the words that you spelled or used incorrectly. (Use a separate piece of paper if you missed more than five words.) Then look up each word in your dictionary, and carefully study its spelling, pronunciation, definition, and history (etymology). Finally, to help fix the word in your memory, write it in a sentence.

Word                          Sentence

_____          _____

_____          _____

_____          _____

_____          _____

_____          _____

## CHECK YOUR ANSWERS

### Master Key Concepts

   I.  A.  qualifications
       B.  functional, performance

  II.  resume
      A.  objective
      B.  education, references

 III.  application
      A.  solicited, attention getter
      B.  midsection
      C.  selling

 IV.  A.  job-inquiry
      B.  accurate
      C.  updates

### Quiz Yourself

1. Functional goals are related to the skills you want to use in your work. For example, if you are a good communicator, your functional goal might be to find a job in which you can use your writing and speaking skills.

   Performance goals are related to the level of achievement you want to attain. These goals might be stated in terms of the organizational level you hope to reach, the amount of money you want to make, and the speed at which you want to advance. (pp. 310-312)

2. The best way to look for a job is to explore as many pathways as possible, taking advantage of the normal recruiting process and looking for opportunities on your own. Options to explore include
   a. On-campus interviews
   b. Advertisements placed by employers in newspapers, professional journals, and other publications
   c. Placement agencies run by private companies, government, and trade associations

   d. Referrals from friends

   e. In-house transfers and promotions   (p. 312)

3. People who read resumes complain about these common faults in the resumes they receive:
   a. Too long
   b. Too short or sketchy
   c. Hard to read
   d. Wordy
   e. Too slick
   f. Amateurish
   g. Poorly reproduced
   h. Misspelled and ungrammatical throughout
   i. Lacking a career objective
   j. Boastful
   k. Dishonest
   l. "Gimmicky"   (pp. 314–316)

4. The qualifications section of your resume should present seven key elements:
   a. Education
   b. Work experience
   c. Activities and achievements
   d. Other relevant facts
   e. Personal data
   f. References
   g. Supporting data   (pp. 317–321)

5. Your resume should present your strongest qualifications first. If you are still in school and have held only part-time or summer jobs, your educational qualifications will probably be your best selling point and should be given prominence. If you have been out of school for several years and have held responsible, full-time jobs related to the position you seek, you should discuss your work experience before describing your education. (p. 322)

6. Application letters are persuasive sales messages. They should therefore be organized according to the direct plan—more specifically, the AIDA plan, to develop attention, interest, desire, and action.   (p. 329)

7. The contents of the opening paragraph of your application letter depend on whether it is *solicited* or *unsolicited*. A *solicited* application letter is one sent in regard to an announced job opening. An *unsolicited*, or "prospecting," letter is one sent to a company that has not announced an opening.   (pp. 329–330)

8. The midsection of an application letter should
   a. Summarize your qualifications that are directly related to the job (or mentioned in the employment ad)
   b. Show how you have put your qualifications to use
   c. Provide evidence of desirable personal qualifications
   d. Tie salary requirements (if requested) to the benefits of hiring you
   e. Refer to your resume   (pp. 331–333)

9. In the closing paragraph of an application letter, you should ask for an interview and make the interview easy to arrange.   (p. 334)

10. The purpose of a job-inquiry letter is to request an application form.   (p. 337)

**Develop Your Word Power**

1. hindrance
2. immediately
3. intelligent
4. C
5. C

6. knowledgeable
7. C
8. inevitable
9. interfere
10. irrelevant

11. B
12. E
13. D
14. A
15. C

16. C
17. A
18. C
19. A
20. C

21. interval
22. inverse
23. introvert
24. intrigue
25. liaison

# Chapter 13

## INTERVIEWING FOR EMPLOYMENT AND WRITING FOLLOW-UP LETTERS

The main point of Chapter 13 is that a job interview gives the company a chance to evaluate you and gives you a chance to evaluate the company. As you read the chapter, think about the attitudes and preparation that contribute to a successful interview. When you finish reading, rehearse a job interview, either mentally or with a friend, until you feel that you can handle any type of interview you may encounter.

### MASTER KEY CONCEPTS

Use the following terms to fill the blanks in the outline. All terms are used, but none is used more than once.

| | | | |
|---|---|---|---|
| acceptance | directed | referral | stress |
| bad-news | evaluation | resignation | thank-you |
| capable | listen | screening | two |
| compatible | questions | | |

I. A good job interview enables the interviewer to find the right person for the job and to convince her or him that the organization is a good one to work for; it also enables the job candidate to find out if the job will be satisfying and to convince the interviewer that he or she is _____ (p. 346) of doing the job.

   A. There are generally three steps in the interview process: a preliminary _____ (p. 346) to eliminate unqualified applicants; an initial _____ (p. 346) by a personnel or recruiting employee; and a final interview by the supervisor or department manager to whom the candidate would report and who is in charge of making the final hiring decision.

   B. An applicant may encounter job interviews (for a soon-to-be-filled opening), _____ (p. 347) interviews (for an indefinite, future opening), screening interviews (to narrow the field of applicants), and selection interviews (to make a final hiring decision); these interviews may be _____ (p. 347) (structured by a checklist or series of prepared questions), unstructured (involving broad, open-ended questions), or _____ (p. 347) (designed to test the applicant's ability to cope with pointed questions, hostility, and criticism).

   C. Employers want to hire people who will fit into the organization and who can perform their work well.

   D. An interview gives the applicant a chance to find out whether the people, the organization, and the work itself are _____ (p. 351) with his or her skills, interests, and goals.

   E. To reduce the natural tension that accompanies a job interview, take steps in advance to handle it successfully: investigate the company and the job, evaluate what you have to offer, develop answers to likely questions, prepare _____ (p. 352) to ask, build your confidence for the interview, polish your interview style, plan to look good, go equipped, and check the route to the interview.

F.  You can create a good impression during the interview if you _____
(pp. 360-361) effectively, discuss salary discreetly, and conclude the interview on a warm and courteous note; make the most of the experience by keeping a record of your performance.

II.  Your job search may require you to write other kinds of messages to employers.
A.  Within two days of each interview, send a _____ (p. 364) note that expresses appreciation, conveys your continuing interest, and asks for a decision.
B.  If you have not heard from the interviewer within _____ (p. 365) weeks, send a note of inquiry based on the assumption that the delay doesn't imply an outright rejection.
C.  If you receive a job offer while you still have interviews scheduled with other companies, write an enthusiastic note requesting more time to make your decision.
D.  Within five days of a job offer that you want to take, send a letter of _____ (pp. 366-367); bear in mind that such a letter is a legally binding contract.
E.  If you receive a job offer that you do not want to accept, send a tactful and sincere letter following the _____ (p. 367) plan; try to leave the door open for future contact in case the job you accept doesn't work out.
F.  If you must quit one job in order to take another, send a letter of _____ (p. 367) that follows the bad-news plan; try to sound positive so that your former employer will willingly supply recommendations in the future.

*Check your answers at the end of this chapter.*

## QUIZ YOURSELF

1.  Briefly describe the three steps in the normal interview process.


2.  An interview for a specific job opening or for employment in the near future is a _____ interview.  An employer may also schedule a _____ interview, which provides a look at a potential candidate for future reference.


3.  What should you do if you are asked an unlawful question in a job interview?


4.  How can you find out whether you are likely to be compatible with your potential co-workers?


5.  What facts should you try to learn about the company and the position for which you are applying before you go to an interview?

6. What are four common weaknesses in personal style that interviewers notice, and how can you overcome them?

7. Give some general pointers on how to discuss salary during a job interview.

8. What organizational plan should you use in writing a thank-you note to a job interviewer?

9. If, after the interview, you are not advised of the decision by the promised date or within two weeks, you might send a _____.

10. How should you organize a letter of acceptance?

*Check your answers at the end of this chapter.*

## BUILD YOUR SKILLS:  ARE YOUR QUESTIONS READY?

In interviewing for a job, you have two objectives:  to create a good impression and to determine whether the job and the organization are right for you.  The questions you ask help you achieve both objectives.

To prepare yourself, make a list of 15 or 20 questions that you would like answered during a typical job interview.

## BUILD YOUR SKILLS:  WHAT'S WRONG WITH THIS FOLLOW-UP LETTER?

A job applicant has drafted this follow-up letter.  What could he do to make it more effective?

1906 Bentley Avenue
Sharon, PA 16146
June 12, 1986

Ms. Elizabeth Monroe
Director of Human Resources
Pennsylvania Power and Light
600 Claremont Boulevard
Sharon, PA 16146

Dear Ms. Monroe:

Talking with you was a real pleasure.  It's exciting to know that even people in large corporations have outside interests like scuba diving and backpacking.  If I'm hired, I look forward to joining you on some of the Sierra Club outings we chatted about.

Please keep me in mind for the position we discussed.  Hope to hear from you soon.

Sincerely yours,

Al Giordano

## EXPAND YOUR KNOWLEDGE: THE ASSERTIVE INTERVIEWEE

Everybody knows that the point of an interview is to give the prospective employer a chance to evaluate the prospective employee. But you should do more in an interview than just meekly answer questions. For one thing, employers usually don't want to hire people who seem to think too little of themselves. For another, the point of an interview is also to give you a chance to evaluate the company.

How can you talk to a prospective employer without seeming to be too wishy-washy? Most of all, go into the interview with the right attitude. If you go in thinking that you won't get the job, you probably won't. Negative assumptions can undermine and defeat you. So develop a positive outlook instead: Believe that you will succeed.

You can boost your confidence by preparing as thoroughly as you can for the interview: putting resume, supporting materials, and your appearance all in order and practicing your interviewing technique over and over. With those basics under control, you can be confident of handling almost anything that arises. After all, an interview is a fairly standard event. If something does come up that you are not prepared for, just do your best—and be yourself. You don't know what specific qualities the interviewer is looking for, and so it makes no sense to try remolding your personality to fit the interviewer's ideal. Instead of worrying about the competition for a job, look on the interview as a chance to make your own unique qualities known.

In your job search, you will eventually have an interview that seems to be bearing fruit; the interviewer will start talking as if you will definitely be joining the company. Many people get so excited by the prospect of a serious job offer that they lose all rationality at this point and leave the interview in a haze of goodwill and eager anticipation. Instead, they should start asking questions that will help them evaluate the job objectively. Here are some that you can reasonably ask the interviewer when the job appears to be within your reach:

- What happened to the last person who had this job?
- May I talk to someone who is doing what I will be doing?
- What is this company like as a place to work?
- Is the company growing, and where is the growth coming from?
- How and by whom will my performance be measured?
- How will the company help me meet the goals we agree on?
- What is the salary range for similar jobs in this organization?
- What other compensation is the company willing to offer?
- If relocation is involved, how much will the company help?
- What will I get in writing?

Don't fear being direct when an interview seems to be going well; most employers will appreciate your hard-headed approach. Those that don't may have personality or organizational problems that will make the job difficult for you. And you are better off asking questions before you take the job. The alternative may be looking for a new one a few months down the road.

*Source*: Adapted from Richard A. Lynch, "10 Questions to Ask Before Accepting a Job," *Money*, February 1985, pp. 109-114.

1. Can you think of any specific "symptoms" that might indicate a company is not for you? What are they?

2. Asserting yourself when the interview is going well is one thing. Taking control when things are going badly is another. What can you do if you and the interviewer seem to be on different wavelengths?

## DEVELOP YOUR WORD POWER

*Spelling Challenge*    Identify the misspelled word in each of the following sentences, and spell it correctly in the space provided.  If all the words in a sentence are spelled correctly, write *C* in the space.

_____    1.  Make sure that your address and phone number are legible.

_____    2.  Sheila will go to almost any lenths to get a promotion.

_____    3.  Tracy is a likeable, energetic young woman.

_____    4.  What is the likelyhood of getting delivery by midweek?

_____    5.  Please send some literture on your new personal computers.

_____    6.  We don't have the luxery of waiting for third-quarter figures.

_____    7.  Gardening—what a wonderful way to spend your leesure time!

_____    8.  All our technicians are fully licenced.

_____    9.  Listen before you jump to conclusions about his limitations.

_____    10.  We have steadily been loosing market share.

*Vocabulary Challenge*    Match the words in the first column with the definitions in the second column.

_____  11.  malign          A.  to show plainly

_____  12.  mandate         B.  to keep to oneself

_____  13.  maneuver        C.  to slander

_____  14.  manifest        D.  to manipulate

_____  15.  monopolize      E.  to authorize

Circle the best definition of the highlighted word in each of the following sentences.

16.  His **Machiavellian** nature finally yielded him leadership.

A.  masculine          B.  cunning          C.  ambitious

17.  We cannot afford to include any **mavericks** on the team for this project.

A.  cowboys          B.  incompetents          C.  loners

18.  My **mentor** was a 50-year-old woman with a reputation for covering her iron fist with a velvet glove.

A.  boss          B.  confidant          C.  adviser

19.  Judy has undergone a **metamorphosis** since taking the Dale Carnegie course.

A.  period of self-doubt          B.  attitude adjustment          C.  complete change

20.  With a **modicum** of training, Andy could become a good manager.

A.  little bit          B.  great deal          C.  modern type

Select one of these words to complete each of the following sentences, and write the word in the space provided.

malleable          mercurial          meticulous          moot          moribund

21.  The proper level of government intervention in the marketplace is a _____ point, but it seems useless to discuss it here.

22. His _____ changes, from calm to anger in moments, unsettle the staff.

23. Tom's _____ nature helps him adjust to many different situations.

24. The employee relations committee has been _____ during the strike.

25. The best accountants are _____ in handling complicated financial reports.

*Follow-up Word Study*    Check your answers at the end of this chapter. In the spaces below, write the words that you spelled or used incorrectly. (Use a separate piece of paper if you missed more than five words.) Then look up each word in your dictionary, and carefully study its spelling, pronunciation, definition, and history (etymology). Finally, to help fix the word in your memory, write it in a sentence.

Word                          Sentence

_____        _____

_____        _____

_____        _____

_____        _____

_____        _____

---

## CHECK YOUR ANSWERS

**Master Key Concepts**

I. capable
    A. screening, evaluation
    B. referral, directed, stress
    D. compatible
    E. questions
    F. listen

II. A. thank-you
    B. two
    D. acceptance
    E. bad-news
    F. resignation

**Quiz Yourself**

1. The interview process consists of three steps:
    a. A preliminary screening (often held on campus) that enables the company to eliminate unqualified applicants
    b. An initial visit to the company, designed to give the personnel officer or department manager an opportunity to narrow the field a little further
    c. A final interview that gives the supervisor a chance to decide whether a particular candidate is the right person for the job   (p. 346)

2. An interview for a specific job opening or for employment in the near future is a *job* interview. An employer may also schedule a *referral* interview, which provides a look at a potential candidate for future reference.   (p. 347)

3. If you are asked an unlawful question and your reply can't hurt you, go ahead and answer the question—but let the interviewer know that you are aware of the law. If your reply might hurt you, react lightheartedly but decline to answer. (p. 350)

4. To find out whether you are likely to be compatible with potential co-workers, do some research about the company and its personnel. Arrange to talk with an employee if you can. Analyze the people you meet during your interviews to determine whether you have similar values, interests, and backgrounds. (p. 351)

5. Before going to a job interview, try to learn these facts about the company:
    a. Company name
    b. Location(s)
    c. Company age
    d. Products and services
    e. Position in the industry
    f. Earnings
    g. Growth
    h. Organization
   Try to learn these facts about the job:
    a. Job title
    b. Job functions
    c. Job qualifications
    d. Career path
    e. Salary range
    f. Travel opportunities
    g. Relocation opportunities   (p. 353)

6. Here are four common weaknesses in personal style that interviewers notice—and how to overcome them:
    a. Shrinking in the presence of authority. To prevent this, project a warm, confident manner from the start. Maintain eye contact; ask questions and acknowledge answers.
    b. Seeming "laid back" and flippant. To dispel this image, try to display real interest. Look alive and attentive. Show enthusiasm.
    c. Talking too much or too little. Ask friends to analyze your conversational style. If they indicate that you are too dominant or too quiet, try to alter the pattern.
    d. Being overwhelming. To avoid being too exuberant, try to use self-restraint in promoting yourself and your ideas. Listen to the interviewer. (p. 358)

7. Don't make money a major talking point. Try to avoid the subject until late in the interview, and let the company representative bring up the topic. If you are asked directly about your salary expectations, say that you would expect to receive the standard salary for the job. If the interviewer doesn't mention salary, you can simply ask what the position pays, but do not inquire about fringe benefits until you have a firm job offer. (pp. 361-362)

8. A thank-you note to a job interviewer should be organized like a routine message, using the direct plan. The main idea (your gratitude for the interview) should come first. (p. 364)

9. If, after the interview, you are not advised of the decision by the promised date or within two weeks, you might send a *note of inquiry*. (p. 365)

10. A letter of acceptance should follow the good-news plan. Begin by accepting the position and expressing thanks. Identify the job you are accepting. Cover any necessary details in the middle section of the letter, and then conclude by saying that you look forward to reporting for work. (pp. 366-367)

## Develop Your Word Power

| | | | | |
|---|---|---|---|---|
| 1. C | 6. luxury | 11. C | 16. B | 21. moot |
| 2. lengths | 7. leisure | 12. E | 17. C | 22. mercurial |
| 3. likable | 8. licensed | 13. D | 18. C | 23. malleable |
| 4. likelihood | 9. C | 14. A | 19. C | 24. moribund |
| 5. literature | 10. losing | 15. B | 20. A | 25. meticulous |

# Chapter 14

## USING REPORTS AS BUSINESS TOOLS

The main point of Chapter 14 is that many types of reports are used in business and that organization and format reflect the purpose of the report. As you read the chapter, think about the way that function influences format. When you finish reading, look for examples of business reports and try to classify them in the categories outlined in the chapter.

## MASTER KEY CONCEPTS

Use the following terms to fill the blanks in the outline. All terms are used, but none is used more than once.

| | | | |
|---|---|---|---|
| accurate | justification | policies | regulatory |
| classified | manuscript | proposals | sensitive |
| directives | nonrecurring | receptive | standardized |
| evidence | plans | recurring | verifiable |

I. A report can be _____ (p. 377) according to who originates it, what subject it covers, when it is prepared, where it is sent, why it is prepared, and how _____ (p. 377) the audience is.

II. A good business report tells readers what they need to know—no more, no less.
   A. So that decisions based on a report will be well founded, make sure that the information in it is _____ (pp. 378-379): provide concrete descriptions, cover all the relevant facts, put the facts in perspective, support conclusions with plenty of _____ (p. 379), provide evidence and conclusions that are valid, and avoid personal biases.
   B. Some subjects are too _____ (p. 379) to be handled in a written document, so be discreet; also bear in mind that most managers like reports that present the main idea first, provide facts, tell the whole story, use language they can understand, and teach them something that makes their jobs easier.

III. Reports provide a formal, _____ (p. 380) link among people, places, and times, regardless of the reports' function, organization, format, and distribution.
   A. Reports for monitoring and controlling operations—_____ (p. 381), management information systems, and personal reports—summarize what is happening and help managers plan the future; they are generally _____ (p. 381) in organization and format, and they are distributed to upper-level management on a routine, recurring basis.
   B. Reports for implementing _____ (p. 386) and procedures—lasting guidelines and one-time _____ (p. 386)—enable managers to communicate the organization's standards and general rules to all employees; to some extent, they follow a standard format, and they may be collected in a special book and updated periodically.
   C. Reports for complying with the requirements of _____ (p. 387) agencies explain what an organization is doing to respond to the rules imposed by various

government agencies; they follow a standard format dictated by the agency and are often _____ (p. 387), periodic documents.

D.   _____ (p. 392) for obtaining new business range from simple letters to multivolume manuscripts and may be presented in a format dictated by the potential client or lender; their organization may also be dictated by the potential client.

E.   Reports for documenting client work—periodic (or interim) progress reports and final reports —keep clients informed about the status of work on a contract; the periodic reports are relatively informal, but the final report is a longer _____ (p. 394) designed to serve as a permanent record of the contract.

F.   Reports for guiding decisions—research reports, _____ (p. 400) reports, and troubleshooting reports—provide managers with a written analysis of the pros and cons of alternatives; they are prepared in response to unique, _____ (p. 400) situations and may be organized according to either the direct or the indirect plan, depending on the audience's probable reaction to their conclusions and recommendations.

*Check your answers at the end of this chapter.*

## QUIZ YOURSELF

1. What is a business report?

2. _____ reports, prepared on your own initiative, require more detail and support than _____ reports, which are prepared at the request of another person.

3. What are the four formats that can be used for reports?

4. What are six specific things a writer can do to ensure the accuracy of a report?

5. What is a "personal report"? Give a few typical examples.

6. Give some general guidelines on the style that should be used for policy procedure reports.

7. Briefly summarize the characteristics of compliance reports.

8. _____ vary in length and complexity, but all are basically attempts to get products, services, or projects accepted by outside business or government clients.

9. Briefly describe the differences in format, style, and organization between interim progress reports and final reports.

10. What are three of the most common decision-oriented reports?

*Check your answers at the end of this chapter.*

## BUILD YOUR SKILLS: CAN YOU CLASSIFY THESE REPORTS?

Take a look at the four reports outlined below, and then classify each report in terms of these six factors:

a. Who (originated the report)?
b. What (subject does it cover)?
c. When (is it prepared)?
d. Where (is it sent)?
e. Why (is it prepared)?
f. How (receptive is the reader)?

If the outline does not provide enough information to enable you to make a decision, use your best judgment and common sense to deduce the answer.

### Report 1: Instrument Division—Monthly Update

I. Summary of monthly activities
   A. New orders
   B. Shipments
   C. Profits

II. Sales by product line
   A. Analytical instruments
      1. New orders
      2. Shipments
   B. Industrial monitoring equipment
      1. New orders
      2. Shipments

    C. Audiometers
      1. New orders
      2. Shipments

III. Problems
    A. Design problems with the Omega system
    B. Production delays in liquid scintillation system

IV. Next month's forecast

## Report 2: Observations on the U.S. Rubber Industry

  I. Basic supply-demand characteristics
    A. Dependence on motor-vehicle industry
    B. Competition from foreign suppliers
    C. Increasing importance of long-life radials

 II. The outlook for tire rubber
    A. Original equipment
    B. Replacement market

III. The outlook for nontire rubber
    A. Basic segments
    B. Five-year forecast
    C. Long-term outlook

IV. Growth opportunities for innovators
    A. Run-flat tires
    B. One-piece integral tires and rims
    C. Twin-tire concept
    D. Liquid-injection molded tires

## Report 3: Optimizing the Organizational Structure

  I. Statement of the problem
    A. Changes in the nature of the company
    B. Need for changes in the company's structure

 II. Scope of work
    A. Design of an optimum organizational structure
    B. Implementation of structure over time

III. Issues for analysis
    A. Strengths and weaknesses of current structure
      1. What functions must be performed?
      2. How well does the present organization accommodate these functions?
    B. Centralization versus decentralization
    C. Organizational alternatives
      1. Line/staff structure
      2. Functional organization

       3. Project-management organization
       4. Matrix organization
   D. Informal organization and corporate "culture"

IV. Methods and procedures
   A. Review of company operations
   B. Interviews with company managers and employees

V. Work plan and schedule
   A. Phase I: Define requirements
   B. Phase II: Analyze alternatives and select optimum structure
   C. Phase III: Implement new structure

VI. Qualifications
   A. Related experience
   B. Staff qualifications

VII. Projected costs

## Report 4: Illegal and Improper Activities

I. Purpose of policy

II. Prohibited transactions
   A. Illegal political contributions
   B. Bribes, payoffs, and kickbacks
   C. Violations of customs law
   D. Violations of tax law
   E. Violations of laws of business conduct
       1. Monopolies or unfair competition
       2. Registration of securities
       3. Labor negotiations
   F. Payment of excessive fees or commissions

III. Actions that require approval from top management
   A. Legal political contributions
   B. Payment of extortion
   C. Any action of questionable legality

IV. Compliance and enforcement
   A. Disclosure of matters set forth above
   B. Disciplinary actions
       1. Demotion
       2. Termination
       3. Legal action

## EXPAND YOUR KNOWLEDGE: THE MANAGEMENT CONSULTANT'S TOOL KIT

Management consulting has boomed recently, as all kinds of organizations turn to outside specialists for help with a variety of problems and decisions. Management consultants are skilled business analysts who are hired to supplement the organization's staff for a particular project.

The assignments that management consultants handle are as varied as business itself. They may suggest ways to reduce overhead expenses, analyze new product opportunities, or diagnose profitability problems. Some specialize in one or two areas; others are generalists. Some work for large consulting firms; others operate independently or with a partner.

Regardless of their orientation, all management consultants need certain talents. They must be able to get to the root of a problem and solve it quickly—while their clients wait. They must also be articulate and versatile enough to sell their solutions to both the plant manager and the company president, without offending either. And they must be able to write well, because reports are an important part of their product.

Management consultants usually supply a potential client with a proposal outlining the work to be done, its objectives, and a target completion date. The proposal also states the fees and expenses to be charged, as well as the tasks to be performed and the critical dates in the project.

When a consultant is hired, the organization supplies a "commitment memorandum" that states why the consultant has been hired and what work will be done. Also, a "project-control memorandum" outlines the roles of the company's project team that will work with the consultant. This team supplies progress reports on the project.

At the conclusion of the project, the management consultant submits recommendations in the form of a written report. This report examines the problem and the proposed solution in depth. It may also explain how to implement the solution and monitor the results. Thus it can serve to guide management decisions long after the work of the consultant is done.

1. Why do you suppose that management consulting has boomed recently?

2. Could you be, would you like to be, a management consultant? Explain your answer.

## DEVELOP YOUR WORD POWER

*Spelling Challenge*    Identify the misspelled word in each of the following sentences, and spell it correctly in the space provided. If all the words in a sentence are spelled correctly, write C in the space.

_____    1.   Would you like a maintainance contract for your new computer?

_____    2.   A company of that size is no longer manageable.

_____    3.   Did you understand what Dave ment?

_____    4.   Drop in sometime for a look at our array of merchendise.

_____    5.   My new company car gets great gas milage.

_____    6.   Let's put all the miselaneous tables in an appendix at the back.

_____    7.   Proofread carefully for mispelled words.

_____    8.   The Operations Department will maintain all the equipment.

_____    9.   Darlene is good at manageing people.

_____   10.   Send now for your set of minature musical instruments!

*Vocabulary Challenge*    Match the words in the first column with the definitions in the second column.

_____   11. obstinate                          A. hateful

_____ 12. obtuse          B. unyielding

_____ 13. odious          C. dull

_____ 14. officious       D. suitable

_____ 15. opportune       E. presumptuous

Circle the best definition of the highlighted word in each of the following sentences.

16. Tampering with the internal mechanism **nullifies** the warranty.

   A. invalidates          B. extends              C. shortens

17. The writing style used in this memo **obscures** the meaning.

   A. clarifies            B. enhances             C. conceals

18. The motto "To the Stars We Aspire" is stamped on the **obverse** of the medallion.

   A. front                B. back                 C. margin

19. An important **omission** from your proposal is a budget.

   A. concept              B. conclusion           C. exclusion

20. Her disappointment at not getting the job is **palpable**.

   A. understandable       B. unjustified          C. obvious

Select one of these words to complete each of the following sentences, and write the word in the space provided.

| multifarious | mundane | nonchalant | noncommittal | nondescript |
|---|---|---|---|---|

21. Underwear was a _____ product until clothing designers started differentiating brands and styles.

22. By remaining _____, she has avoided the appearance of siding with either party in the dispute.

23. Supervisors deal with such _____ concerns as counting supplies.

24. With all his _____ activities, I don't see how he can do another project.

25. I was amazed by your _____ reaction during the massive layoffs.

**Follow-up Word Study**    Check your answers at the end of this chapter. In the spaces below, write the words that you spelled or used incorrectly. (Use a separate piece of paper if you missed more than five words.) Then look up each word in your dictionary, and carefully study its spelling, pronunciation, definition, and history (etymology). Finally, to help fix the word in your memory, write it in a sentence.

Word                      Sentence

_____     _____

_____     _____

_____     _____

_____     _____

## CHECK YOUR ANSWERS

**Master Key Concepts**

I. classified, receptive

II. A. accurate, evidence
   B. sensitive

III. verifiable
   A. plans, standardized
   B. policies, directives
   C. regulatory, recurring
   D. proposals
   E. manuscript
   F. justification, nonrecurring

**Quiz Yourself**

1. A business report is any factual, objective document that serves a legitimate business purpose. (p. 376)

2. *Voluntary* reports, prepared on your own initiative, require more detail and support than *authorized* reports, which are prepared at the request of another person. (p. 377)

3. A report may be prepared in one of four formats:
   a. Preprinted form
   b. Memo
   c. Letter
   d. Manuscript    (p. 376)

4. Here are six guidelines for ensuring the accuracy of a report:
   a. Be concrete.
   b. Report all relevant facts.
   c. Put facts in perspective.
   d. Give plenty of evidence for conclusions.
   e. Be sure evidence and conclusions are valid.
   f. Keep personal biases in check.  (p. 379)

5. Personal reports are a type of monitor and control report. They are prepared by individuals to help keep managers abreast of employee activities. Typical examples include sales-call reports, conference reports, expense reports, performance reviews, and recruiting reports.  (pp. 381–382)

6. Policy procedure reports are comprehensive, detailed documents written in paragraph form according to the direct plan and containing ample introductory and background information. The goal is to hit the right balance between the general and the specific. It is best to keep the policies broad and the procedures as simple as possible.  (pp. 386, 388–389)

7. Here are the characteristics of most compliance reports:
   a. They are prepared for external readers (regulatory bodies) who review many similar documents; they are often recurring reports prepared on an annual basis.
   b. Most follow a standardized format dictated by the regulatory agency.
   c. They are written in a brief style that emphasizes detail as opposed to broad concepts. The language is often legalistic and impersonal.
   d. They are organized generally in direct order and specifically in the order dictated by the regulatory agency. (pp. 387, 390–391)

8. *Proposals* vary in length and complexity, but all are basically attempts to get products, services, or projects accepted by outside business or government clients.  (p. 392)

9. Interim progress reports are often in letter format and are relatively brief, whereas final reports are generally in manuscript format and tend to be longer.

    In terms of style, both are relatively formal; however, interim progress reports require less attention to introductions and transitions.

    Interim progress reports are organized to highlight what was accomplished during a reporting period.  The main headings correspond to the tasks that have been performed.  A closing section usually outlines plans for the coming period.  Final reports, on the contrary, focus on results rather than on progress.  (pp. 394, 398–399)

10. Three of the most common decision–oriented reports are
    a. Research reports
    b. Justification reports
    c. Troubleshooting reports  (p. 395)

## Develop Your Word Power

| | | | | |
|---|---|---|---|---|
| 1. maintenance | 6. miscellaneous | 11. B | 16. A | 21. nondescript |
| 2. C | 7. misspelled | 12. C | 17. C | 22. noncommittal |
| 3. meant | 8. C | 13. A | 18. A | 23. mundane |
| 4. merchandise | 9. managing | 14. E | 19. C | 24. multifarious |
| 5. mileage | 10. miniature | 15. D | 20. C | 25. nonchalant |

## Chapter 15

## GATHERING, ORGANIZING, AND INTERPRETING INFORMATION

The main point of Chapter 15 is that careful research is a necessary foundation to any report. As you read the chapter, think about how researching a business report differs from—and is like—researching a report for school. When you finish reading, plan the research for a business report that you might be required to write sometime during your career.

### MASTER KEY CONCEPTS

Use the following terms to fill the blanks in the outline. All terms are used, but none is used more than once.

| | | | |
|---|---|---|---|
| analytical | factoring | limits | secondary |
| decimal | infinitive | question | suggestions |
| declarative | informational | research | summarize |
| experiments | interpretations | schedules | |

I. The _____ (p. 407) process begins when you define the problem you plan to study in order to set the boundaries of your investigation.
   A. Before beginning a study, be sure that you and the person who authorized the report agree on the _____ (p. 408) of the assignment: what needs to be determined, why the issue is important, who is involved in the situation, where the trouble is located, when it started, how the situation originated.
   B. Write a statement of the purpose of your report, in either _____ (p. 408) form (*"The purpose of this report is to . . ."*), _____ (p. 408) form (*"This report answers the question, What . . .?"*), or _____ (p. 409) form (*"The . . . will be analyzed"*).

II. Once you have defined the problem, you have to break it down into more specific areas for investigation, identifying the questions that you will ask and answer during the course of the study.
   A. Identifying the key issues for investigation—_____ (p. 410) the problem —means breaking the central problem into a hierarchy of narrower and narrower questions; _____ (p. 410) reports, which require little analysis or interpretation, are factored into specific subtopics of the main topic, whereas _____ (p. 411) reports are factored into categories based on problem-solving methods.
   B. Any given problem may be subdivided in many different ways, as long as all the important questions are asked; you can help ensure the logic of your breakdown if you choose a significant, useful basis or guiding principle for the division, if you limit yourself to one basis at a time in subdividing a whole into its parts, if you make sure that each group is separate and distinct, and if you are careful to list all the parts of a whole.
   C. To guide your analysis, you should represent your breakdown of the problem in outline form; to indicate levels of thought, you may use either alphanumeric format (combining Roman numerals, letters, and Arabic numerals) or _____ (p. 413) format, and for each item you may use either descriptive labels or more informative captions or questions.

III. Once the outline is ready, you should establish a work plan that identifies the tasks you will perform in your research, the end products of the research, and a review of _____ (p. 416) and budgets.

IV. The research phase is the most important part of the investigation, because the value of the report depends on the quality of the research.

    A.  Indispensable aids for reviewing _____ (p. 419) sources—information that has been published—are note cards for recording information, libraries and librarians, and such well-known business references as the *Business Periodicals Index*; when you begin to read the same things over and over again, you should leave the library and seek information elsewhere.

    B.  There are three main types of primary research (also known as fieldwork): surveys, which are valid and reliable only if the sampling and questionnaire design are done well; interviews with experts; and _____ (pp. 422-427) and observations.

V. As you collect information, you constantly sift and analyze what you learn in order to draw conclusions and make recommendations.

    A.  When your assignment is to write an informational report containing only facts (no conclusions or recommendations), you still have to point up the significance of the facts and _____ (p. 428) them at the end of the report.

    B.  Analytical reports draw conclusions, which are opinions or _____ (p. 428) based on the information you have obtained.

    C.  Analytical reports may also provide recommendations, _____ (p. 429) about what should be done based on the information you have obtained.

*Check your answers at the end of this chapter.*

## QUIZ YOURSELF

1. What do you accomplish by defining the problem to be investigated during your research?



2. Once you have defined the problem, you have to break it down into more specific areas for investigation. This process is sometimes referred to as outlining the issues, or _____ the problem.

3. Briefly discuss the differences in identifying key issues for investigation in informational reports versus analytical reports.



4. In wording an outline, you must choose between _____ (topical) and _____ (talking) captions. _____ captions label the subject that will be discussed, whereas _____ captions suggest more about the meaning of the issues.

5. What elements should be included in an informal work plan prepared for your own purposes? What elements would you have to add for a formal work plan for a lengthy, formal study?

6. Business research begins with a thorough review of the available literature on the subject. This already published material is known as _____ data.

7. Describe how you would set up a card system for recording your references and taking notes during an investigation.

8. What is the difference between "reliability" and "validity" as used in describing surveys?

9. What seven general guidelines should you follow in developing a questionnaire?

10. Describe the general characteristics of the summary section of an informational report.

*Check your answers at the end of this chapter.*

## BUILD YOUR SKILLS: HOW WOULD YOU ATTACK THE PROBLEM?

If your hometown is like many, it offers few activities for teen-agers. As a result, young people "hang out" and make their own fun. Unfortunately, what starts out as innocent fun sometimes develops into vandalism and rowdiness, which leads to tensions with the adults in the community. All too often, adults react by cutting back on teen-agers' legitimate opportunities to socialize.

Your assignment is to study this problem. The first step is to define it in terms that narrow the focus of your investigation and to develop a clear statement of purpose. Then you are ready to outline the issues you plan to study. Break the general problem into a hierarchy of narrower and narrower questions that have to be answered. The result should be a preliminary outline that you can use to guide your research. Finally, prepare a step-by-step work plan that summarizes your approach for attacking the problem and that provides a schedule for completing the effort.

## EXPAND YOUR KNOWLEDGE:  TECHNIQUES FOR PICKING AN EXPERT'S BRAIN

The key to successful research is often to interview an expert on your subject.  But this may be easier said than done.  Just finding an expert requires patience and persistence—and once found, such a person must be persuaded to help you.

Angela Fox Dunn, whose articles are distributed by the *Los Angeles Times* Syndicate, specializes in profiles of prominent people.  Because these people have many demands on their time, she usually writes to request interviews instead of calling.  What is the secret of her success?  "I always prepare before I make contact.  If I'm lucky, the person is listed in *Current Biography*.  If not, I check the periodical indexes for listings of articles by or about the person.  Nothing pleases people more than knowing that I know about their background and achievements."

With this basic legwork done, Angela is ready to request an interview.  "If a prominent person has paved the way, I mention him or her in my opening sentence," Angela says.  "In my opening, I also focus on the person I'm writing to.  I use praise, not superlatives, and if the person is tops in the field, a known authority, I add a few words of tribute.  I'm subtle, but I let people know that I'm aware of their stature.

"Above all, I don't ramble.  I get to the reason I'm writing as quickly as possible.  Years ago someone gave me 'four magic words' for success in communication.  I have used them in letters and in person.  They are 'I need your help.'  If you can get this idea across simply and sincerely, you'll find you are seldom refused."

Getting an expert to agree to an interview is one thing; the actual interview is quite another.  Here are a few tips for making the most of your opportunity:

- *Know exactly how the expert can help you.*  Do not expect a busy person to do all your work for you.  Use printed sources to get a basic understanding of your subject, and then ask the expert to update your facts or to give you insights into personalities, organizations, or an entire industry.
- *Make a positive first impression.*  Be warm and cheerful, self-confident but not cocky.
- *Consider the person you're talking to.*  You would phrase questions differently for a rock star than for an environmental specialist.
- *Be open.*  State what you're after and why.  Deception in explaining your needs and motives may make your source hesitant to provide information.
- *Do not overstate your knowledge of the subject.*  Experts do not mind your being uninformed and may even help you more if you humbly acknowledge your ignorance.
- *Do not be too quick to accept a no.*  You may have to ask a question several different ways to get an answer.
- *Ask for names of other contacts and other places to look for information.*  If you get nothing else out of an interview, you may as well get a name.  The next person or resource may provide what you need.
- *Be respectful and considerate.*  Let experts know that you realize their time and their good name are precious.
- *Be lavish with your praise and your thanks.*  A well-placed compliment about the person's expertise and insight is bound to come back to you.  And a handwritten thank-you note to a particularly helpful expert may encourage cooperation in the future.

*Source*:  Adapted from Personal interview with Angela Fox Dunn, 1983; "How to Pick an Expert's Brains," *Nation's Business*, February 1982, p. 56.

1. Identify local experts who might be able to provide information for a project you are doing in school.  For example, in connection with Chapter 15 of the book, make a list of professional market researchers who frequently pick other people's brains.  Then write a letter to one of the people on the list and request an interview.

2. If your letter to professional market researchers has produced the desired results, you will soon be interviewing your expert. To prepare yourself, follow Angela Fox Dunn's suggestions. Develop an interview guide in advance so that you will have a specific list of questions ready. To get the most out of the interview, either record the conversation or take notes. Immediately afterward, summarize the gist of the interview in writing. Then analyze the success of the interview. Did you learn all you had hoped to learn? Were you able to cover your questions in the time available? What would you do differently? Finish the project by writing a thank-you note to the person you interviewed.

## DEVELOP YOUR WORD POWER

*Spelling Challenge*     Identify the misspelled word in each of the following sentences, and spell it correctly in the space provided. If all the words in a sentence are spelled correctly, write *C* in the space.

_____     1.   It is hard to maintain employee moral in an uncertain economy.

_____     2.   You should take all nesessary precautions against a takeover bid.

_____     3.   One of your nabers has given us your name.

_____     4.   Niether Tom nor Tim has ever negotiated a contract before.

_____     5.   About nintey people are expected to attend the seminar.

_____     6.   The mar is barely notisable, but we will still give you a discount.

_____     7.   An extraordinary vista awaits you on the nineth green.

_____     8.   Be sure to report on munisiple services as well.

_____     9.   Dick Moore is the nineteenth 60-year-old to be laid off this year.

_____    10.   I couldn't help noticeing that your performance has deteriorated.

*Vocabulary Challenge*     Match the words in the first column with the definitions in the second column.

_____   11. panacea

_____   12. paradox

_____   13. paragon

_____   14. parody

_____   15. perennial

A.   model of excellence

B.   something that lasts

C.   something that seems self-contradictory

D.   cure-all

E.   satirical imitation

Circle the best definition of the highlighted word in each of the following sentences.

16. In general, racism is **passé** in American society.

    A.   unacceptable          B.   outmoded          C.   everywhere

17. How many market tests are **pending**?

    A.   in progress          B.   about to take place          C.   in the planning stage

18. Cathryn's **penetrating** stare seems to help her elicit the truth.

    A.   rude          B.   liquid          C.   keen

19. The **per capita** income in Hartford, Connecticut, is relatively high.

    A.  per person                B.  reported              C.  disposable

20. Her handling of customer complaints is too **perfunctory.**

    A.  perfectionistic          B.  tardy              C.  uninterested

Select one of these words to complete each of the following sentences, and write the word in the space provided.

| perpendicular | perpetual | picayune | pithy | plausible |
|---|---|---|---|---|

21. We should analyze all _____ explanations of O'Grady & Mason's decline.

22. B Street is _____ to 15th Street.

23. We had a _____ stream of accidents until we instituted the safety program.

24. Jorge's _____ comments are few but worth waiting for.

25. Try to focus on the truly important problems instead of the _____.

***Follow-up Word Study***    Check your answers at the end of this chapter. In the spaces below, write the words that you spelled or used incorrectly. (Use a separate piece of paper if you missed more than five words.) Then look up each word in your dictionary, and carefully study its spelling, pronunciation, definition, and history (etymology). Finally, to help fix the word in your memory, write it in a sentence.

Word                    Sentence

_____    _____

_____    _____

_____    _____

_____    _____

_____    _____

## CHECK YOUR ANSWERS

### Master Key Concepts

I. research
    A.  limits
    B.  infinitive, question, declarative

II.  A.  factoring, informational, analytical
    C.  decimal

III.  schedules

IV.  A.  secondary
      B.  experiments

V.  A.  summarize
    B.  interpretations
    C.  suggestions

**Quiz Yourself**

1. By defining the problem to be investigated, you narrow the focus of your investigation and establish its framework. Your definition of the problem helps you decide what information you need to complete your report. (p. 407)

2. Once you have defined the problem, you have to break it down into more specific areas for investigation. This process is sometimes referred to as outlining the issues, or *factoring* the problem. (p. 410)

3. Informational reports are generally broken down into subtopics dealing with specific subjects. These subtopics might be arranged in order of importance, sequentially, chronologically, spatially, geographically, or categorically.

   Analytical reports are generally broken down into categories based on problem-solving methods. The two most common methods are hypotheses and relative merits. (p. 411)

4. In wording an outline, you must choose between *descriptive* (topical) and *informative* (talking) captions. *Descriptive* captions label the subject that will be discussed, whereas *informative* captions suggest more about the meaning of the issues. (p. 413)

5. A simple, informal work plan should include a list of steps that will be taken, an estimate of their sequence and timing, and a list of sources of information.

   A formal work plan should include
   a. A statement of the problem
   b. A statement of the purpose and scope of the investigation
   c. A discussion of the sequence of tasks to be accomplished, together with an indication of sources, research methods, and limitations
   d. A description of end products, such as reports, plans, operating improvements, or tangible products
   e. A review of project assignments, schedules, and resource requirements   (p. 416)

6. Business research begins with a thorough review of the available literature on the subject. This already published material is known as *secondary* data. (p. 425)

7. The card system should contain two types of cards: bibliography cards and note cards. A separate bibliography card should be created for each reference, noting the author's name, the title of the book or periodical, the publisher, and the date and place of publication.

   The note cards should be used for recording information that might be of use. A separate card should be prepared for each point—facts, quotations, and general concepts. The title of the reference and the author's name should appear at the top of each note card, along with a word or two to indicate the general subject of the data. Each card should also indicate the numbers of the pages on which the information was found. (p. 420)

8. A survey is considered "reliable" if the same results would be obtained if the research were repeated at a later date. A survey is considered "valid" if it measures what it was intended to measure and gives a true reflection of the sample group's opinions on a subject. (p. 423)

9. The following guidelines should be applied in developing a questionnaire:
   a. Provide clear instructions so that respondents will know how to fill it out.
   b. Keep it short and easy to answer.
   c. Avoid questions that lead to a particular answer.
   d. Ask only one thing at a time.

    e. Avoid questions with vague or abstract words.

    f. Pretest the questionnaire with a sample group.

    g. Include a few questions that rephrase earlier questions.   (p. 425)

10. The summary section of an informational report should appear at the end of the report (or at the end of each chapter in a long report).  This summary should be organized to correspond with the outline of the report and should be a restatement of the main points already presented.   (p. 428)

## Develop Your Word Power

| | | | | |
|---|---|---|---|---|
| 1. morale | 6. noticeable | 11. D | 16. B | 21. plausible |
| 2. necessary | 7. ninth | 12. C | 17. B | 22. perpendicular |
| 3. neighbors | 8. municipal | 13. A | 18. C | 23. perpetual |
| 4. neither | 9. C | 14. E | 19. A | 24. pithy |
| 5. ninety | 10. noticing | 15. B | 20. C | 25. picayune |

# Chapter 16

## ORGANIZING INFORMATIONAL AND ANALYTICAL REPORTS

The main point of Chapter 16 is that, in general, reports are organized according to their purpose—informational or analytical. As you read the chapter, think about how the direct and indirect organizational plans mesh with the basic outlines for informational and analytical reports. When you finish reading, look at a business report and analyze the effectiveness of the organizational plan that it uses.

## MASTER KEY CONCEPTS

Use the following terms to fill the blanks in the outline. All terms are used, but none is used more than once.

| | | | |
|---|---|---|---|
| arguments | headings | parallel | reasons |
| chronological | informal | periodic | receptive |
| direct | memorandum | present | topics |
| format | outline | previews | transitions |

I. Before you begin to write a report, you generally have to reorganize the _____ (p. 435) that you used to guide your research; you also have to consider such basic issues as length, _____ (p. 435), and structure.
   A. A report may be formatted as a preprinted form, a letter, a _____ (p. 436), or a manuscript; the length depends on the subject and purpose and on your relationship with the reader.
   B. In deciding on a basic structure for your report, you must decide whether to introduce ideas in direct or indirect order and whether to subdivide main ideas around _____ (p. 438) (generally for informational reports) or around conclusions and recommendations or logical _____ (p. 442) (generally for analytical reports).

II. The purpose of informational reports is to explain something in straightforward terms; generally, _____ (p. 438) order is appropriate because the readers are open-minded and receptive, and the most natural structure is that based on subtopics related to the subject matter.
   A. A _____ (pp. 438-439) report, for example, could be formatted as a memo; it should be organized in the same sequence from period to period, perhaps containing an overview of routine responsibilities, a discussion of special projects, plans for the coming period, and an analysis of problems; it should be honest about problems as well as accomplishments.
   B. A personal report on a nonrecurring event could also be formatted as a memo; it should be organized according to the direct plan, with a _____ (p. 439) structure or a topical structure reflecting categories of interest to the reader; it should focus on important information or decisions of interest to management instead of giving a blow-by-blow account.

III. The purpose of analytical reports is to convince the reader to accept certain conclusions and recommendations; if the reader will be _____ (p. 442), the reports are organized to follow the direct plan and to focus on conclusions and recommendations, but if the reader will be skeptical or hostile, the reports use an indirect approach that highlights the reasons behind your position.

   A. When the reader will be receptive, you may use the conclusions and recommendations as the main _____ (pp. 442–443) of the report.

   B. When the reader will be skeptical or hostile, you should use as headings the main _____ (p. 445) why your conclusions and recommendations make sense; four types of logical arguments that can be used in this case are the 2 + 2 = 4 approach (a list of reasons that collectively add up to the main point), the chain reaction approach (if *a* is true, then *b* must be true; if *b* is true, then *c* must be true; and so on), the scientific method (an evaluation of alternative solutions), and the yardstick approach (a list of criteria for evaluating a situation or solution).

IV. In addition to deciding on the length, format, and organization of the report, you have to consider a number of other factors as well.

   A. For brief reports to someone you know well, you can use a relatively _____ (p. 454) style; in formal reports, you should avoid all references to *I* and *you* and any other language that is individualistic, personal, or "unbusinesslike."

   B. Decide whether to write in the past or the _____ (p. 456) tense, and then use it consistently.

   C. The longer the report, the more useful are clues to the structure of the report: the opening introduces the subject, explains why it is important, and _____ (p. 456) the main ideas and the order in which they will be covered; headings and lists help readers scan the report and recognize the relationship among ideas (they should be phrased in _____ [p. 458] form); _____ (pp. 459–460) tie ideas together and keep readers moving along the right track; the ending ties up all the pieces, reminds readers how they fit together, and (in analytical reports) explicitly states the conclusions and recommendations.

*Check your answers at the end of this chapter.*

## QUIZ YOURSELF

1. What are some of the things to consider in deciding on the length of a report?

2. What two issues should you consider in establishing the basic structure of a report?

3. Should informational reports be organized in direct or indirect order? Why?

4. What are the two basic types of analytical reports?

5. What is the five-step sequence of points in an analytical report based on recommendations?

6. When you want readers to concentrate on why your ideas make sense, your best bet is to let _____ provide the structure of the report.

7. Briefly describe four possible organizational plans based on logical arguments.

8. What is the difference between a formal and an informal tone, and when is each appropriate?

9. Is it better to use the past or the present tense in establishing the time perspective of a report?

10. What three things should the opening of a report accomplish?

*Check your answers at the end of this chapter.*

## BUILD YOUR SKILLS:  WHAT'S WRONG WITH THIS OUTLINE?

You have recently been hired by a bank as the administrative assistant to the Vice President of Commercial Loans.  Your boss, the V.P., has asked you to prepare a 10- to 15-page report on the life insurance industry as background information for the bank's board of directors.  Your report is intended to give the board members an overview of the life insurance business so they will be better able to evaluate a loan to finance the start-up of a new insurance company.

Here is your preliminary outline for the report.  Take a close look at it and make any necessary changes before showing it to your boss.

## Overview of the Life Insurance Industry

I. Introduction
   A.  History of the industry
      1.  In Europe
      2.  In the United States
      3.  Role of minority-owned companies
   B.  Size of the industry
      1.  Assets
      2.  Employees
      3.  Income
      4.  Number of companies

II. Structure of the industry
   A.  Mutual companies dominate the industry
      1.  Control 70 percent of assets
      2.  Generate the bulk of premium income
   B.  Stock companies outnumber mutual companies but are less influential
      1.  Generate only 20 percent of premium income
      2.  Account for less than half the insurance in force
   C.  Some life insurance companies carry health insurance too
      1.  Life insurance accounts for 71 percent of premium income
         a.  Ordinary accounts for 43 percent
         b.  Group accounts for 13 percent
         c.  Annuities accounts for 12 percent
         d.  Industrial accounts for 3 percent
      2.  Health insurance accounts for 29 percent of premium income
         a.  Hospital/medical accounts for 21 percent
         b.  Disability accounts for 8 percent
   D.  Distribution channels
      1.  Ordinary agents
      2.  Combination agents
      3.  Independent agents
      4.  Mail order (small share)
   E.  High degree of government regulation
      1.  Restrictions on investment portfolios
      2.  Selling expenses
      3.  Varies from state to state

III. Industry growth
   A.  Ten-year statistics
      1.  New business issued
      2.  Premium income
      3.  Assets
      4.  Insurance in force
   B.  Profit growth
   C.  Future outlook is good
      1.  Growth of 25- to 34-year-old age group
      2.  Higher incomes

IV. Industry outlook
    A.  Negative factors
        1.  Price competition
        2.  National health insurance
        3.  Social Security benefits
        4.  Decline in interest rates
        5.  Increasing overhead expenses
    B.  However, companies have good opportunities
        1.  New products
        2.  New markets
        3.  New sales approaches
        4.  More aggressive investing

V. Profit economics
    A.  Industry has three ways to improve profits
        1.  Higher premium prices
        2.  Changes in mix and volume of sales
        3.  Better return on investment of surplus funds

## EXPAND YOUR KNOWLEDGE: A PLAN FOR SMALL BUSINESSES

Many owners of small businesses have little need for elaborate formal reports. If nothing else, however, most should construct a business plan. Such a plan not only helps guide a new or growing business's development but also is indispensable for seeking financing. Before lenders and investors make a commitment to an unproven entrepreneur, they want to know whether their money has a chance of contributing to the business's success.

The following list of components is only a general guideline for preparing a business plan. For established organizations, only some parts of the plan need to be written down; the rest should at least be in the owner's head, however. But start-up businesses seeking financing generally need to compile all this information. The point in either case is to think through every element of the business, as outlined here:

- *Cover sheet*: name and address of the business, names of the owners
- *Overview*: type of business, legal structure, hours of operation, history of business, market, differences from competition, advantages of location, background of management and chief personnel, management philosophy, relationships with other groups (suppliers, customers, community, and so on), unresolved issues, measurable general objectives (including numbers and dates)
- *Marketing and sales plan*: characteristics and needs of target market, size of market, share of market, market's growth potential, ongoing trends in present and possible markets, position of competitors (size, strengths and weaknesses, market share, growth patterns), channels for communicating with and influencing customers, distribution channels, pricing structure (in relation to both profitability and competitors' prices), plans for customers, avenues for expanding market, sales-force structure (including recruiting, training, compensation, and motivation)
- *Production plan*: existing capacity (whether realized or not), production levels, changes that will improve efficiency, inventory levels (desired and actual), quality-control systems and production standards
- *Development plan*: systems for R & D and new product design, technological improvements being sought, planned expansions or renovations of existing facilities, future technical or service capabilities, planned changes in location

- *Human-resource plan*: existing staff (including strengths and weaknesses), recruiting and training systems, salary structures, fringe benefits, human resources needed for future development, promotion opportunities for existing staff, management philosophy about human resources (especially in relation to technological advances), outside professional resources available
- *Organization plan*: purpose and goals of business, leadership structure, individual responsibilities of owners and management, communication systems, motivational devices, accountability and reporting systems
- *Budgets*: current and projected financial status and plans (annual, quarterly, monthly; for capital improvements and equipment, cash flow, and organizational and departmental operations; balance sheet, break-even analysis, and profit and loss statement), use and expected effect of loans
- *Financial plan*: long-term financial status, long-term financial needs, projected cash flow, projected income
- *Control plan*: system for analyzing budget deviations, inventory-management system, cost-accounting systems, systems for gathering and analyzing operating statistics (on incoming orders, facilities use, quality control, and so on), staff reporting and management systems

One caution about business plans: Although they are valuable, they are no substitute for actually doing business. In other words, do not assume that having a plan will automatically bring success. Some people get so caught up in writing an elaborate plan that they lose sight of the reason for doing one. Others tend to regard the plan as inviolate and refuse to deviate from it if conditions change. Don't make mistakes like these. A business plan is merely a tool for guiding an organization's resources—not a set of laws that can never be challenged.

*Source*:   Adapted from *Business Planning Guide* (Portsmouth, N.H.: Upstart Publishing, 1981); Philip H. Thurston, "Should Smaller Companies Make Formal Plans?" *Harvard Business Review* 61 (September/October 1983):162-188.

1. One good way to develop an understanding of what a business plan is all about is to review one or two of them. Although few companies are willing to share their business plans with outsiders, you can obtain something similar by asking a local stockbroker to provide you with several prospectuses for companies "going public." Analyze these plans from the standpoint of writing style as well as content. How would you characterize their tone and organization?

2. Have you ever thought about starting your own business? Now is as good a time as any to start making the dream a reality. Begin by developing the cover sheet and overview section of a business plan.

## DEVELOP YOUR WORD POWER

*Spelling Challenge*   Identify the misspelled word in each of the following sentences, and spell it correctly in the space provided. If all the words in a sentence are spelled correctly, write *C* in the space.

_____     1.   We carry greeting cards for any ocassion.

_____     2.   When did the accident ocurr?

_____     3.   FastFood, Inc., is the offical caterer to the U.S. team.

_____     4.   How offen will I be required to travel out of town?

_____     5.   The enclosed pamplet will tell you more about our line of shoes.

_____     6.   Please send at least partial payment for the items you ordered.

_____   7. She has made numrous mistakes during her first week.

_____   8. Has it ever occurred to you that you might have hurt his feelings?

_____   9. The section on personal telephone calls has been ommitted from the new edition of the employee manual.

_____  10. He had an oppertunity to apply for the position, but he didn't.


***Vocabulary Challenge***   Match the words in the first column with the definitions in the second column.

_____  11. precaution        A.  bias

_____  12. precedent         B.  harbinger

_____  13. precursor         C.  safeguard

_____  14. predecessor       D.  forerunner

_____  15. predilection      E.  model

Circle the best definition of the highlighted word in each of the following sentences.

16. Give me a week to **ponder** your proposal.

   A.  research              B.  criticize             C.  consider

17. Their good sales figures for the past quarter should **precipitate** a major acquisition.

   A.  dampen               B.  hasten                C.  precede

18. Accounting experience does not **preclude** management experience as well.

   A.  come before          B.  make impossible       C.  coincide with

19. Bonnie works for the most **prestigious** law firm in the city.

   A.  esteemed             B.  tricky                C.  wealthy

20. Alan has a **prodigious** capacity for work.

   A.  professional         B.  modest                C.  immense

Select one of these words to complete each of the following sentences, and write the word in the space provided.

**portfolio**        **premise**        **proficiency**        **profusion**        **prognosis**

21. Past and present customers have supplied a _____ of suggestions, and we are working overtime to evaluate them all.

22. Larry's _____ in computing is what got him the job.

23. What is your _____ for the outcome of the new advertising campaign?

24. Mary's conclusion seemed reasonable, even though it was based on a faulty _____.

25. Ask all those interviewing for the graphic design position to bring a _____ containing samples of their most recent work.


***Follow-up Word Study***   Check your answers at the end of this chapter. In the spaces below, write the words that you spelled or used incorrectly. (Use a separate piece of paper if you missed more than five words.) Then look up each word in your dictionary, and carefully study its spelling, pronunciation, definition, and history (etymology). Finally, to help fix the word in your memory, write it in a sentence.

Word                              Sentence

_____            _____

_____            _____

_____            _____

_____            _____

_____            _____

## CHECK YOUR ANSWERS

### Master Key Concepts

I. outline, format
   A. memorandum
   B. topics, arguments

II. direct
   A. periodic
   B. chronological

III. receptive
   A. headings
   B. reasons

IV. A. informal
   B. present
   C. previews, parallel, transitions

### Quiz Yourself

1. In deciding on the length of a report, the first thing to consider is the wishes of the reader. If he or she has stipulated a certain length, then the report should conform to those instructions. If the question of length is left to your discretion, such factors as the subject, purpose, and nature of the audience should be taken into account.

   If the audience consists of strangers; if they are skeptical or hostile, or if the material is non-routine and controversial, then you have to explain the points in more detail; the resulting report will be relatively long. On the other hand, the report can be brief if the audience is familiar to you and receptive and the information is routine or uncomplicated. Generally, short reports are more common than long ones. (pp. 435-436)

2. Deciding on the basic structure of a report involves two issues:
   a. Which psychological approach is better—direct or indirect order? Should main ideas be presented early, or should they be introduced later in the report, after a discussion of the evidence that supports them?
   b. Which method of subdivision will make the material both clear and convincing? Should the main ideas be categorized according to topics, or should they be grouped as points in a logical argument? (p. 436)

3. Informational reports, which are designed to explain something in straightforward terms, are generally presented in direct order. Because informational reports do not attempt to persuade readers of anything, most readers react to informational reports in an unemotional way. For this

reason, you do not have to worry about introducing ideas gradually to overcome resistance. (p. 438)

4. The two basic types of analytical reports are
   a. Those in which data are analyzed and organized to support conclusions
   b. Those that go one step further and provide specific recommendations as well   (p. 442)

5. An analytical report based on recommendations generally follows this five-step sequence of points:
   a. Discussion of the need for action, presented in the introduction
   b. Brief statement of the benefit that can be achieved, also presented in the introduction
   c. List of the steps (recommendations) required to achieve the benefit, summarized in the introduction
   d. Detailed discussion of each step, giving information on procedures, costs, and benefits (each step corresponding to a main division of the report)
   e. Final summary of the recommendations at the end of the report   (p. 444)

6. When you want readers to concentrate on why your ideas make sense, your best bet is to let *logical arguments* provide the structure of the report.   (p. 445)

7. Here are four possible organizational plans based on logical arguments:
   a. 2 + 2 = 4 approach depends on the accumulation of evidence to persuade readers. The report is organized around a list of reasons that collectively support the main point you are trying to prove. The approach is useful when you have a variety of reasons for your conclusions or recommendations but no single reason that is particularly strong by itself.
   b. Chain reaction approach starts with a point accepted by readers, and then moves from one logical deduction to the next to prove your point. This approach focuses on the rationale for a proposed program, highlighting the problem-solving process as opposed to the solution.
   c. Scientific method evaluates alternative hypotheses to help readers work through the problem and understand the reasons for a solution. This structure runs through all the alternatives —good and bad.
   d. Yardstick approach uses stated criteria to evaluate a situation or a proposed program. It is useful when you want to demonstrate the need for action or the soundness of a proposal or when you want to compare alternatives. Its success depends on the readers' acceptance of the criteria.   (pp. 445-454)

8. An informal tone presupposes a closer relationship with the reader than does a formal tone. Reports with an informal tone use personal pronouns (*I* and *you*) and employ conversational language; reports written in a formal tone avoid the use of personal pronouns and colorful language. They attempt to establish a businesslike, unemotional, objective relationship between the writer and the reader.
   An informal tone is generally appropriate for brief, internal documents. A formal tone is often adopted for longer reports dealing with controversial or complex information, particularly if the audience consists of outsiders.   (pp. 454-456)

9. It is acceptable to use either the past or the present tense, as long as you do not switch back and forth between the two.   (p. 456)

10. The opening of a report should accomplish these three things:
    a. Introduce the subject of the report
    b. Indicate why the subject is important
    c. Give the reader a preview of the main ideas and their sequence   (p. 456)

## Develop Your Word Power

| | | | | |
|---|---|---|---|---|
| 1. occasion | 6. C | 11. C | 16. C | 21. profusion |
| 2. occur | 7. numerous | 12. E | 17. B | 22. proficiency |
| 3. official | 8. C | 13. B | 18. B | 23. prognosis |
| 4. often | 9. omitted | 14. D | 19. A | 24. premise |
| 5. pamphlet | 10. opportunity | 15. A | 20. C | 25. portfolio |

## Chapter 17

## DEVELOPING VISUAL AIDS

The main point of Chapter 17 is that properly selected and crafted visual aids simplify and dramatize the information in a report. As you read the chapter, think about which situations are most appropriate for using the different types of visual aids that are discussed. When you finish reading, look for visual aids in business reports and consumer publications and then analyze how well they simplify and dramatize the accompanying information while still providing an accurate picture of reality.

## MASTER KEY CONCEPTS

Use the following terms to fill the blanks in the outline. All terms are used, but none is used more than once.

| | | | |
|---|---|---|---|
| accuracy | influences | scale | text |
| captions | near | supplement | titles |
| detailed | pie | tables | variables |

I. A visual aid—an illustration in tabular, graphic, schematic, or pictorial form—should be designed to _____ (p. 471) the written word.
   A. Regardless of the type of visual aid used, several guidelines apply: begin with raw data obtained during research, develop visual aids that can present _____ (p. 473) information, aim to emphasize only the key points, maintain a balance between the visual aids and the text, take into account reader preferences for visual aids, and be practical about schedules and budgets.
   B. Different types of visual aids are most useful in certain situations: _____ (pp. 475-476) to present large quantities of detailed, specific information; line and surface charts to show changes over time or the interaction of two _____ (pp. 476-477); bar charts to compare the size of several items at one time, to show changes in one item over time, to indicate the composition of several items over time, and to show the relative size of parts of a whole; _____ (p. 479) charts to show the relative size of parts of a whole; flow charts and organization charts to illustrate physical or conceptual relationships; maps to show geographic information; and drawings, diagrams, and photographs to show how something looks or operates.

II. Visual aids should be tied very closely to the _____ (p. 482), so that readers can more easily interpret them.
   A. Introduce illustrations in the text, and explain their significance.
   B. Place visual aids _____ (p. 483) the point they illustrate.
   C. Choose _____ (pp. 483-484) and _____ (pp. 483-484) that convey a complete message, for the benefit of those who focus on the visual aids and merely skim the text.

III. Visual aids may be prepared at any point in the report-writing process—before, during, or after writing the text—but be sure that enough time is reserved to prepare them properly.

IV. The final step in creating effective visual aids is to review them.
   A. Don't include any visual aid that will not be useful to readers.
   B. Be sure that the visual aids are easy to find (perhaps by listing them on a separate page right after the table of contents) and easy to understand.
   C. Check the _____ (pp. 485–486) of numbers, plotted lines, scales, and the format and content of source notes, as well as the wording of headings, titles, and labels.
   D. Ensure that visual aids create an honest visual impression by using an undistorted _____ (p. 486) and by revealing any outside _____ (p. 486) on the results shown.

*Check your answers at the end of this chapter.*

## QUIZ YOURSELF

1. What are some of the reasons that United Airlines uses pictures and charts in its annual reports?

2. What are the six guidelines to follow in planning the visual aids for a report?

3. What type of visual aid would you use to present detailed statistical or financial data? What type would you use to dramatize key points?

4. What is a "text" table?

5. If you are comparing trend lines in successive charts, you owe it to your readers to maintain the same _____ in all the charts.

6. What are some of the creative things you can do with bar charts?

7. Ideally, the biggest slice of a pie chart is placed at the _____ position.

8. What are three ways to make a strong connection between the text and the visual aids?

9. What is the difference between a descriptive title and an informative title?

10. In a graph or chart, you can make your sales appear to soar by compressing the _____, but you will mislead your readers in the process.

*Check your answers at the end of this chapter.*

## BUILD YOUR SKILLS:  CHOOSE THE RIGHT VISUAL AID FOR THE SITUATION

You are preparing a report on the mail-order market for books.  Which visual aid would you use to portray each of the following points?

1. You want to show that mail-order purchases accounted for 13 percent of all books purchased this year.

2. You want to show that the mail-order book market consists of two segments:  book clubs and other forms of mail order.  You want to show the relative size of the two segments over the past five years, as well as the size of the total book market.

3. You want to show statistics on the people who buy mail-order books.  You have data on their gender, age, education, and annual income, which you want to display for both book-club purchases and other mail-order purchases.

4. You want to show that of all the books bought this year, 27 percent were purchased at a discount.  You want to contrast this to the fact that 49 percent of all book-club books were purchased at a discount, whereas 40 percent of all other mail-order books were discounted.

5. You want to contrast the types of books purchased through retail outlets, book clubs, and other mail-order sources.  You have compiled data on the source of purchases for various categories of fiction (mysteries, romances, westerns, science fiction, adventure, classics, and so on), as well as various nonfiction categories (references, histories, health/diet, religious, home and garden, cookbooks, finance and investments, biographies, art, and so on).

## EXPAND YOUR KNOWLEDGE:  PICTURES THAT TELL THE WRONG STORY

Visual aids and statistics are a valuable tool to report writers, because they invest facts with credibility and drama.  But readers beware.  The following flaws could hide significant problems with the facts that the report is based on:

- *Overwhelming facade*:  Don't let dazzling photographs, charming drawings, and expensive covers and paper blind you to the content of a report.  These niceties are intended to make the facts more palatable, but nothing says you have to suspend all judgment.

- *Apples-and-oranges graphs*:  A series of graphs on the same subject should use similar scales—or clearly indicate that a change has been made.  Otherwise, you cannot sensibly compare the graphs' ups and downs.

- *Chopped-off graph*:  The vertical (upright) axis of a graph is supposed to start with 0 at the base.  But when all the numbers being plotted are significantly above 0, some people erroneously chop off the lower part of the axis and use a higher number at the base.  As a result, the plotted line appears to be much more dramatic than warranted by the facts.

- *Souped-up graph:* One way to solve the problem of a boring, undramatic graph is to change the units of measurement. If the vertical axis is compressed by making the gradations smaller, the line seems to rise and fall much more vigorously. Unfortunately, changes over time are sometimes minor, and no amount of fiddling with the graph will affect the truth—only your perception of the truth.

- *One-dimensional picture:* When pictures are used in a line or bar chart, beware. For instance, if number *A* is represented by a house 1 inch tall, number *B*, which is twice number *A*, should not be represented by a house 2 inches tall. That's because the houses are multidimensional, and their true size is measured by multiplying their height by their width. To be fair, number *A* should be represented by one little house 1 inch tall, and number *B* should be represented by two little houses 1 inch tall.

- *Well-chosen average:* Most so-called averages are the mean, which is derived by adding a string of numbers and dividing by the number of numbers. But the median, which is the number in the exact middle of the group, may also be presented as the average. A clever writer may select the most advantageous of these averages; the clever reader looks for information to clarify which one has been used.

- *Ever-impressive decimal:* Numbers carried out to decimal places look good, but don't let yourself be unduly impressed by them. Would a secretary, average or otherwise, type 5.3 letters a day? It would be more useful to say that a secretary types about five letters a day. By the same token, there is no point in using a decimal figure if the statistic is based on approximate numbers or people's guesses.

- *Sample with built-in bias:* When you read statistics based on a sample, you should also study the procedures used to select the sample so you can judge for yourself whether it has been selected fairly. For example, consider the statement that a company's average profit for the past three years is $1 million. What this statistic does not say is that the company's profit three years ago was $3 million; 2 years ago, $1 million; and last year, $1 million. In all likelihood, the author of the statistic was trying to beautify last year's dismal results by selecting a more favorable sample.

- *Insignificant difference:* Before choosing one option over another on the basis of a rather small statistical difference, look for a number that represents the "probable error." For example, say that 52 percent of a survey sample prefer higher quality, 48 percent prefer lower prices, and the probable error is ±3 points. That means 49 to 55 percent may prefer higher quailty and 45 to 51 percent may prefer lower prices. Because these ranges of numbers overlap, it is foolhardy to choose to offer higher quality over lower prices; if anything, the results show that the sample is evenly divided.

- *Semiattached figure:* Someone with a difficult point to prove may borrow credibility from an unrelated statistic. For example, the claim that "nine out of ten track stars wear Mercury shoes" may be used to convince a small retailer of the value of stocking Mercuries. What the statistic does not say is that the typical jogger does not need shoes of the same high quality—and price—and will not be so easily fooled.

- *Unwarranted assumption:* Do not let someone confuse you about cause and effect. So what if statistics show that those who graduate with high grade-point averages are more likely to become managers than those who graduate with lower grades? The discrepancy may only show that high academic achievers tend to be channeled into management-training programs and receive more attention from supervisors who have high expectations. Some of those who graduated with lower grades may actually have more native management ability but never get the chance to prove it.

*Source:* Adapted from Darrell Huff, "How to Lie with Statistics," in *Strategies for Business and Technical Writing,* ed. Kevin J. Harty (New York: Harcourt Brace Jovanovich, 1980), pp. 241-248;

Rudolf Flesch, *The Art of Clear Thinking* (New York: Harper & Row, 1951), pp. 157-159; Robert Lefferts, *How to Prepare Charts and Graphs for Effective Reports* (New York: Barnes & Noble Books, a division of Harper & Row, 1981); J. C. Mathes and Dwight W. Stevenson, *Designing Technical Reports: Writing for Audiences in Organizations* (Indianapolis, Ind.: Bobbs-Merrill Educational Publishing, 1976), pp. 185-189.

1. Develop your own powers of critical thinking by looking for examples of misleading pictures. Over the next week, collect at least five visual aids or statistical descriptions that are likely to be misinterpreted by an unwary reader. What, specifically, is wrong with each of your examples?

2. Pick a major story of national significance from the front page of a recent issue of the local newspaper. Now obtain at least four other versions of the same story from other sources, such as *U.S.A. Today,* the *New York Times, The Wall Street Journal, Time,* and *Newsweek.* How do the different publications handle the story? Are the same facts presented? How are the various articles illustrated? Can you honestly pick the "truest" version? How?

## DEVELOP YOUR WORD POWER

***Spelling Challenge***    Identify the misspelled word in each of the following sentences, and spell it correctly in the space provided. If all the words in a sentence are spelled correctly, write C in the space.

_____    1.  Do you percieve any differences between this loaf and that one?

_____    2.  Julie is persistant and should eventually find a job she wants.

_____    3.  Try to persuade Mr. Mitchell to send full payment tomorrow.

_____    4.  Do you have any phisical problems that may affect your work?

_____    5.  Greg's preferrence is the oak finish.

_____    6.  The urge to avoid all taxes is quite prevalent.

_____    7.  I would have preferred to discuss this matter in private.

_____    8.  In about a week, we will install the permenent awning.

_____    9.  Your visit Monday was a pleasent surprise.

_____    10.  Having some of the new models is preferrable to having none.

***Vocabulary Challenge***    Match the words in the first column with the definitions in the second column.

_____  11.  prohibitive          A.  exciting

_____  12.  provisional          B.  repetitive

_____  13.  provocative          C.  forbidding

_____  14.  redundant            D.  negligent

_____  15.  remiss               E.  temporary

Circle the best definition of the highlighted word in each of the following sentences.

16.  Dr. Jepson has been a **prolific** writer.

    A.  productive          B.  antiabortion          C.  wordy

17. The new lobby will **protrude** into the courtyard.

    A. meld               B. project            C. flow

18. What does the letter from their attorney **purport**?

    A. say                B. recommend       C. signify

19. Jeff's career has been his **raison d'être**.

    A. constant problem      B. means of support      C. reason for being

20. Remember to **recapitulate** at the end of your presentation.

    A. summarize           B. surrender         C. retrench

Select one of these words to complete each of the following sentences, and write the word in the space provided.

    **propensity**        **protégé**        **proxy**        **rendezvous**        **repertoire**

21. Sylvia has a _____ for accepting more work than she can handle.

22. What other skills do you have in your _____?

23. You will be my _____ during my absence.

24. Miss Blackmer's _____ is being groomed to take over when she retires.

25. They have scheduled a _____ for discussing the details face to face.

*Follow-up Word Study*   Check your answers at the end of this chapter. In the spaces below, write the words that you spelled or used incorrectly. (Use a separate piece of paper if you missed more than five words.) Then look up each word in your dictionary, and carefully study its spelling, pronunciation, definition, and history (etymology). Finally, to help fix the word in your memory, write it in a sentence.

Word                    Sentence

_____      _____

_____      _____

_____      _____

_____      _____

_____      _____

## CHECK YOUR ANSWERS

### Master Key Concepts

| | | |
|---|---|---|
| I. supplement | II. text | IV. C. accuracy |
|   A. detailed |   B. near |      D. scale, influences |
|   B. tables, variables, pie |   C. titles, captions | |

**Quiz Yourself**

1. United Airlines uses pictures and charts to visually depict the highlights of the company's performance. By using illustrations, charts, and graphs, the company is able to present key information in easily understood and easily accepted ways. At the same time, the visual aids make the report more attractive and interesting. (pp. 469-471)

2. These are the six guidelines to follow in planning visual aids:
    a. Begin with raw data.
    b. Develop visual aids that present detailed information.
    c. Develop visual aids that emphasize key points.
    d. Try to achieve a reasonable balance between the illustrations and the text.
    e. Take into account your reader's preferences.
    f. Be practical about the resources available for producing visual aids. (p. 472)

3. A numerical table would be the best choice for presenting detailed statistical or financial information; a more graphic or pictorial format would be better for highlighting key points. (pp. 475-481)

4. A "text" table is, in essence, a part of the paragraph that is typed in tabular format. It is introduced with a sentence that leads directly into the tabulated information and does not have a formal title. (p. 475)

5. If you are comparing trend lines in successive charts, you owe it to your readers to maintain the same *scale* in all the charts. (pp. 476-477)

6. Here are some of the creative options available with bar charts:
    a. Draw the charts either vertically or horizontally.
    b. Show both positive and negative quantities.
    c. Subdivide the bars to show the composition of something.
    d. Double the bars for comparisons.
    e. String a series of bar charts together.
    f. Convert the bars into symbols (pictograms). (p. 478)

7. Ideally, the biggest slice of a pie chart is placed at the *12 o'clock* position. (p. 479)

8. To make a strong connection between the text and the visual aids,
    a. Introduce each visual aid in the text.
    b. Place the visual aid as close as possible to the point you are trying to illustrate.
    c. Reinforce the connection by repeating the important textual point in the title or the caption of the visual aid. (pp. 482-484)

9. A descriptive title identifies the topic of the visual aid; an informative title calls attention to the conclusion that ought to be drawn from the data. (p. 484)

10. In a graph or chart, you can make your sales appear to soar by compressing the *horizontal (or time) scale*, but you will mislead your readers in the process. (p. 486)

**Develop Your Word Power**

| | | | | |
|---|---|---|---|---|
| 1. perceive | 6. C | 11. C | 16. A | 21. propensity |
| 2. persistent | 7. C | 12. E | 17. B | 22. repertoire |
| 3. C | 8. permanent | 13. A | 18. C | 23. proxy |
| 4. physical | 9. pleasant | 14. B | 19. C | 24. protégé |
| 5. preference | 10. preferable | 15. D | 20. A | 25. rendezvous |

# Chapter 18

## COMPLETING THE FORMAL REPORT

The main point of Chapter 18 is that a formal report has an accepted format and sequence of parts. As you read the chapter, think about how the parts correspond to the parts of reports that you have written for school. When you finish reading, check the guidelines in this chapter against a few formal business reports.

## MASTER KEY CONCEPTS

Use the following terms to fill the blanks in the outline. All terms are used, but none is used more than once.

| | | | |
|---|---|---|---|
| appendixes | evidence | prefatory | substance |
| Arabic | format | punctuation | typographically |
| convincing | longer | Roman | 2 inches |
| double-spaced | organization | style | |

I. The _____ (p. 493) and more formal a report, the more separate pieces it has.

  A. The _____ (pp. 494-497) parts, which precede the text of the report, consist of a cover, a title fly (optional), a title page, a letter of authorization (optional), a letter of acceptance (optional), a letter of transmittal (optional), a table of contents, a list of illustrations (optional), and a synopsis (optional).

  B. The text of the report consists of three basic parts: the introduction, which establishes the background, purpose, _____ (pp. 498-499), and tone of the report; the body, which presents the _____ (p. 499) obtained during the study; and the summary, conclusions, and recommendations, which is longer and more detailed for reports organized by the indirect plan than for those organized by the direct plan.

  C. The supplementary parts at the end of the report may include _____ (p. 500) containing material related but not central to the main part of the report, a bibliography listing sources, and an index.

II. An attractive _____ (p. 501) enhances the effectiveness of a report.

  A. All margins should be at least 1 inch; the top margin of the first page of all prefatory and supplementary parts, of the report text, and of chapters within the text should be _____ (p. 501); an extra ½ inch should be left on the side at which the report will be bound.

  B. Differentiate first-, second-, and third-level headings _____ (p. 502), so that readers can use them as a clue to the relationship among ideas; whatever system you use for headings, be consistent throughout the report.

  C. Most reports, especially long ones, should be _____ (p. 502), although letters of authorization, acceptance, and transmittal should be single-spaced; indent paragraphs in double-spaced sections five spaces, but use block style in single-spaced sections; center the copy on the title page both horizontally and vertically.

D.  Number the pages of the prefatory parts with lower-case _____ (p. 502) numerals centered 1 inch from the bottom (but do not number the title page); number all pages in the text of the report with _____ (pp. 502-503) numerals placed 1 inch from the top at the right-hand margin for all pages except those that begin chapters—unless the report is bound at the top, in which case the numbers should be centered 1 inch from the bottom of the page.

III.  Review all reports before submitting them, preferably after a day or two of not working on them.
  A.  Go over the report once to check the organization and the _____ (p. 503), with the idea being to make sure it is clear, accurate, and _____ (p. 503).
  B.  Go over the report a second time to check the finer points of _____ (p. 503) and mechanics, such as word choice, grammar, _____ (p. 503), and typographical accuracy.

IV.  If a week or two go by and you still have not received a response to your report, you might politely inquire whether the report has arrived and offer to answer questions; if the reaction is disappointing, be philosophical and try to learn from the experience.

*Check your answers at the end of this chapter.*

## QUIZ YOURSELF

1. List the components that might be included in a long formal report.

2. What is the difference between a letter of authorization, a letter of acceptance, and a letter of transmittal?

3. An _____ synopsis summarizes the main ideas of the report in the order in which they appear in the text. A _____ synopsis states what the report is about in only moderately greater detail than the table of contents; the actual findings of the report are omitted.

4. What eight topics might you cover in the introduction to a long formal report?

5. What are the differences among a summary, a conclusion, and a recommendation?

6. What types of information might be included in an appendix?

7. What is a guide sheet?

8. Should reports be single-spaced or double-spaced?

9. Discuss the rules for numbering pages.

10. How much time should you allow for editing a report?

*Check your answers at the end of this chapter.*

## BUILD YOUR SKILLS: YOU BE THE EDITOR

The following pages are taken from a report on the U.S. market for home health care. The report was prepared by Jack Williams, a former hospital administrator who is starting a company to provide home-health-care supplies through retail outlets. Jack prepared this report as a means of attracting potential financial backers. He has asked you to critique the report for him and to make any necessary improvements. Here is the introduction of the report, which is intended to give the reader an overview of the market and the role of Jack's proposed company.

### The Market for Home Health Care

This is a report on the market for home health care, which is a large and growing market. Already, 28 million people in the United States are over 65; by 1995, over 34 million Americans will be over 65 years old. These people tend to be big health-care consumers. In fact, people over 65 require twice as much health care as the rest of us.

The U.S. government, in its divine wisdom, has committed us to paying the medical bills of these old people. But the fact is, the country can't really afford to pay the price. Medicare and Medicaid are rapidly growing broke.

The solution to this problem is to encourage these old folks to stay out of hospitals and nursing homes and get the care they need at home. The cost of caring for a person at home is a fraction of the cost of caring for a person in a nursing home or hospital. For this reason, the government will probably pass laws that require it to reimburse people for their home-health-care expenses.

I figure that the current market for home-health-care services is about $2.6 billion. By 1988, the market will be $5.2 billion, and by 1995, the market will be a whopping $10 billion.

As more and more old folks get their health care at home, they will need equipment and supplies. For example, hospital beds, wheelchairs, walkers, traction devices, pads and cushions, toilet devices, and other nondisposable things should make up a $1.8 billion market by 1988.

Disposable supplies are another big segment, which should develop into a $3.6 billion market by 1988. In this category are such items as tapes, dressings, disinfectants, antiseptics, splints, restraints, curettes, adult diapers, diagnostic kits, and the like.

A smaller segment of the market consists of sales of nutritional items for people who are unable to eat the normal way. This segment should have sales of about $190 million in 1988.

Finally, the home-health-care services market consists of such services as chemotherapy, kidney dialysis, and respiratory therapy. This segment will have sales of about $350 million in 1988.

My proposed company would initially be involved in segments I and II above (durable equipment and disposable supplies). I plan to open retail stores that will sell and rent these supplies. The stores will be located in areas with a high concentration of old people, preferably next door to clinics or medical buildings.

The rest of this report explains the need for a company like mine, the strategy I would use to make my operation successful, and the way you can participate in the great home-health-care boom by investing with me.

Data taken from "Home Health Care Revenues to Top $24 Billion by 1995," *Predictions from Predicasts* (Cleveland: Predicasts Research Division, October 1984), p. 1.

## EXPAND YOUR KNOWLEDGE: IN BRIEF

The synopsis at the beginning of a report is a small but significant element. Some readers are interested only in the synopsis (and perhaps the conclusions and recommendations at the end), because they have little time to read a long report or little interest in all the details that contribute to your findings. Even those readers who are willing to read the whole report tend to read the synopsis first. If it is poorly written, they may read no further or read with skepticism. However, a well-written synopsis gets readers thinking about the subject as you perceive it and helps them understand why it is important. Here are some guidelines to help you write a synopsis that does the job:

- *Include enough specific information about your investigation and/or analysis to satisfy the needs of a busy manager.* Do not assume that the manager will remember all the details of the assignment. Briefly recall the problem that led to the assignment and the limits that were set. Then cover the basics in the same general order that they are presented in the report.
- *Make the synopsis a self-contained unit, a complete report-in-miniature.* Write so that someone who does not have time to read the whole report can get the most important details from reading just the summary. Or so that the summary can stand alone if it is circulated independently. If possible, eliminate references to parts of the report and to the report itself (such phrases as "this report contains").

- *Keep your synopsis short.* Synopses vary in length, depending on the length of the entire report, the ease with which the contents can be summarized, and the amount of detail that must be included in the synopsis. Some executives expect a synopsis to be a page long or a paragraph long or some other specific length corresponding to their needs or attention span; you may want to check existing reports or company style manuals for guidelines on this point. Usually, however, a synopsis should be no more than a tenth the length of the entire report—much shorter for a very long report. Aim to make your synopsis as short as possible while still covering all the important details.

- *Write your synopsis in fluent, easy-to-read prose.* Assume that readers are not familiar with jargon or are not experts in the subject of the report. Apply all the principles of writing clear, concise sentences and paragraphs to the synopsis, just as you would in writing any other letter, memo, or report.

- *Keep the tone and emphasis of the synopsis consistent with the tone and emphasis of the report.* Do not put any information or analysis into the synopsis that is not in the report. Make sure that your conclusions and recommendations are presented in the same way, with the same qualifications, in both places.

Although you will usually write the synopsis of your report last, take care to write it well. Schedule plenty of time for a first-class writing job and an objective review. The payoff may be that readers pay more attention to the whole report.

*Source:* Adapted from Christian K. Arnold, "The Writing of Abstracts," in *Strategies for Business and Technical Writing*, ed. Kevin J. Harty (New York: Harcourt Brace Jovanovich, 1980), pp. 213-217.

1. Can you boil things down to the bare essentials? Spend the next three minutes looking at your surroundings. Then summarize what you have seen in one paragraph, so that a complete stranger will get a reasonable idea of your environment.

2. With practice, you can improve your ability to synopsize. Each day for the next week, read a different article from a recent issue of a business magazine like *Fortune* or *Business Week*. Select articles of roughly the same length—three to five pages. After reading each article, write a 250-word synopsis. Keep track of how long it takes you to write these synopses.

## DEVELOP YOUR WORD POWER

*Spelling Challenge*    Identify the misspelled word in each of the following sentences, and spell it correctly in the space provided. If all the words in a sentence are spelled correctly, write *C* in the space.

_____    1.    We should establish a prosedure for handling returns.

_____    2.    Dr. Stein is a promenent psychologist.

_____    3.    At the next meeting, let's persue the idea of reorganizing.

_____    4.    Your losses in the second quarter may be bigger than you realise.

_____    5.    How many responses did we receive?

_____    6.    Try to avoid a recurence of that unfortunate episode.

_____    7.    All moving parts are replacible within 30 days of purchase.

_____    8.    It is my priviledge to recommend Samuel Sharpe for the award.

_____   9.   The questionnaire has 50 items on two pages.

_____   10.   I didn't reconnize any of the names on the list.

**Vocabulary Challenge**   Match the words in the first column with the definitions in the second column.

_____   11.  repugnant         A.   firm

_____   12.  resilient         B.   severe

_____   13.  rigorous          C.   doubtful

_____   14.  skeptical         D.   offensive

_____   15.  steadfast         E.   buoyant

Circle the best definition of the highlighted word in each of the following sentences.

16.  We recommend **retention** of all register receipts for at least five years.

   A.   analysis              B.   keeping              C.   memorization

17.  A new vacation policy is **retroactive** to January 1.

   A.   effective to a past date     B.   scheduled for review     C.   effective to a future date

18.  In **retrospect,** we can be proud of our modest gains during that period.

   A.   looking back          B.   all due modesty      C.   conclusion

19.  He has **reverted** to his old habit of smoking.

   A.   referred              B.   returned             C.   become hostile

20.  Her **savoir faire** is an asset in dealing with clients.

   A.   nice appearance       B.   bubbly personality   C.   diplomacy and tact

Select one of these words to complete each of the following sentences, and write the word in the space provided.

   **reprimand**       **reproach**       **respite**       **stalemate**       **stigma**

21.  Christmas Day is only a brief _____ in the hectic Christmas shopping season.

22.  With time, you will overcome the _____ of bankruptcy.

23.  Until we resolve this _____, we cannot negotiate further.

24.  Robert's handling of the situation is beyond _____.

25.  A formal_____ should make our extreme displeasure clear.

**Follow-up Word Study**   Check your answers at the end of this chapter. In the spaces below, write the words that you spelled or used incorrectly. (Use a separate piece of paper if you missed more than five words.) Then look up each word in your dictionary, and carefully study its spelling, pronunciation, definition, and history (etymology). Finally, to help fix the word in your memory, write it in a sentence.

Word                          Sentence

_____       _____

_____       _____

_____       _____

_____       _____

_____       _____

---

## CHECK YOUR ANSWERS

---

### Master Key Concepts

I. longer
   A. prefatory
   B. organization, evidence
   C. appendixes

II. format
   A. 2 inches
   B. typographically
   C. double-spaced
   D. Roman, Arabic

III. A. substance, convincing
    B. style, punctuation

### Quiz Yourself

1. The following components might be included in a long formal report:

| Prefatory Parts | Text of the Report | Supplementary Parts |
|---|---|---|
| Cover | Introduction | Appendixes |
| Title fly | Body | Bibliography |
| Title page | Summary | Index |
| Letter of authorization | Conclusions | |
| Letter of acceptance | Recommendations | |
| Letter of transmittal | | |
| Table of contents | | |
| List of illustrations | | |
| Synopsis | | |
| (p. 493) | | |

2. A letter of authorization is written by the person who requests the report. It generally discusses the problem, scope, time and money limitations, special instructions, and due date for the report. A letter of acceptance is a reply to the letter of authorization, written by the person who is in charge of doing the study. The letter of acceptance confirms the arrangements for doing the work. A letter of transmittal conveys the report from the writer to the reader. This letter often is merely a brief statement that effectively says, "Here is the report you asked for." However, in some situations, the letter of transmittal might be used to make certain comments "off the record" to some, but not all, of the audience. Or it might call attention to important points, make comments on side issues, suggest follow-up work, or convey helpful information about the background of the report. If the report does not have a synopsis, the transmittal letter might summarize the major findings, conclusions, and recommendations. (pp. 494-495)

3. An *informative* synopsis summarizes the main ideas of the report in the order in which they appear in the text. A *descriptive* synopsis states what the report is about in only moderately greater detail than the table of contents; the actual findings of the report are omitted. (p. 497)

4. The introduction of a long formal report might cover these eight topics:
   a. Authorization: who asked for the report and who prepared it
   b. Problem/purpose: what the report is supposed to accomplish
   c. Scope: what is and is not covered in the report
   d. Background: conditions leading up to the report

e. Sources and methods: how the research was conducted

f. Definitions: explanations of unfamiliar terms

g. Limitations: factors affecting the quality of the report

h. Report organization: sequence of topics to be covered  (pp. 498-499)

5. A summary states the key findings of the report, paraphrased from the body and presented in the order in which they appear in the body.  A conclusion is the writer's analysis of what the findings mean.  A recommendation is a personal opinion, based on the writer's conclusions, about the course of action that should be taken.  (p. 499)

6. An appendix contains materials related to the report but too lengthy or bulky to include or not of direct or vital interest to all readers.  Some typical items that might be placed in an appendix are sample questionnaires and cover letters, sample forms, computer printouts, statistical formulas, and a glossary of terms.  (p. 500)

7. A guide sheet is a piece of paper that a typist uses to locate the center of the paper and the proper positions for margins.  The guide sheet, marked in dark ink, is placed behind each sheet of paper that the typist types on.  With the dark lines showing through, the typist can correctly position the typing on the page.  (p. 502)

8. Both single and double spacing are acceptable; however, long or technical reports are often double-spaced for reading ease.  If the report is double-spaced, all paragraphs should be indented five spaces.  In single-spaced reports, the paragraphs are usually not indented, and one blank line is left between them.  (p. 502)

9. Every page in the report is counted, but not all pages have numbers shown on them.  Prefatory parts are numbered in lower-case Roman numerals, beginning with ii.  (No number appears on the first page, normally the title page.)  These Roman numbers are centered 1 inch from the bottom of the page and have no dashes or periods around them.  The text of the report is numbered with unadorned Arabic numerals.  If the report is bound on the left, the numbers appear in the upper-right-hand corner; if the report is bound on the top, the numbers are centered 1 inch from the bottom of the page.  In either case, page 1 is numbered on the bottom center of the page.  (pp. 502-503)

10. Most good writers spend about as much time editing a report as they do on initial composition. In addition, many writers allow an extra day or two between completing the draft and beginning the editing process so they can approach the job of editing with a fresh perspective.  (p. 503)

## Develop Your Word Power

| | | | | |
|---|---|---|---|---|
| 1. procedure | 6. recurrence | 11. D | 16. B | 21. respite |
| 2. prominent | 7. replaceable | 12. E | 17. A | 22. stigma |
| 3. pursue | 8. privilege | 13. B | 18. A | 23. stalemate |
| 4. realize | 9. C | 14. C | 19. B | 24. reproach |
| 5. C | 10. recognize | 15. A | 20. C | 25. reprimand |

# Chapter 19

## CONDUCTING INTERVIEWS AND MEETINGS

The main point of Chapter 19 is that the success of interviews and meetings relies to a great extent on the participants' listening skills. As you read the chapter, think about the different kinds of interviews and meetings and how the "you" attitude and self-confidence might help someone participate successfully. When you finish reading, think about an interview or meeting that you have participated in, categorize the problems that came up, and speculate on the actions or attitudes that could have solved those problems (or, if the interview or meeting was a total success, analyze why).

## MASTER KEY CONCEPTS

Use the following terms to fill the blanks in the outline. All terms are used, but none is used more than once.

| | | | |
|---|---|---|---|
| active | conversation | open-end | persuasive |
| agenda | critical | participation | semantic |
| closed-end | emergence | perception | training |
| content | flexibility | | |

I. Although being able to listen well is just as important as being able to express oneself well, few of us have undergone the _____ (p. 536) and practice necessary to become good listeners.

   A. Listening is a four-part process consisting of reception (the act of hearing), attention (the act of focusing on certain messages), _____ (p. 537) (the act of interpreting and absorbing what we hear), and retention (the act of storing information for later retrieval).

   B. Your effectiveness as a listener may be limited by three barriers: physical, which prevent you from hearing the message; psychological, which impede your ability to perceive and retain what you hear; and _____ (p. 538), which limit your ability to interpret the speaker's message.

   C. You can be a better listener by learning to listen for _____ (p. 538), to listen critically, to listen empathically, and to listen actively; you can also train yourself to be open to an exchange of information, which will lead to higher-quality decisions, and an exchange of feelings, which will build understanding and mutual respect.

II. An interview is a planned, purposeful _____ (p. 539) that involves at least two people; so important are interviews in the business world that your ability to handle them effectively will influence your success.

   A. Different kinds of interviews require different listening skills: job interviews, information interviews (for obtaining facts), _____ (p. 542) interviews (such as sales calls), and exit interviews (when employees leave) focus on the exchange of information and call for content and _____ (p. 540) listening skills; counseling interviews (for resolving employee problems), conflict-resolution interviews (for reducing tensions between two or more groups), disciplinary interviews, and evaluation interviews involve the exchange of feelings and require empathic and _____ (p. 540) listening.

148

B. Before conducting an interview, you should plan questions that will elicit the information you need, will motivate the other person to respond honestly, and will build a good relationship: _____ (p. 545) questions invite the interviewee to offer an opinion, not just a yes-or-no answer; direct open-end questions are more pointed than open-end questions and suggest a response; _____ (p. 546) questions require yes-or-no answers and short responses; restatement questions invite the interviewee to expand on an answer, to clarify points, and to correct misunderstandings.

C. To obtain the information you need from an interview and to build a good relationship at the same time, you can create a pleasant, relaxed environment for the interview; keep the interview on track but still have some _____ (p. 546); counter hostility by expressing understanding, making the other person aware of her or his resistance, evaluating objections fairly, and holding your arguments until the other person is receptive; and sum up the results before closing on a friendly note.

D. After the interview, write down your thoughts and important facts, and write a brief thank-you note to the other person, if appropriate, that summarizes the outcome.

III. Meetings are held to solve problems, make decisions, and share information.

A. The interaction among the people attending a meeting—especially decision-making meetings—goes through four phases: orientation, conflict, _____ (p. 549) (of a consensus), and reinforcement; the best results occur when participants focus on the group's goals instead of their own.

B. The key to running effective meetings is to do some advance planning: justify the need for getting a group together, determine the purpose (whether to share information or to reach a decision), select participants (roughly seven) who can make an important contribution and who are key decision makers, set the _____ (p. 552) and distribute it to participants beforehand, and prepare the location for the participants' comfort and convenience.

C. The leader must encourage _____ (pp. 552–553), focus attention on what needs to be accomplished, and establish the flow and timing of the discussion; the leader's duties include appointing someone to take notes, keeping the discussion focused on the agenda, encouraging those who are quiet and controlling those who are too domineering, summarizing ideas as the meeting progresses, asking for a decision, clarifying points of agreement or conflict, assigning responsibilities, circulating the minutes after the meeting, and reminding participants of decisions, schedules, and responsibilities.

*Check your answers at the end of this chapter.*

## QUIZ YOURSELF

1. What happens during the perception phase of the listening process?

2. How does a semantic barrier affect the listening process?

3. What general guidelines should you follow to become a better listener?

4. Define the term *interview*.

5. What types of interviews are dominated by the exchange of information? What types involve the exchange of feelings?

6. What is a persuasive interview, and what listening skills are important in this situation?

7. _____ interviews are conducted to correct personnel problems that are interfering with work performance; _____ interviews are designed to correct behavior that is contrary to the organization's rules and regulations.

8. In planning the questions for an interview, what three general goals should you bear in mind?

9. What are the four phases of a decision-making meeting?

10. What are some of the common roles taken by participants at a meeting?

*Check your answers at the end of this chapter.*

### BUILD YOUR SKILLS: PLAN YOUR HIGH-STAKES INTERVIEW

To develop your ability to handle challenging interviews, try your hand at planning your strategy for asking for a raise. Use a current or past job as a frame of reference, or invent a job. Write down your plan for conducting the conversation with your boss. Include a list of questions you should ask, points you want to make, and responses you can give to your boss's possible objections.

## EXPAND YOUR KNOWLEDGE: HOW TO NEGOTIATE LIKE A PRO

The point of many business interviews and meetings is to negotiate something: a job offer, a raise in pay, a new office or assignment, a contract for work, a purchase. What all these situations have in common is that they bring together two or more parties with competing needs and interests who nevertheless must come to some agreement. The process by which that agreement is reached is called negotiating.

A lot of people are afraid of negotiating. True, some "hard-ball" types don't consider a negotiation successful unless they win and the other party loses. This sort of negotiation is understandably somewhat intimidating. Most people, however, approach a negotiation with much the same feeling: a simple desire to get what they need. They do not have any particular desire to win at the other party's expense.

How can you negotiate successfully? Try some of these tactics:

- *Know what you need and what you would like.* The minimum acceptable outcome—what you need —is the ammunition you keep in reserve. But aim for the ideal solution; you just might get it. The secret is to have confidence that your needs are legitimate and that your desires are justified.

- *Accentuate the positive*: Always negotiate for something positive, never against something negative. A positive attitude is easier for the other party to accept—and therefore more effective. Also remember that negotiation is a compromise; you will get some of what you want, and the other party will get some of what it wants. Assume that both parties can find some common ground, and plan on doing your best to reach it.

- *Prepare, prepare, prepare.* Learn all you can in advance about the other party's strengths, weaknesses, goals, and motives. Don't assume that the other party's goals are the same as yours. If hard data about the other party isn't available, develop some reasonable hunches. Then get all the facts so that you can explain why your position is a good deal for everyone. The more facts you have, the more convincing you will be. Finally, rehearse the negotiation with a colleague who can play the role of the other party.

- *Be ethical.* Don't risk losing your credibility by being tricky or deceitful. The other party is probably just as worried as you are about being taken advantage of. But if you demonstrate that you can be trusted, you probably will be.

- *Negotiate from physical as well as moral strength.* You need to be rested and alert to do your best in a situation like this. A comfortable environment is important too, so do what you can to find suitable seating and to regulate the temperature and lighting to your liking.

- *Use the "you" attitude to encourage the other party's cooperation.* Avoid being judgmental; adopt a helpful, cooperative stance; look for the real meaning behind the other party's words. Then, when it's time to present your proposal, try to put it in terms of benefits to the other party. If you can, let the other party seem to come up with the best ideas and to get the better deal.

- *Present yourself as a human being.* You are an individual with your own style, just as the other party is. Be yourself. Don't be afraid to let the other party know that you have a life beyond the negotiating table.

- *Stay flexible.* Examine the issue from every possible angle. You may come up with a compromise that is fairer to both parties than your original solution. Remember, too, that money isn't everything. Focusing too much on the financial aspects of the issue may cause you to neglect other, more important points.

- *Remain cool, calm, and collected.* Don't let yourself be rushed; set your own pace. If the other party tries to push for a quick agreement or bully you into accepting a solution you won't be happy with, stand your ground. And if you are faced with someone who seems determined to provoke you, don't overreact. Remain the capable professional that you are, and keep on negotiating.

- *Be a gracious winner.* You can win the battle but lose the war, meaning a future relationship with the other party, if you gloat over your victory. Remember that the other party has not only needs for a certain outcome of negotiations but also the human need to save face. Exercise your tact.

- *Get any agreement in writing.* In the process of writing out the agreement, issues are often clarified. And signing on the dotted line cements the negotiated agreement.

The ability to negotiate successfully enhances your job satisfaction and may increase your financial rewards, so give it your best effort.

*Source*: Adapted from David D. Seltz and Alfred J. Modica, *Negotiate Your Way to Success* (New York: New American Library, 1980), pp. 183-200; Kay Cassill, *The Complete Handbook for Freelance Writers* (Cincinnati: Writer's Digest Books, 1981), pp. 220-221; and Herb Cohen, *You Can Negotiate Anything* (Secaucus, N.J.: Lyle Stuart, 1980).

1. Everyday life is full of situations that involve negotiation—although few people are conscious of "bargaining" with friends or relatives. But the next time you are in a situation that involves two opposing views—yours and someone else's—try to negotiate like a pro. The issue may be which movie to attend, where to go for dinner, who cleans what, or any of a host of other routine decisions. Do you find that behaving like a professional negotiator gives you an edge in convincing the other person to agree with you?

2. Identify a time in your life when you have been involved in an important negotiation—perhaps buying a car, convincing your parents to let you do something, or making housing arrangements with friends. Was the outcome totally satisfactory? Did you consciously or unconsciously apply any of the principles of negotiation listed here? If you had it to do over again, what would you do differently?

## DEVELOP YOUR WORD POWER

*Spelling Challenge*   Identify the misspelled word in each of the following sentences, and spell it correctly in the space provided. If all the words in a sentence are spelled correctly, write C in the space.

_____  1.  Seize the opportunity to profit from others' mistakes!

_____  2.  The most sensable course is to build slowly.

_____  3.  These serviceable tablecloths will give you many years of wear.

_____  4.  Our sales representatives receive a strait commission.

_____  5.  Compare the strenth of Grit detergent with that of your current brand.

_____  6.  This policy supercedes your old one.

_____  7.  Donna desperately wants to succede in sales.

_____  8.  The replacement we are sending is similiar to the umbrella you bought.

_____  9.  Keep yesterday's receipts seperate from today's.

_____  10. Each day has a certain rythem from start to finish.

*Vocabulary Challenge*   Match the words in the first column with the definitions in the second column.

| | |
|---|---|
| _____ 11. tacit | A. implied |
| _____ 12. tedious | B. succinct |
| _____ 13. tenacious | C. persistent |
| _____ 14. terse | D. hackneyed |
| _____ 15. trite | E. monotonous |

Circle the best definition of the highlighted word in each of the following sentences.

16. Be careful not to **subvert** your own authority by appearing too playful.

    A. undermine        B. increase        C. mock

17. Five temporary clerks will be **sufficient** during the holidays.

    A. enough        B. employed        C. absent

18. Professor Buckalew will be one of the panelists at the **symposium**.

    A. inquiry        B. trade show        C. conference

19. This move will require us to **synchronize** many people and things.

    A. weed out        B. coordinate        C. notify

20. Include a **synopsis** at the beginning of the report.

    A. outline        B. introduction        C. summary

Select one of these words to complete each of the following sentences, and write the word in the space provided.

    **superficial**    **superfluous**    **susceptible**    **symbolic**    **synonymous**

21. Unfortunately, our sophisticated new equipment is _____ to breakdown.

22. See if you can flesh out this _____ analysis.

23. The name Pearson's is _____ with value.

24. The statue in front of the building is _____ of our role in the world of health care.

25. Jane already realizes her mistake; your criticism is _____ .

*Follow-up Word Study*   Check your answers at the end of this chapter. In the spaces below, write the words that you spelled or used incorrectly. (Use a separate piece of paper if you missed more than five words.) Then look up each word in your dictionary, and carefully study its spelling, pronunciation, definition, and history (etymology). Finally, to help fix the word in your memory, write it in a sentence.

Word                      Sentence

_____      _____

_____      _____

_____      _____

_____      _____

_____      _____

# CHECK YOUR ANSWERS

## Master Key Concepts

I.  training
    A. perception
    B. semantic
    C. content

II. conversation
    A. persuasive, critical, active
    B. open-end, closed-end
    C. flexibility

III. A. emergence
     B. agenda
     C. participation

## Quiz Yourself

1. Perception is the act of interpreting and absorbing what you hear.  During this phase of the listening process, you fit the speaker's message into your own frame of reference, depending on your values, beliefs, ideas, expectations, roles, needs, and personal history.  Perception is the most complex and influential component of listening and the point where the speaker's meaning is most likely to be distorted.   (p. 537)

2. A semantic barrier is a source of misunderstanding that arises from differences in the way the speaker and the listener use language.  If two people have different vocabularies because of educational, professional, social, ethnic, racial, or age differences, they have trouble grasping the nuances of each other's comments.  The words used imply slightly different things to speaker and listener.  In extreme cases, the speaker's words may be totally incomprehensible to the listener.  (p. 538)

3. Follow these general guidelines to become a better listener:
   a. Clear your mind of barriers that may interfere with effective listening.
   b. Select surroundings conducive to listening.
   c. Be alert and attentive.
   d. Be positive:  assume that you will benefit from listening.
   e. Maintain eye contact with the speaker.
   f. React responsively, and provide feedback to the speaker.
   g. Listen for central themes; be alert to both words and gestures, facts and feelings.
   h. Interrupt only to ask clarifying questions.
   i. Pay attention to body language.
   j. Do not be put off by emotional words or ideas.
   k. Delay evaluation until you have had time to consider the entire exchange.  (pp. 538-539)

4. An interview is a planned conversation with a specific purpose involving at least two people. (p. 539)

5. Job interviews, information interviews, persuasive interviews, and exit interviews are dominated by the exchange of information.  The exchange of feelings is important in counseling interviews, conflict-resolution interviews, disciplinary interviews, and evaluation interviews.  (pp. 540-545)

6. A persuasive interview is one in which you try to convince the other person of something.  The objective is to "sell" a product, a service, or an idea of some sort.  The person conducting the interview presents information designed to convince the listener that the product, service, or idea is good and satisfies the listener's needs.  The listener must exercise critical and content

listening skills to determine whether the interviewer's facts and conclusions are correct; the interviewer must listen empathically in order to draw out the other person's feelings and learn about her or his needs. (pp. 540, 542)

7. *Counseling* interviews are conducted to correct personnel problems that are interfering with work performance; *disciplinary* interviews are designed to correct behavior that is contrary to the organization's rules and regulations. (pp. 542-543, 544)

8. In formulating the questions for an interview, you should bear in mind that the purpose of the questions is threefold:
   a. To get information
   b. To motivate the interviewee to respond honestly and appropriately
   c. To create a good working relationship with the other person (p. 545)

9. The four phases of a decision-making meeting are
   a. The orientation phase, during which the participants become acquainted and agree on the purpose
   b. The conflict phase, when participants air their views and weigh pros and cons
   c. The emergence phase, during which a consensus develops
   d. The reinforcement phase, when the group assigns responsibilities and develops commitment to the solution (p. 549)

10. The following roles tend to be taken in any meeting:
   a. Climate maker: creates a productive atmosphere
   b. Coordinator: ties things together
   c. Gatekeeper: guides the flow of information
   d. Harmonizer: reduces tension
   e. Information giver: provides facts
   f. Information seeker: asks for facts
   g. Initiator: gets the process moving
   h. Opinion giver: states opinions based on experience
   1. Opinion seeker: asks others for their opinions
   j. Standard setter: focuses the group's attention on a good decision
   k. Summarizer: ties up loose ends (p. 549)

## Develop Your Word Power

| | | | | |
|---|---|---|---|---|
| 1. C | 6. supersedes | 11. A | 16. A | 21. susceptible |
| 2. sensible | 7. succeed | 12. E | 17. A | 22. superficial |
| 3. C | 8. similar | 13. C | 18. C | 23. synonymous |
| 4. straight | 9. separate | 14. B | 19. B | 24. symbolic |
| 5. strength | 10. rhythm | 15. D | 20. C | 25. superfluous |

# Chapter 20

## GIVING SPEECHES AND ORAL PRESENTATIONS

The main point of Chapter 20 is that speeches and oral presentations require just as much preparation and skillful execution as a formal report does. As you read the chapter, think about the parallels between these "oral reports" and their written cousins. When you finish reading, analyze the strengths and weaknesses of someone else's speech or oral presentation, and then list ways that the weaknesses could have been overcome.

## MASTER KEY CONCEPTS

Use the following terms to fill the blanks in the outline. All terms are used, but none is used more than once.

| | | | |
|---|---|---|---|
| briefings | interaction | presentation | theme |
| credibility | letters | question-and-answer | three |
| eye | memos | report | transparencies |
| impromptu | models | | |

I. Regardless of the career you pursue, sooner or later you are likely to be asked to deliver a speech or _____ (pp. 557–558).

   A. Short speeches, which last for 15 minutes or less, resemble _____ (p. 558) and _____ (p. 558) in breadth of content and organization; some examples are introductions (which set the stage for people, events, or concepts), _____ (p. 559) (which describe projects, procedures, programs, or activities), recognition speeches (which acknowledge someone's contribution and reinforce the audience's morale), and welcoming speeches (which build enthusiasm, establish rapport, outline an event, and explain the ground rules).

   B. Formal presentations lasting an hour or more cover complex subjects, involve extensive audience _____ (p. 559), and require visual aids; although similar in some respects to formal reports, oral presentations allow immediate interaction with the audience but do not permit the audience to consult what has gone before.

II. In general, developing a formal presentation requires you to use the same structural pieces that are used in a formal _____ (p. 560) and to use similar kinds of visual aids; however, there are some differences.

   A. The process of developing a presentation takes place in four steps: develop a _____ (pp. 560–561), a single sentence that summarizes who should do what and why after your presentation is complete; develop an outline with _____ (p. 561) or fewer main points and only the most essential facts for backup; establish the time frame (you can orally deliver about 1 paragraph per minute, or 20 to 25 pages of typed, double-spaced text per hour); and decide on the appropriate style, ranging from casual and participative for small, decision-oriented presentations to formal for large, important events.

   B. Long presentations consist of the same basic pieces as formal reports do: an introduction that identifies the topic, outlines the main points, arouses interest, and establishes

_____ (p. 564) with the audience; a body that is streamlined and simple, relies heavily on transitions to summarize and preview ideas, and is interwoven with such pace-changing devices as visual aids, specific examples, and audience interaction; a final summary that reviews the main points, emphasizes information that will help the audience make a decision or understand the subject, is memorable, and will motivate the audience to accept your ideas; and a _____ (pp. 565–566) period (at the end for large, hostile, or unfamiliar groups, during the presentation for small groups trying to reach a decision).

    C. Presentations accompanied by visual aids are more interesting and more likely to be understood and remembered by the audience; the most common visual aids used in presentations are handouts, chalkboards and other boards, flip charts, _____ (p. 568) projected on a screen in full daylight, opaque projections (showing typed or printed material on a screen), slides projected on a screen in a darkened room, and such other props as samples, _____ (p. 568), audiotapes, filmstrips and movies, and videotapes.

II. The final step in preparing for a presentation is to practice your delivery.
    A. Depending on your personal style and the situation, you may choose to deliver a memorized speech, to read a speech from prepared text, to speak from an outline or notes, or to make _____ (p. 570) comments (without advance preparation).
    B. The best way to improve your delivery is to practice such techniques as projecting enthusiasm, using your voice and body to arouse the audience's interest, and maintaining _____ (p. 570) contact; you can also learn to overcome stage fright and to handle tough audiences if you accept the fact that many people have these problems and that most members of the audience are silently wishing you success.

_Check your answers at the end of this chapter._

## QUIZ YOURSELF

1. What are three general characteristics of short speeches?

2. What are the four most common types of short speeches?

3. How do long, formal presentations differ from short speeches and from major reports?

4. In developing a theme for your presentation, what three questions should you ask yourself?

5. What is involved in establishing the time frame for a speech or presentation?

6. In general, when would you cultivate a casual, informal style in a presentation, and when would you use a more formal approach?

7. Briefly describe some of the most commonly used visual aids for oral presentations.

8. Briefly describe the four delivery modes. When might you use each approach?

9. What are four items you should check on before giving a presentation?

10. List at least five things you can do to overcome stage fright.

*Check your answers at the end of this chapter.*

## BUILD YOUR SKILLS:  PLAN YOUR FIVE-MINUTE SPEECH

You have been asked to prepare a five-minute speech about your school to present to a group of high school seniors who are deciding which college to attend.  You don't know any of the students, but you have been told that they are 25 high achievers from Des Moines, Iowa, who are visiting your campus as well as others.  Write out a plan for this speech.

## EXPAND YOUR KNOWLEDGE:  A MASTER'S VOICE

When an audience cannot hear the speaker or is lulled into inattention by the quality of the speaker's voice, the communication process is impeded.  An authoritative and compelling voice is not easy to develop, but you can improve the way you sound by diligent practice.

**Producing Words**

Most people have trouble concentrating on the content of a speech when the speaker has problems with pronunciation (correctness) or articulation (distinctness). To improve your pronunciation, make sure you know the correct way to say every word that is likely to be used in your speech. If in doubt, consult the pronunciation key in a dictionary. You could also look up every word you read in daily life that you don't know how to pronounce. Listen to the speech of others as well for pronunciations that you are not familiar with; when you look up these words, you may find that you are right and the other person is wrong, but at least you will know.

You can begin attacking any articulation problems you may have by trying these exercises:

- Sit about 15 feet away from a friend in an unoccupied room. Then converse in a whisper. Your friend will not be able to understand what you are saying unless you articulate carefully.
- Say these sounds rapidly while exaggerating your lip movements: *oo, ee, oo, ah, oo, ee, oo, ah.* Then, exaggerating your lip and tongue movements, say these sounds: *pppppp pah, pppppp pay, pppppp pee, bbbbbb bah, bbbbbb bay, bbbbbb bee, tttttt tah, tttttt tay, tttttt tee, dddddd dah, dddddd day, dddddd dee.*
- Make a list of the sounds that you have trouble articulating. While you say words that contain these sounds, record your voice and look in a mirror. Watch how your lips, jaw, and tongue move as you articulate the words correctly and incorrectly; close your eyes and feel the differences too. Finally, listen critically to the tape.
- Make a list of the common words that you tend to articulate carelessly, such as *jist* and *git.* Every week, select one or two of these words and make a point of articulating them correctly in your everyday conversations.

Your accent may cause problems too, but only if it differs considerably from what your audience is used to. People with unusually heavy accents—foreign or domestic—may find it worthwhile to consult a speech therapist for help in developing a general American accent.

**Producing Tones**

The first step in developing your ability to produce tones that can reach and excite an audience is to record your voice. Try some general conversation, an extemporaneous speech, and prose and poetry reading. When you play back the tape, take notes about the loudness of your voice, the variety in your voice's rate and pitch, and its tone of pleasantness.

If the loudness of your voice seems to be a problem, try some of these exercises:

- Practice speaking louder or softer (as necessary) in your everyday conversations.
- Speak from the front of an unused classroom with a friend sitting 2 feet away, then in one of the front rows, then in the middle of the room, then in the back row. Your friend can use hand signals to tell you when your voice is too soft or too loud. Remember that your goal in speaking to an audience is to project your voice to the back row.
- While talking normally, observe in a mirror the amount of space between your upper and lower teeth. Observe the jaw movements and the space between your teeth that produce the appropriate voice volume.

Here are some exercises for developing vocal variety:

- To learn how to vary your speaking rate, count or recite the alphabet at different speeds.
- Read aloud several literary passages. Speak slowly when reading the serious passages; speak more quickly when reading the lighter passages.

- Draw slash lines to indicate appropriate pauses between groups of words in a literary passage. Then read the passage, pausing at each slash line. When you finish, draw a different set of slash lines and read again; notice how the meaning seems to change.
- Practice using volume for variety. Read a passage, count, or recite the alphabet in several different ways: starting out with a soft voice that gradually becomes louder, starting loudly and ending softly, and then emphasizing selected words or phrases by speaking either more loudly or more softly than the normal volume.
- Limber up the pitch you use in speaking by counting in different tones; start with the lowest note your voice can comfortably reach, and progress to the highest note—as if you were doing vocal scales. Then start counting from the highest note and progress to the lowest note. Finally, experiment with pitch as you read a literary passage.

If you need to improve the tone of pleasantness in your voice, try these:

- Pretend that you are different sorts of people as you count or recite the alphabet: a conceited snob; someone sincere and genuine; a bitter, malicious person; a caring friend; a listless, lifeless person; a healthy, vigorous, enthusiastic person; someone who is insensitive and intolerant; a sensitive, obliging, helpful person.
- To come across as an interesting speaker, you must be an interesting person. As you conduct your life, try to become more aware of the things you see, hear, smell, taste, and touch. Become more sensitive to ideas, feelings, and beauty. Your discoveries will help you put more meaning into your words.

*Source*:    Adapted from Milton Dickens, *Speech: Dynamic Communication*, 3rd ed. (New York: Harcourt Brace Jovanovich, 1974), pp. 172-187; John A. Grasham and Glenn G. Gooder, *Improving Your Speech* (New York: Harcourt Brace Jovanovich, 1960), pp. 303-310; Louise M. Scrivner and Dan Robinette, *A Guide to Oral Interpretation: Solo and Group Performance*, 2nd ed. (Indianapolis, Ind.: Bobbs-Merrill Educational Publishing, 1980), pp. 76-87.

1. The quality of your voice depends to a great extent on how well you breathe. To test your breath control, take a deep, deep breath, and then gradually exhale, letting the air hiss out through slightly pursed lips. Time yourself. How long does it take you to exhale?

2. How articulate are you? Test yourself on these tongue twisters:

> Betty Botta bought some butter.
> "But," she said, "this butter's bitter.
> If I put it in my batter,
> It will make my batter bitter.
> But a bit of better butter
> Will make my bitter batter better."
>
> So she bought a bit of butter—
> Better than the bitter butter —
> And it made her bitter batter better.
> So 'twas better Betty Botta
> Bought a bit of better butter.

> Theophilus Thistle, the successful thistle sifter, in sifting a sieve full of unsifted thistles, thrust three thousand thistles through the thick of his thumb. Now if Theophilus Thistle, the successful thistle sifter, in sifting a sieve full of unsifted

thistles, thrust three thousand thistles through the thick of his thumb, see that thou, in sifting a sieve full of unsifted thistles, thrust not three thousand thistles through the thick of thy thumb.  Success to the successful thistle sifter.

Luke Luck likes lakes.
Luck's duck likes lakes.
Luke Luck licks lakes.
Luke's duck licks lakes.
Duck takes licks
In lakes Luke Luck likes.
Luke Luck takes licks
In lakes Luck's duck likes.

## DEVELOP YOUR WORD POWER

*Spelling Challenge*    Identify the misspelled word in each of the following sentences, and spell it correctly in the space provided.  If all the words in a sentence are spelled correctly, write C in the space.

1.  Reserve the meeting room for next Wensday.

2.  For a long report, a table of contents is useful.

3.  A deposit is unecessary for orders under $50.

4.  This year our researchers discovered a twelfth-century townsite.

5.  While I'm on the road, you can reach me threw the main office.

6.  Midday tempratures are in the high 70s.

7.  The store needs a through, floor-to-ceiling cleaning.

8.  We are truely sorry for any inconvenience you have experienced.

9.  After only a week, the thermometer is no longer useable.

10.  Store your valuables in our security vaults.

*Vocabulary Challenge*    Match the words in the first column with the definitions in the second column.

___ 11. ulterior
___ 12. uncompromising
___ 13. unilateral
___ 14. unprecedented
___ 15. urbane

A.  one-sided
B.  firm
C.  unparalleled
D.  sophisticated
E.  concealed

Circle the best definition of the highlighted word in each of the following sentences.

16.  After working with Richard for five years, I have learned to cope with his **vagaries.**

   A.  abstractions        B. bad moods        C. whims

17.  The **vicissitudes** of the restaurant business parallel the state of the general economy.

   A.  ups and downs       B. fads             C. truths

18. Before our new product line comes out, we will be **vulnerable** to the competition.

    A. bothersome          B. attractive          C. defenseless

19. Many of our customers are **wary** because they have been disappointed.

    A. combative          B. tired          C. on guard

20. Many new inspectors are overly **zealous**.

    A. sensitive          B. diligent          C. trained

Select one of these words to complete each of the following sentences, and write the word in the space provided.

    **vacillating**        **vapid**        **versatile**        **vigilant**        **vindictive**

21. Protect your home with a _____ watchdog.

22. We have enough specialists; let's try to find someone who is _____.

23. Don't be in a hurry to write up a contract for a _____ client; his mind will change before the ink is dry.

24. A _____ commercial is unlikely to build anyone's enthusiasm.

25. Julia is _____ and will not hesitate to pay you back for insulting her.

*Follow-up Word Study*    Check your answers at the end of this chapter. In the spaces below, write the words that you spelled or used incorrectly. (Use a separate piece of paper if you missed more than five words.) Then look up each word in your dictionary, and carefully study its spelling, pronunciation, definition, and history (etymology). Finally, to help fix the word in your memory, write it in a sentence.

Word                 Sentence

_____     _____

_____     _____

_____     _____

_____     _____

_____     _____

## CHECK YOUR ANSWERS

**Master Key Concepts**

I. presentation
    A. letters, memos, briefings
    B. interaction

II. report
    A. theme, three
    B. credibility, question-and-answer
    C. transparencies, models

III. A. impromptu
        B. eye

**Quiz Yourself**

1. Short speeches have three general characteristics:
   a. They deal with simple, straightforward subjects.
   b. They involve relatively little audience interaction.
   c. They do not require many visual aids.  (p. 558)

2. The four most common types of short speeches are
   a. Introductions
   b. Briefings
   c. Recognition speeches
   d. Welcoming speeches  (pp. 558-559)

3. Unlike short speeches, long, formal presentations often last an hour or more. They may deal with complex and controversial subjects and frequently involve a good deal of interaction between the speaker and the audience. They often are accompanied by visual aids, some of which may be quite elaborate.

   In contrast to written reports, oral presentations permit the audience and the speaker to interact immediately. As a consequence, oral presentations can be used to deal with subjects and situations that require collaboration between the speaker and the audience. In presentations where collaboration occurs, the speaker has less control over content than the writer of a major report does. In other words, presentations are less predictable than reports and require more flexibility on the part of the author/speaker.

   Oral presentations also differ from written reports in terms of the needs of the audience. Listeners are more likely to lose the thread of an argument than are readers, who can backtrack to refresh their memory. As a consequence, listeners are likely to miss important points unless the speaker takes special pains to present the material so that the audience can tune in and out without getting lost.  (pp. 559-560)

4. In developing a theme for your presentation, ask yourself these three questions:
   a. What are the key issues involved in this subject?
   b. How do I want the audience to react to these issues?
   c. What is the audience's existing attitude and level of knowledge?  (p. 560)

5. In establishing the time frame for a speech or presentation, first figure out approximately how many points you want to cover in a given period of time. For example, if you want to cover three points in 5 minutes, your speech should be about three paragraphs long (375 to 450 words), and you should spend about 1 minute on each point, leaving yourself 1 minute each for the introduction and conclusion.

   Thinking about the relationship between the number of points on your outline and the amount of time available for your presentation will prevent you from trying to cover too much material in too little time or, alternatively, from running out of things to say when you are 15 minutes into a presentation that is scheduled to last 30 minutes.  (pp. 562-563)

6. You should use a casual, informal style for your presentation if you are addressing a group of ten or fewer who are trying to reach a decision. To achieve this style, you could hold the presentation in a small conference room and seat the audience around a table. You could also use simple visual aids and invite the audience to interject comments throughout the presentation. Your remarks should be delivered in a conversational tone with the aid of a few notes, if necessary.

   If you are addressing a large audience for a significant event or ceremonial occasion, you should establish a more formal tone. You could do this by holding the meeting in an auditorium or a convention hall, where the audience sits in rows. You might also use slides or a film to dramatize your message. Ask the audience to hold all questions until you have concluded your remarks. Use detailed notes or a complete script to guide your delivery. (p. 563)

7. The most commonly used visual aids are
   a. Handouts: papers that the audience can refer to after the presentation to remind themselves of important ideas. Handouts may be given to the audience before or after the presentation.
   b. Boards: chalkboards, magnetic boards, flannel boards, and white boards. All can be used to illustrate points during a presentation.
   c. Flip charts: large sheets of paper, attached at the top like a tablet and propped against an easel. The speaker can either prepare the charts in advance or create them on the spot as the presentation progresses.
   d. Transparencies: transparent sheets of film, with information written or drawn on them, that can be projected on a screen in full daylight. Transparencies are generally prepared in advance, but they can be modified with pens during the presentation.
   e. Opaque projections: images of any regular typed or printed material that can be cast on a screen with the use of a special projector.
   f. Slides: mounted pieces of film showing either text or visual material that are projected on a screen in a darkened room. Slides must be prepared in advance; showing slides tends to limit audience interaction. (pp. 566-568)

8. The four delivery modes and their characteristics are as follows:
   a. Memorizing: committing all or part of the speech to memory, word for word. This is not generally a good way to deliver an entire speech or presentation, but it is often an effective technique for the introduction, the conclusion, or special quotations or stories.
   b. Reading: delivering a prepared script by reading it verbatim. Reading is an appropriate approach when precise wording is necessary and is often used for delivering policy statements and technical papers. Reading has the disadvantage of limiting eye contact and interaction with the audience.
   c. Speaking from notes: speaking in a conversational way with the help of notes, transparencies, or an outline. This method permits eye contact and audience interaction and gives the speaker flexibility to deviate from the planned material. Notes are used for most decision-making presentations and for many brief speeches.
   d. Impromptu speaking: delivering remarks spontaneously, without any advance preparation. Impromptu speaking is not recommended for long, formal presentations, but it is appropriate for responding to questions during a meeting. (pp. 569-570)

9. In checking the location for your presentation, make sure that these four items are ready:
   a. Seating arrangements
   b. Electrical outlets
   c. Light switches and dimmers
   d. Equipment required for visual aids, such as flip chart easels, chalkboards, chalk, and erasers (p. 570)

10. Here are some things you can do to overcome stage fright:
    a. Select a topic that interests you, and prepare your material thoroughly.
    b. Rehearse several times.
    c. Think positively.
    d. Be realistic about stage fright; it's natural.
    e. As you prepare to begin speaking, tell yourself that you are ready.

f. Take a few deep breaths before you begin speaking.
g. Memorize your first sentence.
h. Drink a little water if your throat is dry.
i. Use the podium for security if need be.
j. Establish eye contact with individuals in the audience.
k. Don't panic if you feel that the audience is bored; involve them in the action.
l. Use visual aids to maintain and revive audience interest.   (pp. 570–573)

## Develop Your Word Power

1. Wednesday
2. C
3. unnecessary
4. twelfth
5. through
6. temperatures
7. thorough
8. truly
9. usable
10. C
11. E
12. B
13. A
14. C
15. D
16. C
17. A
18. C
19. C
20. B
21. vigilant
22. versatile
23. vacillating
24. vapid
25. vindictive

## INTERNATIONAL BUSINESS COMMUNICATION

The main point of Component Chapter A is that communication with people in other countries requires special sensitivity and enhanced skills. As you read the chapter, think about not only the language barriers that often exist but also the cultural barriers that affect relations even with people from other English-speaking countries. When you finish reading, seek opportunities to communicate with people from another part of the world and take note of the accommodations you must make in order to communicate well.

## MASTER KEY CONCEPTS

Use the following terms to fill the blanks in the outline. All terms are used, but none is used more than once.

| | | | |
|---|---|---|---|
| body | ethnocentric | monetary | respond |
| cultural | feedback | nonverbal | time |
| differences | formal | oral | written |

I. International business communication, like all communication, has three goals: to tell the audience exactly what you mean, to get the audience to _____ (p. 578) as you intended, and to build mutual respect between you and the audience.

II. The more _____ (p. 578) there are between the people communicating, the more difficult communication is.
   A. Much business communication is conducted in English, but when you must communicate with people who do not know English, you must overcome the language barrier by either learning their language, using a translator or interpreter, or teaching them your language; _____ (p. 579) communication is usually less of a problem than _____ (p. 579) communication.
   B. _____ (p. 580) differences that manifest themselves in unconscious assumptions and _____ (p. 580) communication patterns are responsible for many misunderstandings in international business dealings; among the areas that are most different from culture to culture are religion and values, roles and status, decision-making customs, concepts of _____ (p. 581), concepts of personal space, _____ (p. 581) language, and social behavior and manners.
   C. _____ (p. 582) reactions—judging people from other cultures according to our own standards—exacerbate the problems that may arise from language and cultural differences; through trying to understand cultural differences and reacting to foreigners as individual human beings, many of these problems can be overcome.

III. By being aware of these barriers and consciously trying to overcome them, you can improve your effectiveness as an international business communicator.
   A. In written communication, use the same basic guidelines presented in this book: in letters, use clear and simple language, adopt a somewhat more _____ (p. 583)

tone than usual, use either the block or the modified block style, and be tolerant of cultural differences; in memos and reports, concentrate on being clear, be somewhat more formal than usual, and check in advance (if possible) for special reporting requirements and reader expectations; in other documents, use the _____ (p. 584) units and system of measurement used in the other country.

B.  When the situation calls for face-to-face communication, learn in advance about the other person's culture through books, magazines, and other references; learn at least a few words of the language; be alert to cultural differences and try to overcome them by keeping an open mind, listening carefully, clarifying your words with examples and repetition, inviting _____ (p. 587), concentrating on words more than on nonverbal communication, and confirming any understanding both at the end of the conversation and in writing later.

*Check your answers at the end of this chapter.*

## QUIZ YOURSELF

1. What are some of the ways that you might become involved in international business?

2. Describe a situation in which it might be practical for an organization to overcome a language barrier by teaching other people to speak English.

3. Which forms of written communication from North American firms to foreign countries are most likely to require translation?

4. What language barriers might you encounter in a conversation with a person from an English-speaking country?

5. Briefly explain why cultural differences give rise to misunderstandings in international business communication.

6. Give an example of how the North American focus on efficiency and productivity might be inappropriate in another culture.

7. Give an example that illustrates how a gesture that is meaningful in one country can be misconstrued by a person from another culture.

8. Briefly discuss the implications of ethnocentrism.

9. Give some tips on how to achieve clarity in letters written in English to people from other cultures.

10. What are some of the things you should try to learn about another country before taking a business trip there?

*Check your answers at the end of this chapter.*

## BUILD YOUR SKILLS: PLAN YOUR BUSINESS TRIP ABROAD

Your boss has asked you to spend two weeks scouting for business opportunities in a foreign country. Your assignment is to find a good location for a new resort hotel. Where you go is up to you, so pick a country that you have never seen before and plan your two-week trip. Make a list of all the things you will need to do or learn before you go.

## EXPAND YOUR KNOWLEDGE: THE GO-BETWEENS

Relatively few American businesspeople are fluent in the languages of the countries with which they do business. Therefore, they must often conduct their intercultural transactions with the aid of translators (written communication) and interpreters (spoken communication). Vic Petrelli, who spent six years as an overseas project manager with Aramco, has had plenty of firsthand experience with these go-betweens.

For the most part, Vic negotiated contracts for electric-power projects in Saudi Arabia. "That meant that I had to deal with Saudi Arabian contractors and government bureaucrats, as well as Pakistani engineers," Vic recalls. "Usually the Pakistanis served as interpreters, because they could speak better English than the people I had to negotiate with. Most of the world's engineering students learn English as a base language. It's similar to what I had to go through when I was younger; then German was the predominant language in the technical books."

But schooling in the English language is not always enough. "Head and hand movements and facial expressions are quite different from culture to culture," Vic notes. "Some quite expensive problems arose from those differences. I was in Al-Hasa, the world's largest oasis, which has about 150,000 people. The electric-power system was being run by a group of Pakistani engineers, and the top three in the group could speak English. My job was to get a transmission line strung through the oasis to serve 62 villages. An American engineer with another company agreed to install the wire, which was to be supplied by the Pakistani company, while installing a separate high-voltage line. I explained to the Pakistanis that this procedure would save us about six months of work and a lot of money, and they seemed to agree that they would put the wire aside so it would be ready when the other work was done.

"The Pakistanis have a side-to-side head movement that looks to a Westerner like a sign that they understand. But what it really means is maybe. Pakistanis will never say anything negative to a westerner, true or not true. I was getting this head movement from the Pakistanis and thought everything was ready to go, but when the American contractor showed up to start work, 22 miles of wire was missing. So I went to the chief Pakistani engineer, who had seemingly agreed to put the wire aside. He said the wire had been used about a week before to energize some villages. I thought we had fully communicated, but because of cultural differences we had not."

You might think that written communication would present fewer problems. But such was not the case, according to Vic: "All of our contracts had to be translated from English into Arabic. Well, almost all. The technical passages were in English, preceded by a statement something like this: 'Due to the technical nature of this contract, the following passage won't be translated into Arabic.' There are simply no Arabic words for many of the technical terms.

"We also ran into problems with some of the general paragraphs because of cultural differences. The connotations of our words just could not be properly translated into Arabic. Also, Americans expect contract language to be precise, but in most Middle Eastern cultures, nothing is laid on the table. They like to see as much remain in the gray area as possible to reduce the possibility of losing face if something goes wrong. That can cause some huge problems, especially when you're trying to manage the contract after it's been signed. You might be trying to say that 'According to Paragraph X, you're supposed to be doing this,' but what the other people are seeing in the Arabic contract is 'You don't necessarily have to do this.' "

As if learning to communicate with people from Pakistan and Saudi Arabia wasn't enough, Vic also had to interact with Germans, Filipinos, and Japanese. He had the most trouble communicating with the Japanese, who were part of a Japanese-European consortium working on a big engineering project in Saudi Arabia. "I had meetings with the Japanese engineers, who had to explain their electrical system to me. Hardly anyone in Japan speaks English at all, except for the international salespeople and business leaders—and even they sometimes have trouble with English. The engineers learn their engineering from Japanese textbooks, so the engineers and I had to discuss the electrical system through an interpreter, using electrical symbols that were different from the ones that westerners use."

Vic has learned a few things about the world of translation and interpretation in his years overseas: "Most managers and salespeople involved in international business speak English; in some countries, English is taught in school as the language of business. But the more technical the subject, the more necessary it is to have an interpreter. The sales department of an international company usually has someone who can interpret—especially into English, maybe into several other languages.

"The best quality for an interpreter to have is to really like people and to be good at working with them. To overcome cultural differences, an interpreter has to 'read' everything—the words themselves, gestures, eye movements, everything. Engineers tend to be a bit introverted, which further impedes communication—unless the interpreter is adept at reading nonverbal cues. The broader the interpreter's background knowledge, of course, the better off he or she is, because a good general background helps the interpreter put things in perspective. And the more the interpreter knows about what is being talked about, the easier it is to explain in two languages."

Vic has a few simple tips for those who work with interpreters. First, he says, "speak in as many one- and two-syllable words as possible. Using legalistic phrases and flowery speech will do nothing but confuse the interpreter. At the same time, you have to present a clear picture of what you want. The interpreter may actually be able to help you organize your thinking to make communication easier."

Vic's second suggestion is to ask the interpreter to repeat every passage in English before passing it on in another language. "If the interpreter summarizes the idea for you—'Is this what you mean?'—everybody benefits."

The third suggestion applies more to your own behavior: "Be careful not to offend the other party. Be as open and as friendly as possible. Any gruffness of manner or stern look can be interpreted in many different ways, depending on the culture. People tend to start talking to the interpreter and forget that the other person over there is the one receiving the message. Most westerners also tend to have too strong a personality. They come on like they're handling a large meeting. But with that stern, heavy look about them, they intimidate people from many other cultures into not really conversing.

"I was in a meeting with an Arab contractor who could read only the Arabic portion of the contract. Our department had a Lebanese interpreter who went to the meeting with us. Step by step, we went through the technical description of what the contractor was going to have to do. The process took hours. It was extremely important, though, that both parties understand what was going to have to be done. I tried to keep my explanations to the interpreter as simple as possible and to paint as clear a picture as possible. Then the interpreter summarized for me his understanding of each passage before explaining it in Arabic to the contractor. Then he would ask if there were any questions and translate those. This back-and-forth process was slow and tedious, but it was the only way to be sure that the Arabic contractor and I were talking about the same thing."

1. How could Vic Petrelli have avoided the problem of the missing 22 miles of wire?

2. How difficult is it to become an interpreter? What is the typical background of people in this profession? Does the job pay well? To answer these questions, write to some of the organizations that employ interpreters: Peace Corps, United Nations, and United States State Department. Ask about the qualifications and compensation of interpreters.

## DEVELOP YOUR WORD POWER

Use the spelling and vocabulary words from previous chapters to complete this crossword puzzle.

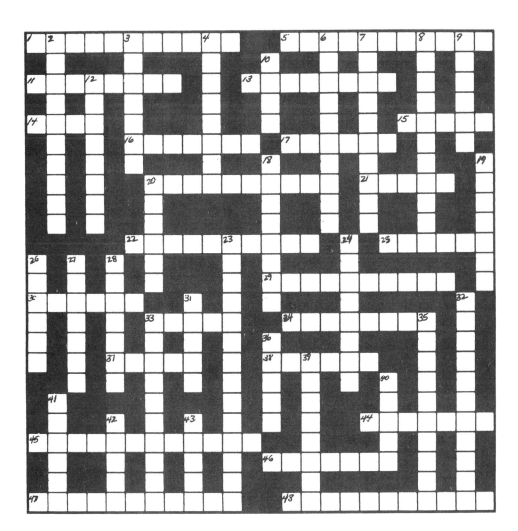

### Across

1. measure of heat
5. not harmonious
11. correctness
13. unconnected
14. debatable
15. to happen
16. diligent
17. to force
20. sense of right and wrong
21. unimpressed
22. vengeful
25. beat
29. probability
30. mental state
33. to scold
34. precise
37. entire range
38. urges
44. superficial
45. discontented
46. extinct
47. upkeep
48. to adjust

### Down

2. trespasses
3. to understand clearly
4. severe
6. to go around
7. conspicuous
8. inessential
9. helpful
10. skillful
12. concealed
18. reasonable
19. predicament
20. option
23. mail
24. satisfies
26. death
27. alien
28. distance in miles
31. in position number 9
32. fake
33. contrast
35. stressed
36. concise
39. productive
40. skepticism
41. stain
42. implied
43. frequently

---

## CHECK YOUR ANSWERS

---

### Master Key Concepts

I. respond

II. differences
   A. written, oral
   B. cultural, nonverbal, time, body
   C. ethnocentric

III. A. formal, monetary
    B. feedback


### Quiz Yourself

1. Here are some of the ways that you might become involved in international business:
   a. Your company may employ foreign workers.
   b. Your company may import goods or services from foreign suppliers.
   c. Your organization may export its products or services.
   d. Your organization may have foreign subsidiaries or joint ventures.
   e. Your international transactions may require dealings with foreign governments.
   f. You may work in this country for a company that is headquartered abroad.  (p. 577)

2. Many multinational companies offer English-language training programs for their foreign employees. Tenneco, for example, instituted an English-language training program for its Spanish-speaking employees in a New Jersey plant. The classes concentrated on practical English for use on the job. According to the company, these classes were a success: accidents and grievances declined, and production improved.  (p. 578)

3. The following types of written communication are likely to require translation:
   a. Advertisements
   b. Warranties
   c. Repair and maintenance manuals
   d. Product labels
   e. Policy and procedure manuals and benefit plans used by foreign subsidiaries of North American companies
   f. Reports passed between foreign subsidiaries and North American headquarters   (p. 579)

4. In talking with a person from an English-speaking country, you would encounter some differences in vocabulary and idiomatic expressions, as well as differences in pronunciation.  (p. 579)

5. Misunderstandings are especially likely to occur when the people communicating have different backgrounds. Party A encodes a message in one context, using assumptions common to people in his or her culture; Party B decodes the message using a different set of assumptions. The result is confusion and, often, hard feelings.

We assume—wrongly—that other people are like us. We ignore the fact that people from different cultures differ in many ways—in their religion and values, their ideas of status, their decision-making habits, their attitude toward time, their use of space, their body language, and their manners. (pp. 580-581)

6. The North American belief that modern, labor-saving methods are superior to old-fashioned, labor-intensive methods is inappropriate in a country where unemployment is an extremely serious problem. In such a country, the method that requires the most workers may well be the most beneficial to society. (p. 580)

7. Here are two examples that illustrate how a gesture that is considered meaningful in one country can be misconstrued by a person from another culture:
    a. A North American crosses his legs so that the sole of his shoe is showing, unaware that this gesture is viewed as an insult by an Egyptian businessperson.
    b. An American saleswoman thinks nothing of it when an Arab businessperson runs his hand backward across his hair. She fails to recognize the gesture as a romantic invitation. (p. 581)

8. Ethnocentric people are prone to stereotyping and prejudice. They generalize about entire groups of people on the basis of sketchy evidence, and then develop biased attitudes toward the group. As a consequence, they fail to see people as they really are. They ignore the personal qualities of individuals. (p. 582)

9. In writing letters to people from other cultures,
    a. Use short, precise words.
    b. Rely on specific terms; avoid abstractions.
    c. Stay away from slang, jargon, buzzwords, idioms, acronyms, and North American product names.
    d. Use short paragraphs.
    e. Use many transitional devices.
    f. Use numbers, visual aids, and preprinted forms. (pp. 582-583)

10. Before taking a business trip to another country, try to learn about its history, religion, politics, and customs. In addition, find out about such practical things as weather conditions, health-care facilities, money, transportation, communications, and customs regulations. Even though you may not have time to master the language, do try to learn a few words and phrases. (pp. 585-586)

## Develop Your Word Power

## Component Chapter B

## GRAMMAR AND USAGE GUIDE, WITH EXERCISES

The main point of Component Chapter B is that the misuse of language can impede communication. As you read the chapter, think about the ways that errors in grammar, punctuation, mechanics, and vocabulary may contribute to misunderstandings. When you finish reading and doing the exercises, analyze your weak points and work to overcome them.

### MASTER KEY CONCEPTS

Use the following terms to fill the blanks in the outline. All terms are used, but none is used more than once.

| | | | |
|---|---|---|---|
| abbreviations | ellipsis | mood | punctuation |
| antecedents | exclamation | phrases | quotation |
| capitals | grammar | possessive | semicolons |
| clauses | hyphens | prepositions | verbs |
| dashes | mechanics | proper | |

I. _____ (p. 590) is the way that words are combined into sentences; sentences are composed of parts of speech, the most basic of which are nouns, pronouns, _____ (p. 591), adjectives, and adverbs.

    A. Nouns name a person, a place, a thing, or an idea; to use nouns correctly, you must learn the difference between _____ (p. 591) nouns and common nouns, the method of making a noun plural, and the method of making a noun possessive.

    B. Pronouns are words that stand in for nouns; to use pronouns correctly, you must learn how to deal with multiple _____ (p. 592), how to select gender-neutral pronouns, how to select the correct case for pronouns, and when to use possessive pronouns.

    C. Verbs describe an action or a state of being; to use verbs correctly, you must know about verb tenses, irregular verbs, transitive and intransitive verbs, the voice of verbs, and the _____ (p. 596) of verbs.

    D. Adjectives modify (tell something about) nouns and pronouns.

    E. Adverbs modify verbs, adjectives, and other adverbs.

    F. Nouns, pronouns, verbs, adjectives, and adverbs are linked together in sentences by four other parts of speech: _____ (p. 598), conjunctions, articles, and interjections.

    G. Whole sentences contain, at minimum, a subject and a predicate; to be able to construct whole sentences, you must know about commands, the difference between _____ (p. 599) and _____ (p. 599) in longer sentences, sentence fragments, fused sentences, sentences with linking verbs, and misplaced modifiers.

II. _____ (p. 602), when used properly to mark different sorts of sentences and sentence elements, keeps readers from losing track of your meaning.

    A. Periods are used at the end of sentences that are not questions, after _____ (p. 602), and in money expressions.

B.   Question marks are used after any direct question that requires an answer.

C.   _____ (p. 602) points are used after highly emotional sentences.

D.   _____ (p. 602) are used to separate closely related independent clauses, items in a series that already contain commas, and independent clauses when the second one begins with a transitional word or phrase.

E.   Colons are used after salutations in a letter and at the end of a sentence or phrase introducing a list, a _____ (p. 603), or an idea.

F.   Commas separate the items in a series, separate an opening phrase or dependent clause from an independent clause, follow an introductory statement, surround parenthetical phrases or words, separate adjectives modifying the same noun, separate some abbreviations (such as *Inc.* and *Jr.*) from the words they identify, separate days from years in dates, separate quotations from the rest of the sentence, and separate words and phrases whenever needed to prevent confusion or an unintended meaning.

G.   _____ (p. 604) are used around parenthetical comments that represent a sudden turn in thought, around parenthetical comments that require emphasis, and around parenthetical phrases that contain commas.

H.   _____ (pp. 604-605) are used to separate the parts of compound words, to separate the parts of compound adjectives that come before the noun (but not after the noun), and to divide words at the ends of lines.

I.   Apostrophes are used in the _____ (p. 605) form of nouns and in contractions.

J.   Quotation marks surround words that are repeated exactly as they were said or written, set off the titles of newspaper and magazine articles, and indicate special treatment for words and phrases.

K.   Parentheses surround comments that are entirely incidental and dollar amounts in legal documents.

L.   _____ (p. 606) points are used to indicate that material has been left out of a direct quotation.

M.   Underscores and italics provide emphasis and indicate the titles of books, magazines, and the like.

III. A number of small details known as _____ (pp. 606-607) demonstrate a writer's polish and reflect on the organization's professionalism.

A.   _____ (p. 606) are used at the beginning of sentences, as the first letter of proper nouns and adjectives, for official titles, and as the first letter of salutations and complimentary closes.

B.   Abbreviations are used mainly in tables, graphs, lists, and forms.

C.   Numbers from one to ten are generally spelled out, and numbers over ten are generally indicated with Arabic numerals; for handling numbers in other situations, many other rules exist.

IV. Use of the right word in the right place is a crucial element in business communication.

A.   Frequently confused words are sets of words that sound similar but are spelled differently; be careful not to mistake one for another.

B.   Frequently misused words tend to be misused for reasons other than sound.

C.   Frequently misspelled words are commonly used words that are difficult to spell for a variety of reasons.

D.   Transitional words and phrases are useful for showing the relationship between two sentences or clauses.

*Check your answers at the end of this chapter.*

## QUIZ YOURSELF

1. _____ is nothing more than the way words are combined into sentences, and _____ is the way language is used by a network of people.

2. In general, which nouns are capitalized, and which are not?

3. Explain what an antecedent is, in grammatical terms, and name two types of antecedents that cause confusion.

4. List the six verb tenses, and briefly describe how they are regularly formed.

5. Name the two voices of verbs, and explain when each should be used.

6. What are the five most important parts of speech, and what are the four other parts of speech that link them together in sentences?

7. Because it does not have both a subject and a predicate, the group of words known as a _____ can never be written as a sentence; a group of words that does contain both a subject and a predicate, known as a _____, can be written as a sentence if it is an independent thought.

8. Explain what sentence fragments and fused sentences are and why both are unacceptable.

9. How can you test the appropriateness of inserting a comma between adjectives modifying the same noun?

10. In the absence of a different company style, you should generally spell out all numbers from _____ to _____ and use Arabic numerals for the rest.

*Check your answers at the end of this chapter.*

### BUILD YOUR SKILLS:  CAN YOU CORRECT THE ERRORS IN THIS MEMO?

The following memo contains errors in grammar, punctuation, mechanics, and spelling.  Find them and correct them.

TO:            All employees

FROM:          Martin Smores, V.P. Administration

SUBJECT:       Educational Refund Plans

It is the policy of this company to encourage employees to continue there education in fields which are related to their current work, or deemed in the companies best interests in the soul judgement of the Company.

To be eligible for the program, full-time employment is required.

Only course work taken at accredited schools and colleges by a nationally recognized accrediting agency are eligible for refunds under the plan.

An employee wishing to participate in the refund plan will obtain written approval from their supervisor prior to enrollment in courses.

All initial costs associated with taking courses will be born by the employee.

Upon completion of courses, evidence of course completion such as grades received and receipts for bills paid must be submitted to the company.

When the requirements of the refund plan having been met, costs will be reimbursed as follows:

Tuition costs and labratory fees—100%
Required textbooks—50%

### EXPAND YOUR KNOWLEDGE: WRITING WITH STYLE

In writing, there are two kinds of style.  One is a set of guidelines for handling certain grammatical elements—as in "house style" and "style manual."  The other is an individualized pattern of word choice, sentence construction, and paragraph organization—a sort of personalized "signature"—that each writer develops.  In most business writing, you are expected to suppress this individual style; you are, after all, representing your organization and not yourself.  You can never totally eliminate your outlook from your writing, however.  You can only learn to make the most of it.

#### Word Choice

- *Use the best word you can think of.*  The word that most accurately says what you mean is probably harder for you to identify and use correctly than for a reader to recognize in context.  So develop your vocabulary, and eschew only pompous words and unnecessary jargon.
- *Use figures of speech appropriately.*  In one sense, your ability to come up with a clever metaphor or simile is a mark of style.  This sort of style, however, is to be avoided in business writing.  The same goes for slang and the breezier idioms.  You can exercise plenty of creativity by selecting solid, objective words and putting them together for maximum impact.
- *Use contractions knowledgeably.*  In formal writing, contractions should be avoided.  But in informal writing that includes contractions, you can gain impact by sometimes using a complete phrase instead—for example, *will not* instead of *won't*.

## Sentence Construction

- *Repeat words, phrases, and constructions for emphasis.* Awkward repetition is a sign of ignorance. Deft repetition is a sign of sophistication.
- *Place modifiers as close as possible to the words they modify.* In long, complicated sentences, it is easy to get lost. Help your readers by telling them the how and the why as soon as you tell them who or what. If you end up with verbal spaghetti, you probably need to rewrite—perhaps making more than one sentence out of the mess.
- *Use a variety of sentence structures.* Some sentences should be simple and short. When your ideas are a bit more complicated, you can use complex sentences. Other thoughts naturally go together, and you can use compound sentences to show that they are related.
- *Begin sentences in different ways.* Most sentences begin with the main clause, consisting of a subject and a predicate and a few modifiers. For variety, however, and to show how your ideas are related, you should occasionally begin sentences with more complicated modifying words, phrases, and clauses. Just don't overdo any one device.
- *Make sure that every sentence has its own logic.* If you're talking about a series of things or ideas, put them in logical order. In compound and complex sentences, give the main idea the stronger position; in other words, do not subordinate the main idea. Also, make sure that the ideas in a compound sentence are truly related.

## Paragraph Organization

- *Vary the placement of your topic sentences.* Every paragraph must somewhere state exactly what its point is, but that statement does not always have to come first.
- *Use sentence structure to build a rhythm in your paragraphs.* Short, punchy sentences have impact. But they tend to become boring if used exclusively, so you should build paragraphs with sentences that are long and short, simple and complex and compound.
- *Vary the length of your paragraphs.* Paragraphs that are all about the same length also become monotonous. You can make some paragraphs short, with only three or four sentences, and add a couple of sentences to the paragraphs that require more development. Remember that although longer paragraphs may sometimes be necessary, long paragraphs tend to bore readers.

The more you write, the more you will be able to refine these and other techniques. You will eventually notice, however, that they all have one purpose: to make your ideas clear and interesting to readers.

1. Style is a mix of elements, involving choices between passive and active, formal and informal, bland and colorful language. In the following situations, what mix of elements would be appropriate?
   a. You are a newly hired researcher, with a relatively low position in the organization. You are writing your first memo to your boss.
   b. You are the vice president of a large corporation and must announce to the employees that, because of disappointing financial performance, your company will not be offering generous raises this year.
   c. You have been asked to take charge of the company picnic. You are writing a memo for general distribution announcing the time, place, and program for the event.
2. One good way to learn how to control your style is to study other writers who have a clear "voice." Analyze the writing style of these writers:
   a. Ernest Hemingway (twentieth-century American novelist)
   b. Samuel Johnson (eighteenth-century English essayist)
   c. An unknown reporter for the *New York Times*

## DEVELOP YOUR WORD POWER

Use the spelling and vocabulary words from previous chapters to complete the crossword puzzle.

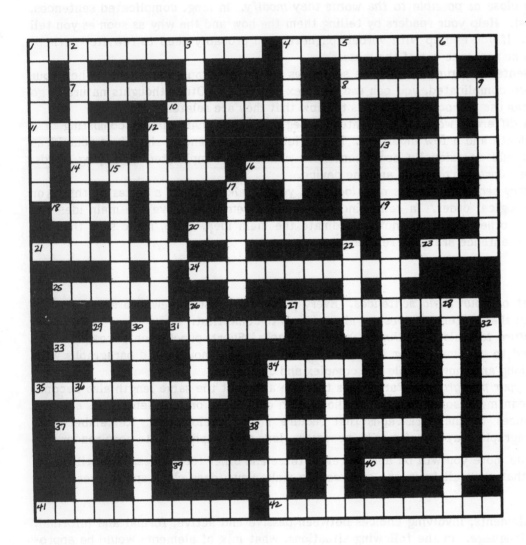

### Across

1. noninterference
4. insolent
7. intended
8. trifling
10. verbal attack
11. to examine
13. adviser
14. friendly
16. to cause
18. skillful
19. option
20. opinionated
21. bodily
23. on guard
24. unending
25. yearly
27. discord
31. death
33. representative
34. frequently
35. book of words in a language
37. sincerely
38. frivolously amusing
39. shortage
40. person under the care of someone influential
41. up and down
42. not committing oneself

### Down

1. praiseworthy
2. right away
3. clothing
4. indirect criticism
5. advantageous
6. to try to equal or excel
9. very
12. capable of being put on credit
15. plotting
17. between seventh and ninth
22. outmoded
26. arousing longing
28. discreet
29. debatable
30. equivalent
32. workable
34. event
36. habitual

---

## CHECK YOUR ANSWERS

---

### Master Key Concepts

I. grammar, verbs
  A. proper
  B. antecedents
  C. mood
  F. prepositions
  G. phrases, clauses

II. punctuation
  A. abbreviations
  C. exclamation
  D. semicolons
  E. quotation
  G. dashes
  H. hyphens
  I. possessive
  L. ellipsis

III. mechanics
  A. capitals

### Quiz Yourself

1. *Grammar* is nothing more than the way words are combined into sentences, and *usage* is the way language is used by a network of people. (p. 590)

2. Common nouns, which refer to general classes of things, are not capitalized; proper nouns, which refer to particular persons, places, and things, are capitalized. (p. 591)

3. An antecedent is a noun in the beginning of a sentence that corresponds to a pronoun later in the sentence. Both multiple antecedents and unclear antecedents cause confusion if not handled knowledgeably. (p. 592)

4. These are the six verb tenses and how they are regularly formed:
  a. Present: the basic form
  b. Past: the basic form with an *ed* ending
  c. Future: *will* or *shall* followed by the basic form
  d. Present perfect: *have* or *has* followed by the past tense of the main verb
  e. Past perfect: *had* followed by the past tense of the main verb
  f. Future perfect: *will have* followed by the past tense of the main verb (pp. 594–595)

5. Verbs have two voices, active and passive. The active voice is preferable in most sentences, because it allows fewer words to be used and is more direct. But when the writer doesn't know (or doesn't want to say) who performed the action, the passive voice becomes necessary. (p. 596)

6. These are the five most important parts of speech:
  a. Nouns
  b. Pronouns
  c. Verbs
  d. Adjectives
  e. Adverbs
The following four parts of speech link them together in sentences:
  f. Prepositions
  g. Conjunctions
  h. Articles
  i. Interjections (p. 598)

7. Because it does not have both a subject and a predicate, the group of words known as a *phrase* can never be written as a sentence; a group of words that does contain both a subject and a predicate, known as a *clause*, can be written as a sentence if it is an independent thought.   (p. 599)

8. A sentence fragment is an incomplete sentence (a phrase or dependent clause) written as though it were a complete sentence.  A fused sentence combines two independent thoughts without showing any point of separation.  Because sentence fragments and fused sentences do not clearly express a single thought, they are easily misinterpreted by the reader. (pp. 599–601)

9. To test the appropriateness of inserting a comma between adjectives modifying the same noun, try reversing the order of the adjectives.  If the order cannot be reversed, leave out the comma.  A comma also is not used when one of the adjectives is part of the noun.  (p. 603)

10. In the absence of a different company style, you should generally spell out all numbers from *one* to *ten* and use Arabic numerals for the rest.  (p. 607)

**Develop Your Word Power**

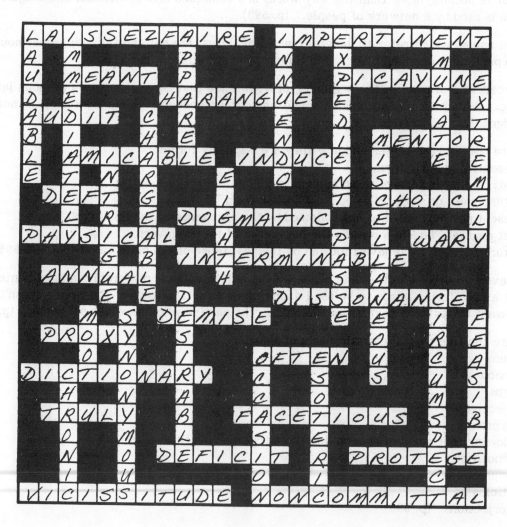

# Component Chapter C

## FORMAT AND LAYOUT OF BUSINESS CORRESPONDENCE

The main point of Component Chapter C is that conscientious attention to format and layout makes letters and memos more effective by helping them get to the right person, makes an impression of professionalism, and tells the recipient who wrote them and when. As you read the chapter, think about how the various elements of format and layout contribute to these goals. When you finish reading, study some business correspondence that you have received for real-life variations on the patterns recommended in this chapter.

## MASTER KEY CONCEPTS

Use the following terms to fill the blanks in the outline. All terms are used, but none is used more than once.

| | | | |
|---|---|---|---|
| agendas | complimentary | mailing | reference |
| attention | correspondence | memo–letters | salutation |
| block | heading | minutes | simplified |
| centered | letterhead | paper | thirds |

I. Readers unconsciously judge business _____ (p. 619) on the basis of appearance: neatness, professionalism, and reading ease.

   A. High-quality _____ (pp. 619–620) of a standard size and color is especially important in letters and other correspondence directed to outsiders.

   B. Most letters are written on _____ (p. 620) stationery, which has the company name and address and other information printed at the top; internal documents, such as memos and standardized reports, are often typed on printed forms designed to highlight the required information in minimal space.

   C. To make the best impression, letters should be _____ (p. 620) on the page with good-size margins all around; the proper spacing should be used after all punctuation; and the typing should appear clean, dark, and neat.

II. Regardless of their content, letters have certain standard parts and optional additional parts and are generally arranged in one of three basic letter styles.

   A. Business letters typically have seven standard parts: heading, usually in the form of a letterhead; date; inside address identifying the recipient of the letter; _____ (p. 623), a greeting to the recipient; body, or main message; _____ (p. 623) close, a word or two of courtesy to conclude the letter; and typewritten name of the sender.

   B. Depending on the requirements of the letter, any combination of these additional letter parts may also be used: addressee notations indicating special handling required for delivering the letter; _____ (pp. 624–625) line identifying the recipient when the inside address does not include the name of a specific person; subject line telling the recipient what the letter is about; second-page heading for long letters; company name, should be included in the signature block if it does not appear in the letterhead; _____ (p. 626) initials indicating who typed and who composed the letter; enclosure notation indicating the inclusion of additional materials; copy notation indicating the names of those who are receiving copies of the letter, preferably in order of rank or in alphabetical order; _____ (p. 627) notation indicating special mailing procedures; and postscript, which is an afterthought or a message requiring special emphasis.

C. The three most common styles for formatting a business letter are the _____ (pp. 627, 628) style, in which each part of the letter begins at the left margin; the modified block style, in which all items begin at the left except for the date, complimentary close, and typewritten name, which start in the center of the page; and the _____ (pp. 627, 630) style, in which the salutation and complimentary close are eliminated.

III. Envelopes should match the company letterhead and should be sized to accommodate the stationery.

A. Envelopes contain two blocks of copy—the sender's name and address and the recipient's name and address—both of which should conform to U.S. Postal Service standards.

B. An 8½ x 11-inch piece of paper can be folded in _____ (p. 634) lengthwise to fit in a standard No. 10 envelope; if it must be sent in a smaller envelope, it should first be folded in half and then in thirds.

IV. Clarity, careful arrangement, and neatness are important in internal memos, whether they are typed on preprinted forms or on plain paper; the _____ (pp. 634-635) identifies the date, writer, recipient, and subject; the complimentary close is eliminated.

V. Two types of documents are used in connection with meetings: _____ (pp. 635-636) are outlines of the topics that will be covered in a meeting, and _____ (pp. 636-637) are the official notes of what has occurred during the meeting.

VI. Special time-saving message formats reduce the amount of time spent typing and writing messages: _____ (p. 637) are printed like memos but provide space for an inside address so the message can be folded and sent in a window envelope; short-note replies are responses written at the bottom of original documents instead of on a new piece of paper; "letterhead" postcards bear the organization's name and address and may also be preprinted with a list of responses that the "writer" can check off.

*Check your answers at the end of this chapter.*

## QUIZ YOURSELF

1. What items of information are frequently provided in a company's letterhead? Why might a company decide to limit the number of items included in the letterhead?

2. What are the seven standard parts of a letter?

3. Give a couple of examples of an acceptable complimentary close.

4. Letters that have a restricted readership or that must be handled in a special way should include such _____ as "Personal," "Confidential," or "Please Forward."

5. What do these notations mean?
   a. cc
   b. pc
   c. c
   d. bc
   e. bcc
   f. bpc

6. Letters may be classified according to the style of punctuation they use. _____, or mixed, punctuation uses a colon after the salutation (a comma if the letter is social or personal) and a comma after the complimentary close. _____ punctuation uses no colon or comma after the salutation or the complimentary close.

7. What format is used in typing an envelope?

8. What order should be used for the names on a memo's distribution list?

9. What are the items that typically appear on an agenda?

10. Organizations that often deal by mail with individuals frequently have _____ preprinted with a list of responses; the "writer" merely checks the appropriate response.

*Check your answers at the end of this chapter.*

## BUILD YOUR SKILLS:  FIX THE FORMAT

Your secretary is on vacation, and a high school student is filling in.  You assumed that everyone knows how to format a business letter, but you were wrong.  The student presented the following letter for your signature.  Using arrows to show where things should be moved and little boxes to show where blank lines should be left (one for each line), mark the letter for retyping.

### ECO-CARE DISPOSAL SERVICES, INC.
**2572 North Pine**
**Davenport, Iowa  52804**
**319/287-3892**

June 21, 1986

Ms. Marybeth Cosentino

Subject:  Dumpsters for new apartment buildings

Hagedorn Property Services, Inc.

2809 Fair Avenue, Suite 101

Davenport, Iowa 52803

Dear Ms. Cosentino:

Congratulations on finishing the new Davenport Gardens complex.  We look forward to helping you keep it clean and tidy.

Your dumpsters have been ordered from the factory and should arrive sometime next week.

As soon as the dumpsters arrive, I will call you to set up delivery to Davenport Gardens.

Keep us in mind as you put the finishing touches on the complex.  We'd be pleased to send over one of our experienced clean-up crews if you find the scheduled completion date approaching too quickly.

gw

Sincerely,

Lou Shafer, Manager

Residential Services

PS:  After only a little negotiation, the factory agreed to use the custom paint color you asked for.  The plant manager liked it so much that he supposedly has repainted his office Davenport Beige!

pc:  Dana Evans, Traffic Department

## EXPAND YOUR KNOWLEDGE:  HOW TO CREATE A WINNING IMPRESSION

"When clients come to us for letterhead, what they really want is a corporate-image program," says Tom Michael, head of Graphic Designers, Inc. "They want a trademark or logo—a symbol, word, or mark—that they can use to identify their company and to distinguish it from others." Tom's firm has designed corporate-image programs for such clients as Honda, Johnson & Johnson, Bristol-Meyers, Warner Brothers, and the Bank of America. Some clients want Tom's company to design only the bare essentials, such as letterhead and envelopes. Others want him to go a step further and show them how their trademark can be used in ads and on signs, T-shirts, shopping bags, trucks, uniforms, and other items.

"Letterhead is often the only introduction that an outsider has to a company," Tom observes. "It represents the company—and tells a lot about it." The key factors, according to Tom, are color, continuity, and white space. "Color has real psychological impact. Warm colors, for example, tend to stimulate and excite an active response." Continuity refers to the harmony of the design elements—for example, how the logo design and the type style used for the company's name hold together. White space can be used to focus attention on a given design element. "If you surround a block of type with white space," Tom points out, "the type appears to be in a spotlight."

Placement of the heading must also be considered, because many companies have preferences for setting up a typewritten page. Some want more space at the top or prefer to have the address at the bottom. "The trend in letterhead design today is toward simplicity and clarity. Most companies prefer a clean, uncluttered look. Most companies also print their letterhead on two different grades of paper, using the premium-quality letterhead only when appropriate."

And how does Tom go about designing a logo for letterhead and other items? "I start by finding out what the client is currently using for its symbol," he explains. "That symbol tells me how the public now perceives the company and what the client may once have liked as a logo." Tom then asks the client what image the company wants to convey. Does it want to seem traditional? High tech? Does it want to inspire confidence, build trust? Says Tom: "A logo is a very personal statement about a company—one that it can't afford to change frequently."

Tom also feels that it is important to consider the end uses of the company logo. Will it be read quickly? Must it be highly visible? What type style would suit it best? "The type I'd use for a cosmetics company," he notes, "would be quite different from what I'd use for a motorcycle manufacturer."

After discussing these matters with the client, Tom does some independent research. He examines the logos that the client's competitors are using and learns something about the industry. All this information influences the type of image that he creates for the company. Then Tom starts sketching. When he comes up with a solution that seems to work, he shows it to the client. If the client approves, Tom produces the finished artwork.

Tom has this final bit of advice for those who balk at the expense of hiring a professional designer: "If your company wants to look like a winner, it's usually worth paying the price for quality design and printing. It may make a real difference in the level of response you get."

1. Go to a stationery store and ask to look through the catalogs of personalized and letterhead stationery. Pick something appropriate for the following businesses:
   a. An advertising agency
   b. A Wall Street law firm
   c. A pet store
   d. An interior decorating store
   What qualities of each design make it appropriate for the business?

2. Leaf through an issue of *Fortune* or some other business magazine and study the logos in the ads. Which of them appeal to you? What are the common denominators of your favorites?

## DEVELOP YOUR WORD POWER

Use the spelling and vocabulary words from previous chapters to complete the crossword puzzle.

### Across

1. administration
5. something out-dated
11. breakable
14. to invalidate
16. being
17. person under the care of someone influential
22. discontented
23. pause
24. predicament
26. to spend
31. directing
33. brings about
35. dull
37. beat
40. obvious
41. skillful
42. place
43. trite saying
44. right away
45. to deal in broad concepts

### Down

1. to promise
2. wavering
3. in position number 9
4. effectiveness
5. to prevent
6. to publicize
7. obstacle
8. unconcerned
9. diplomacy and tact
10. one or the other
12. keen insight
13. primary
15. debatable
17. outmoded
18. social blunder
19. contact person
20. succinct
21. 4 times 10
25. intended
27. trifling
28. uninformed guess
29. supposition
30. faultfinding
32. proper to be recommended
34. cure-all
36. shortage
38. pertaining to everyday concerns
39. representative

---
### CHECK YOUR ANSWERS
---

## Master Key Concepts

I. correspondence
  A. paper
  B. letterhead
  C. centered

II. A. salutation, complimentary
    B. attention, reference, mailing
    C. block, simplified

III. B. thirds

IV. heading

V. agendas, minutes

VI. memo-letters

## Quiz Yourself

1. Letterhead is typically printed with the name and address of the company. It may also contain the company's telephone number, cable address, product lines, date of establishment, officers and directors, slogan, and symbol (logo). A company might decide to limit the amount of information printed on the letterhead in order to avoid a cluttered appearance, save space, and prevent the stationery from becoming outdated.  (p. 620)

2. The seven standard parts of a letter are
  a. Heading
  b. Date
  c. Inside address
  d. Salutation
  e. Body
  f. Complimentary close
  g. Typewritten name   (p. 621)

3. The complimentary close should reflect the relationship between the writer and the reader. Currently, the trend seems to be toward using one-word closes, such as *Sincerely* or *Cordially*.  (p. 623)

4. Letters that have a restricted readership or that must be handled in a special way should include such *addressee notations* as "Personal," "Confidential," or "Please Forward."  (p. 624)

5. These notations have the following meanings:
  a. cc—carbon copy
  b. pc—photocopy
  c. c—copy
  d. bc—blind copy
  e. bcc—blind carbon copy
  f. bpc—blind photocopy  (pp. 626-627)

6. Letters may be classified according to the style of punctuation they use. *Standard*, or mixed, punctuation uses a colon after the salutation (a comma if the letter is social or personal) and a comma after the complimentary close. *Open* punctuation uses no colon or comma after the salutation or the complimentary close.  (p. 627)

7. Envelopes should be typed in block form and single-spaced. If a No. 10 envelope is used, the block identifying the recipient should begin 4 inches from the left side and 2-1/2 inches from the top; if a No. 6-3/4 envelope is used, the recipient's address should begin 2-1/2 inches from the left edge and 2 inches from the top. (p. 631)

8. The names on a memo's distribution list should generally be listed in alphabetical order; however, some organizations prefer to list people in order of their rank in the organization. (p. 635)

9. Most agendas follow this order:
   a. Call to order
   b. Roll call
   c. Approval of agenda
   d. Approval of minutes
   e. Chairperson's report
   f. Subcommittee reports
   g. Unfinished business
   h. New business
   i. Announcements
   j. Adjournment (p. 636)

10. Organizations that often deal by mail with individuals frequently have *letterhead postcards* preprinted with a list of responses; the "writer" merely checks the appropriate response. (p. 637)

**Develop Your Word Power**

# Component Chapter D

## DOCUMENTATION OF REPORT SOURCES

The main point of Component Chapter D is that documenting your work gives it credibility, gives readers the means for checking your findings and pursuing the subject further, and is the accepted way to give credit to the people whose ideas you have drawn on. As you read the chapter, think about how the recommended formats and practices would help someone trying to look up references for further information. When you finish reading, practice documenting several types of reference works.

## MASTER KEY CONCEPTS

Use the following terms to fill the blanks in the outline. All terms are used, but none is used more than once.

| author–date | content | key-number | reference |
|---|---|---|---|
| bibliography | copyright | publication | source |
| consecutively | fair use | punctuation | title |

I. Under the _____ (pp. 638-639) laws, you must acknowledge the source of direct quotations and paraphrased passages but need not cite the source of general knowledge; the _____ (p. 639) doctrine requires you to obtain written permission from the copyright holder if, generally speaking, your use of the material would prevent the author from selling it.

II. _____ (p. 639) notes documenting quotations and paraphrased passages generally appear at the end of a document; _____ (pp. 639-640) notes elaborating on the text are usually presented at the bottom of the page they refer to.
   A. Notes are referenced and typed according to several stylistic conventions: the placement of a note is indicated with a superscript, the superscripts are numbered _____ (p. 640) throughout a document, direct quotes over three lines long are set off as extracts, and notes are single-spaced and separated by a double space.
   B. Regardless of their precise form, all source notes comprise the author's name, the _____ (p. 641) of the work, and such _____ (p. 641) information as the publisher's name and location, the publication date, and the page reference; to save time, later references to the same source may use a shortened format.
   C. Source notes referring to books, periodicals, newspapers, unpublished material, and other material differ in detail.

III. A _____ (p. 643), arranged in alphabetical order by author's last name, serves as a reading list for those who want to do further research; it should include all the sources referenced in notes as well as additional references that may be useful to readers.
   A. A single bibliography may be placed at the end of the report, or separate bibliographies may be prepared for each chapter; a bibliography may be subdivided according to subject matter or type of reference.

B.  The major difference between notes and bibliography entries is in the _____ (p. 644); bibliography entries for books, periodicals, newspapers, and unpublished and other material are all different to a certain extent.

IV.  A couple of simplified methods—known as _____ (p. 645) citations—have been developed for handling notes and bibliographies: the _____ (p. 645) system provides an end-of-report list of references and refers to them in the text by author's last name and publication date; the _____ (p. 645) system identifies items in the reference list by Arabic numeral and then uses this number in parentheses with a colon and the page number.

V.  For additional details on preparing bibliographies and notes, consult one of the style books available in the reference sections of libraries or in bookstores.

*Check your answers at the end of this chapter.*

## QUIZ YOURSELF

1.  Discuss the fair-use doctrine.

2.  _____ notes are used to document quotations and paraphrased passages. _____ notes are used to supplement the text with asides about a particular issue or event or to direct the reader to another section of the report or to a related source.

3.  Notes are signaled with _____—Arabic numerals placed just above the line of type.  They are numbered _____ throughout the report—or, for very long reports, throughout each chapter.

4.  If a book has four or more authors, how do you handle the author's name in a source note?

5.  What punctuation is used to set off publication information in a source note referring to a book?

6.  In general, what is the difference between the formal and the informal style in shortened note references?

7. What information should be included in a reference to a letter, a speech, or an interview?

8. An _____ bibliography comments on the subject matter and viewpoint of the source, as well as on its usefulness to readers.

9. Describe the two basic methods for handling reference citations.

10. List five style books that provide additional information on the format for notes and bibliographies.

*Check your answers at the end of this chapter.*

## BUILD YOUR SKILLS: COMPILE A BIBLIOGRAPHY

To hone your ability to prepare a bibliography, compile one on the subject of marketing products in underdeveloped countries. Use a mix of reference types, including books, business journals, popular magazines, academic papers, and newspapers. Include at least 20 entries, presented in acceptable format and arranged in the proper order.

## EXPAND YOUR KNOWLEDGE: HOW TO TAKE BETTER NOTES FASTER

Unless you have adequate resources at your fingertips, research usually means taking notes while you conduct an interview or scan books at the library. This time-consuming procedure becomes a lot quicker if you know one of the many shorthand systems, such as Gregg, Speedwriting, or Century 21. But if you don't, you still can save time by using some of the following shortcuts:

- Use such common abbreviations as 1, 2, 3, 1st, 2nd, 3rd, &, %, #, *dept., co.,* and *acct.*
- Use such "natural" abbreviations as *bus (business), dif (difference),* and *pix (pictures).*
- Write what you hear, such as *hi* instead of *high.*
- Leave out vowels whenever possible, as in *Lv t vls wnvr posbl.*
- Abbreviate suffixes: *attribun (attribution),* *commemorv (commemorative),* *radl (radical),* *monumt (monument).*
- Use letters for common short words, such as *b (be, been, but, buy, by), c (can), d (would), e (ever, every), f (for, from), h (had, he, him), l (well, will), n (in, not), o (on, own), p (please, up), r (are, our), t (to, too), u (under), v (of, have, very), w (with), x (extra), y (why), z (was, as).*
- Use a standard abbreviation for common phrases, such as *lb (will be)* and *db (would be), nvrls (nevertheless)* and *nnls (nonetheless), tb (to be)* and *tk (to come), vb (have been)* and *vn (have not), zlz (as well as)* and *zz (as soon as).*

- Underscore the last letter to add *ing* or *thing* as a word ending, as in smil̲ (smil*ing*).
- Form the past tense of a regular verb by writing a hyphen at the end, as in *stay-* (stayed).
- Use an apostrophe at the end of any word ending in *ness*, as in *kind'* (kind*ness*).

Once you have practiced these techniques a few times, your note taking will go much faster. Remember, however, that putting notes on paper is only half the battle. The other half, which is equally critical, is to translate them when the need arises. You can save yourself the trouble of going back to the source by reading over your notes as soon as you get back to your office. While your memory is fresh, write out words that you think you might not recognize in a couple of days or weeks. To be really safe, you might even want to type out all your notes for future reference.

*Source*: Adapted from Rudolf Flesch, *The Art of Clear Thinking* (New York: Harper & Brothers, 1951), p. 154; Joe M. Pullis, *Principles of Speedwriting Shorthand*, Regency Edition (Indianapolis, Ind.: Bobbs-Merrill Educational Publishing, 1984), pp. 433-436, 447-450, 455-459.

1. Analyze your own class lecture notes. How useful are they? Are you able to decipher them later? Have you included too much? Not enough? Is the relationship among ideas clear? What can you do to improve in the future?

2. Try to come up with your own "shorthand" techniques to augment those listed here. For example, during any given research effort, certain concepts are mentioned repeatedly. Can you abbreviate these common terms in some way?

## DEVELOP YOUR WORD POWER

Use the spelling and vocabulary words from previous chapters to complete the crossword puzzle.

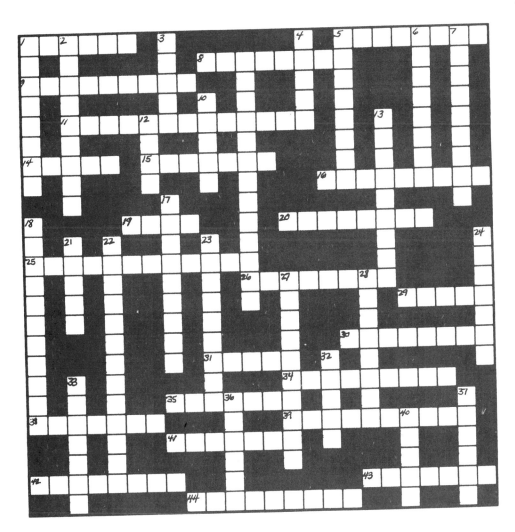

### Across

1. hateful
5. genuine
8. well known
9. polite
11. directly
14. frequently
15. pertinent
16. agility
19. to leave out
20. severe
25. beneficial
26. indirect criticism
29. social blunder
30. something given stress
31. implied
34. being
35. facts behind a conclusion
38. to authorize
39. conspicuous
41. take advantage of
42. admits
43. person under the care of someone influential
44. aware

### Down

1. event
2. flooded
3. skepticism
4. concise
5. pamphlet
6. to struggle
7. heterogeneity
10. severity
12. dash
13. case for samples
17. analysis
18. something outdated
21. to prevent
22. possessing understanding
23. group formed for a purpose
24. direct opposite
27. in position number 19
28. opinionated
32. in position number 9
33. pertaining to everyday concerns
36. to slander
37. pleasant
40. uninvolved

---

## CHECK YOUR ANSWERS

---

### Master Key Concepts

I. copyright, fair use

II. source, content
   A. consecutively
   B. title, publication

III. bibliography
   B. punctuation

IV. reference, author-date, key-number

### Quiz Yourself

1. The fair-use doctrine says that you cannot use other people's work without written permission if your use might unfairly prevent the author from benefiting in some way—say, by selling a copy of the work or by receiving a royalty payment for it. In such cases, even if you credit the source in your report, you must obtain written permission from the copyright holder to reprint the material. You should probably get permission to use
   a. More than 250 words from a book
   b. Any piece of artwork
   c. Any dialogue from a play or line from a poem or song   (p. 639)

2. *Source* notes are used to document quotations and paraphrased passages. *Content* notes are used to supplement the text with asides about a particular issue or event or to direct the reader to another section of the report or to a related source.   (pp. 639-640)

3. Notes are signaled with *superscripts*—Arabic numerals placed just above the line of type. They are numbered *consecutively* throughout the report—or, for very long reports, throughout each chapter.   (p. 640)

4. If a book has four or more authors, the first author's name is spelled out in full (with the first name first). This is followed by the Latin *et al.* or the more informal *and others*, with no comma after the author's name.   (p. 641)

5. In a source note, publication information for books is set off in parentheses. The first item following the opening parenthesis is the name of the city in which the publisher is located. A colon follows the name of the city, after which the name of the publisher appears (often in shortened form). A comma separates the publisher's name from the publication date. The closing parenthesis follows the date.   (p. 641)

6. The formal style for shortened references uses the Latin abbreviations *ibid., op. cit.,* and *loc. cit.* to indicate previously cited sources. The informal style uses the author's last name, a short form of the title, and the page number where the information can be found.   (pp. 641-642)

7. In referencing a letter, a speech, or an interview, begin with the name, title, and affiliation of the "author"; then describe the nature of the communication, the date, possibly the place, and (if appropriate) the location of any files containing the reference.   (p. 643)

8. An *annotated* bibliography comments on the subject matter and viewpoint of the source, as well as on its usefulness to readers.   (p. 643)

9. There are two basic ways to handle reference citations:

    a. The author-date system uses regular bibliography style for the list of references. In the text, reference to a given work is documented by noting the author, date of publication, and page number, set off in parentheses within the text.

    b. The key-number system also uses regular bibliography style for the list of references, but each reference is numbered in sequence in Arabic numerals, followed by a period. (Sometimes the "bibliography" is arranged in order of the appearance of each source in the text, rather than in alphabetical order.) In the text, references are documented with two numbers separated by a colon; the first is the number assigned to the source, the second is the page number. (p. 645)

10. These five references provide additional information on preparing notes and bibliographies:

    a. *Form and Style: Theses, Reports, Term Papers*, by William Giles Campbell and Stephen Vaughan Ballou

    b. *The Chicago Manual of Style*, by University of Chicago Press

    c. *MLA Style Sheet*, by Modern Language Association

    d. *A Manual for Writers of Term Papers, Theses, and Dissertations*, by Kate L. Turabian

    e. *U.S. Government Printing Office Style Manual*, by U.S. Government Printing Office  (p. 645)

**Develop Your Word Power**

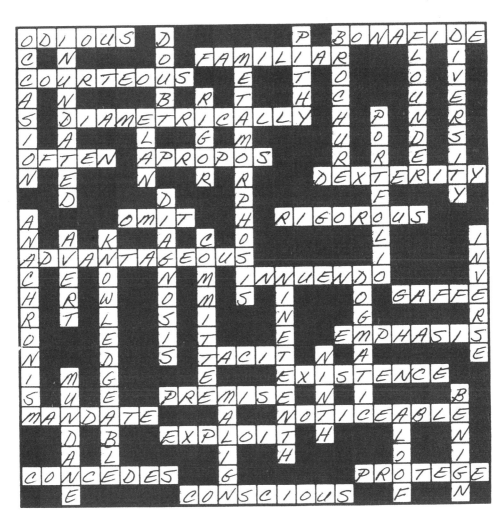

**Lesson 1**

**SENTENCES**

What is a sentence? Saying that it is a word or group of words that starts with a capital letter and ends with a period is only partly right. Sentences also require a subject (someone or something) and a predicate (doing or being):

> Rosemarie conducts the meeting.

In this sentence, <u>Rosemarie</u> is the subject, the someone or something; <u>conducts</u> is the predicate that explains what Rosemarie does.

Subjects are usually nouns or pronouns, and predicates are verbs. However, subjects and predicates may take many different forms. In the following sentences, the subject is underlined once and the predicate is underlined twice:

> <u>He</u> <u>quit</u>.
>
> <u>She</u> <u>was</u> ready to start legal proceedings.
>
> <u>Deborah and Stephen</u> <u>worked</u> together on the BNA account.
>
> The <u>typing pool</u> <u>copied and collated</u> the report.
>
> <u>They</u> <u>are working</u> on a new business plan.
>
> <u>Has</u> <u>he</u> <u>had</u> any trouble with the audit?
>
> <u>Give</u> us your analysis.

In the last sentence in this list, the subject, <u>you</u> is understood; therefore, only the predicate is present. Some sentences with an understood subject—for example, <u>Stop!</u>—contain only one word.

Some sentences use a certain type of predicate—usually a form of the verb <u>is</u>—to link the subject with a word that further describes it:

> The <u>man</u> <u>is</u> happy.

Occasionally this order is inverted, especially in questions:

> Happy <u>is</u> the <u>man</u>.
>
> <u>Is</u> the <u>man</u> happy?

Regardless of the order of the words, these statements are sentences—because they have both a subject and a predicate.

The most basic sentences consist of a subject and a predicate in a simple one-two pattern: <u>They</u> <u>paid</u>. But sentences are usually more complicated. Many sentences also have modifiers that further describe the subject or predicate; they often have an object as well, someone or something that is acted on by the subject of the sentence. For example:

> In most cases, new <u>customers</u> promptly <u>pay</u> bills.

In this sentence, bills is the object. Customers pay what? They pay bills. In addition, new modifies the subject, and promptly and in most cases modify the predicate. If you took away all these extra words and were left with only Customers pay, you would still have a sentence.

In the following exercises, underline subjects once and predicates twice:

1. He found a tactful way to tell her.

2. While adding the column, she noticed a couple of errors.

3. The letter gave him a clue to their thinking.

4. Her favorite activity in her new job was analysis of letters from customers.

5. Were his methods fair?

6. Tracy and Susanne were awarded the top positions.

7. Take one.

8. We are sending the replacement postpaid.

9. Under the desk was a wastebasket.

10. Were his supplies all in order?

Some sentences contain more than one subject-predicate set:

Ben discovered the faulty typewriter, and he was the one who took it to be fixed.

Notice the comma separating the two subject-predicate sets. You could split the one long sentence into two shorter sentences at this comma, and each of the new sentences would have a subject and a predicate. But be careful. Not every sentence containing a comma can be broken in two:

Looking around for a replacement, we found Judy.

Only the latter part of this statement has a subject and a predicate and could therefore stand alone as a sentence. The same is true of the following statement:

Because she had the experience, she got the job.

Although the first part of this statement has a subject and a predicate (she had), it could not stand alone; because she had the experience actually modifies the predicate, tells why she got the job.

In the following exercises, circle all the complete sentences:

11. Show me how to do it.

12. Writing and speaking to perfection.

13. Michael, Betty, and Tom, without whom we would not have succeeded.

14. In an emergency, use it to signal passing motorists.

15. Spending enough to make it worthwhile.

16. With everyone else on vacation, she became responsible for completing the report.

17. Since he became a supervisor.

18. Punctuate correctly, and then retype.

19. When our company first got into the ice-cream business, profits were spectacular, and soon we became too confident.

20. Expenses down, profits up.

Including too much in one sentence is just as serious a problem as leaving out a subject or predicate. The following sentence pastes together too many ideas:

> When she was offered the job, she immediately wrote a letter accepting it and then sat down to list the things she had to do to start work the following Monday, including buying a new dress and shoes, and then she decided to take a break so she could call some of her friends to tell them about her good fortune.

This account is easier to understand when broken into shorter sentences. For example:

> When she was offered the job, she immediately wrote a letter accepting it. Then she sat down to list the things she had to do to start work the following Monday, including buying a new dress and shoes. Then she decided to take a break so she could call some of her friends to tell them about her good fortune.

Although a sentence may contain more than one subject-predicate set, you must be careful not to use a comma to combine what should be two separate sentences:

> He sat down at his desk to prepare a reply, meanwhile his supervisor talked to the customer on the phone.

A solitary comma is not strong enough to link, these two subject-predicate sets. A comma teamed with a linking word such as *and, but, for, nor, or, so,* or *yet* would solve the problem. But if you did not want to add any words, you could use stronger punctuation:

> He sat down at his desk to prepare a reply. Meanwhile, his supervisor talked to the customer on the phone.

> He sat down at his desk to prepare a reply; meanwhile, his supervisor talked to the customer on the phone.

If you were willing to add, to take out, and rearrange words, you could find many other solutions to the problem too.

Correct the sentences in the following exercises by crossing out extra words and inserting only periods and capital letters—not by adding any words or other punctuation:

21. The best part of the day had gone, she decided to try something less demanding.

22. Thank you for your prompt payment, whenever you need cleaning services for your offices, give us a call.

23. After I thought about your performance, I decided to let you take over while I am gone, I hope everything goes well in my absence.

24. Give him the report, he will know what to do with it.

25. Jackie and Bob reported exceptional sales this past month, and they surely deserve some reward, and I know they would like a cash bonus.

If you have had trouble with the exercises in this section, you may want to consult a grammar book on the following subjects:

| | | | |
|---|---|---|---|
| clauses | complex sentences | phrases | sentence fragments |
| comma splices | compound sentences | run-on sentences | simple sentences |

You might also wish to consult section 1.7, "Whole Sentences," in Component Chapter B, "Grammar and Usage Guide, with Exercises," in *Business Communication Today.*

## Lesson 2

### PARTS OF SPEECH: NOUNS

Words that stand for a person, a place, an idea, or a thing are called nouns. Here are some examples of common nouns:

| | | | |
|---|---|---|---|
| industry | assistant | compiler | administration |
| markup | lunch | fitness | downtown |

A word preceded by *a, an,* or *the* in a sentence is usually a noun; so is a word that ends in *ation, ism, ity, ment,* or *ness.*

Nouns may be used in sentences as subjects or objects. That is, the person, place, idea, or thing that is being or doing (subject) is represented by a noun. So is the person, place, idea, or thing that is being acted on (object). In the following sentence, the nouns are underlined:

The secretary typed the report.

The secretary (subject) is acting in a way that affects the report (object).

In this more complicated sentence, *installer* is used as a subject, and *carpeting* and *customer* are used as objects:

The installer delivered the carpeting to the customer.

Notice that *carpeting* is the object of the main part of the sentence (is acted on by the installer), whereas *customer* is the object of the phrase *to the customer.* Nevertheless, both *carpeting* and *customer* are objects.

In the following exercises, underline the subjects and circle the objects:

1. The technician has already repaired the machine for the client.
2. An attorney will talk to the group about incorporation.
3. After her vacation, the buyer prepared a third-quarter budget.
4. The new typewriters are serving our department very well.
5. Accuracy overrides speed in importance.

Some nouns are actually composed of two or more words. *Data base,* for example, is considered a single noun; in fact, you may see it spelled as one word in some places. A few of the many other nouns that combine two or more words:

| | | |
|---|---|---|
| vice president | profit-and-loss statement | administrative assistant |
| coffee maker | attorney general | hanger-on |

The way to tell if word groups like these should be considered single nouns is to try separating the parts. Can the parts be used alone, or do you need both parts to talk about the same thing? Is the word group used as a single unit to mean something distinct? For example, a coffee maker is never called just a maker; nor can it correctly be called a coffee pot.

So far, all the examples have been common nouns—that is, they refer to general classes of things. In business, however, you will often need to refer to specific examples of buildings, companies, people, and so on. Thus you will often need to use proper nouns, which are always capitalized:

| | | |
|---|---|---|
| Crandall Corporation | Tuesday | President Abraham Lincoln |
| Eleanor Kramer | Wyandotte Building | Crest (toothpaste) |

Underline the common and proper nouns in the following exercises:

6. Perhaps the client will provide more time.

7. Has the messenger delivered a package without a label?

8. Give the balance sheet to Melissa.

9. The climate for investment might improve.

10. With a wink and a nod, the assistant ushered the visitor into the office.

11. The clerks gave up their break so they could discuss the new policies with the manager.

12. We'd like to order more satchels for Craigmont Stores.

13. Tarnower Corporation donates a portion of its profits to charity every year.

14. Which aluminum bolts are packaged?

15. Please send a dozen of the following: stopwatches, canteens, headbands, wristbands, and white shoelaces.

When you refer to more than one person, place, idea, or thing of a certain class, you must use the plural form of the noun. Most plurals are formed by adding *s* to the end of the singular form, as in *pencils* and *special offers*. Many nouns, however, are irregular and therefore form the plural in a different way. For example, when a word gains an extra syllable by being made plural, you should add an *es* instead of just an *s*:

| | | |
|---|---|---|
| boss/bosses | batch/batches | Harris/Harrises |

Words ending in *ay, ey, oy,* or *uy* form the plural by adding *s*, but words ending in a consonant and a *y* form the plural by changing the *y* to *i* and adding *es*—except when the word is a proper name:

| | | |
|---|---|---|
| day/days | party/parties | Henry/Henrys |

Similarly, nouns that end in *ao, eo, io, oo,* and *uo* form the plural by adding *s*:

| | | |
|---|---|---|
| video/videos | duo/duos | tattoo/tattoos |

Some nouns that end in a consonant and *o* form the plural by adding *s*, others by adding *es*:

| | | |
|---|---|---|
| veto/vetoes | tomato/tomatoes | memo/memos |

But some words ending in a consonant and *o* may form the plural by adding either *s* or *es*, like *zeros* and *zeroes*. Because of all this variation, you should consult a dictionary whenever you are in doubt about forming the plural of any word that ends in a consonant and an *o*.

Most words that end in a single *f* form the plural by changing the *f* to *v* and adding *es*:

| | | |
|---|---|---|
| shelf/shelves | loaf/loaves | wharf/wharves |

Then there are the words that form the plural by changing radically:

| | | |
|---|---|---|
| man/men | foot/feet | salesperson/salespeople |

Some words derived from Greek and Latin roots form the plural by changing an *is* ending to *es*:

analysis/analyses crisis/crises diagnosis/diagnoses

But other frequently used foreign plurals are treated more like English words in business writing. For example, instead of using *appendices* or *maxima*, you may use *appendixes* or *maximums*.

Finally, some words are the same in both singular and plural form:

data scissors deer headquarters

The only way to tell if these words are singular or plural is to study the rest of the sentence.

When trying to make a plural out of a noun that is actually a combination of words, you must figure out which word in the group is most important. Then you can make a plural out of that word and leave the other in its singular form:

data bases vice presidents attorneys general

These are just a few examples. You can save yourself the embarrassment of using the wrong plural form by consulting a dictionary whenever you have any doubts. If it says nothing about the plural of the word, just add an *s*. Otherwise, use the form specified in the dictionary.

Supply the plural form of each of the nouns in the following exercises:

16. copy _____ Copies _____

17. bonus _____ bonuses _____

18. son-in-law _____ sons-in-laws _____

19. folio _____ folios _____

20. Amy _____ Amys _____

21. sheaf _____ sheaves _____

22. child _____ children _____

23. parenthesis _____

24. supply _____ supplies _____

25. mess _____ messes _____

If you need more help with nouns, consult a grammar book on the following subjects:

| | | |
|---|---|---|
| collective nouns | objects | proper nouns |
| common nouns | plural nouns | subjects |
| compound nouns | | |

You might also check section 1.1 "Nouns," in Component Chapter B, "Grammar and Usage Guide, with Exercises," in *Business Communication Today.*

## Lesson 3

## PARTS OF SPEECH: PRONOUNS

These are the pronouns that substitute for nouns referring to specific people or things:

| | Subject | Object | Possessive |
|---|---|---|---|
| Singular | I | me | my, mine |
| | he, she, it | him, her, it | his, her, hers, its |
| Plural | we | us | our, ours |
| | they | them | their, theirs |
| Singular and Plural | you | you | your, yours |
| | who | whom | whose |

Your choice of a pronoun from this list depends on whether the person or thing represented by the pronoun is acting, is being acted on, or possesses something. If acting, the pronoun is standing in for the subject of a sentence or phrase; if being acted on, the pronoun is standing in for the object of a sentence or phrase; if possessing something, the pronoun is showing the ownership. (Notice that none of the possessive pronouns, not even *its*, has an apostrophe.)

Study the pronouns in these sentences, noting whether they are subjects (S), objects (O), or possessives (P):

Who (S) gave the receipts to her (O)?

She (S) looked at my (P) resume.

They (S) returned the defective parts to us (O).

Our (P) major concern is your (P) satisfaction.

He (S) sent me (O) a check for $239.28.

To whom (O) will you (S) give the assignment?

I (S) will sell them (O) to you (O) at a discount.

If a noun is singular, the pronoun that stands in for it is also singular. If a noun is plural, the pronoun that stands in for it is also plural:

The ledger sat on the desk.
It sat on the desk.

The desks were delivered Tuesday.
They were delivered Tuesday.

A plural pronoun may also be used to stand in for two or more singular nouns:

Put the typewriter and adding machine into the empty office.
Put them into the empty office.

Complete the following exercises by replacing the underlined nouns with the correct pronouns:

1. To <u>which retailer</u> will you send <u>your merchandise</u>?

2. Have you given <u>John and Nancy</u> a list of parts?

3. <u>The main office</u> sent the invoice to <u>Mr. and Mrs. Litvak</u> on December 5.

4. The company settled <u>the company's</u> accounts before the end of the year.

5. <u>Which person's</u> umbrella is this?

6. <u>Peter</u> gave <u>Martin</u> a great pep talk.

7. I saw Bill at the conference, and <u>Bill</u> gave me a directory for <u>the conference</u>.

8. Where did Mr. Schiller get <u>Mr. Schiller's</u> new car?

9. Tell the Randolphs about <u>the Randolphs's</u> obligations.

10. When do you want Meg and Robert to take <u>Meg's and Robert's</u> break?

Replacing nouns with pronouns streamlines a sentence:

> Roy gave <u>Roy's</u> pencil to Terri so <u>Terri</u> could add the figures.
> Roy gave <u>his</u> pencil to Terri so <u>she</u> could add the figures.

In some sentences, however, you must sometimes reuse a noun for clarity, even though you could substitute a pronoun.  For example:

> Tom told Richard that <u>he</u> would be going to the meeting.

Who will be going to the meeting, Tom or Richard?  Readers will be less confused if you use the appropriate noun again:

> Tom told Richard that Richard would be going to the meeting.

(This problem may also be solved by rewriting the sentence.)

In the following exercises, cross out nouns and write pronouns above them wherever appropriate:

11. Customers always receive what customers expect from Blomberg's.

12. Janet and Anne are preparing a report for Janet and Anne's boss that tells the boss about Janet and Anne's results for the first quarter of the year.

13. Bob broke the chair, and so now Bob has to fix the chair.

14. When Mara spoke at the last gathering of the company's sales representatives, Mara gave the sales representatives a complete picture of the company's operations.

15. Tell Edward to turn in Edward's expense account before the expense account is overdue.

What pronoun should you use when referring to a group?  Use a singular pronoun if the focus is on the group as a single unit, a plural pronoun if the focus is on individuals within the group:

The <u>staff</u> completed <u>its</u> report on time.

The <u>staff</u> turned in <u>their</u> reports at various times.

In the first sentence, the staff is working together on a report and is therefore seen as a unit, requiring a singular pronoun. In the second sentence, staff members are preparing individual reports, and thus a plural pronoun is required.

In most cases, companies are considered as units. Therefore, a singular pronoun is usually used to stand in for the name of a company:

<u>Starbright Enterprises</u> has lower prices than <u>its</u> competitors.

<u>Flyway Airlines</u> has just had <u>its</u> best year ever.

Another problem area for business communicators is indefinite pronouns. Words like *everyone*, *neither*, and *each* are singular, referring to one person or thing, and so require a singular pronoun:

<u>Neither</u> Elizabeth nor Connie has reached <u>her</u> potential yet.

<u>Each</u> display area has <u>its</u> limitations.

Words like *many* and *several*, however, take plural pronouns:

<u>Many</u> employees have requested <u>their</u> holidays already.

Still other indefinite pronouns—such as *all, any, most,* and *some*—may be either singular or plural, depending on the context:

<u>Some</u> is still left in <u>its</u> container.

<u>Some</u> are already asking for <u>their</u> bonuses.

Write the correct pronouns in the following exercises:

16. The typing pool is preparing guidelines for _____ clients.

17. Few of the sales representatives turn in _____ reports on time.

18. The board of directors has chosen _____ officers.

19. Several of the account executives have told _____ clients about the new program.

20. Mondo Taco, Inc., plans to expand_____ operations dramatically over the next two years.

21. Has everyone supplied _____ Social Security number yet?

22. Give the staff _____ raises early this year.

23. All can voice _____ opinions here.

24. City Securities has just announced _____ year-end dividends.

25. Either of the new products would readily find _____ niche in the marketplace.

You can learn more about pronouns by looking in a grammar book under the following headings:

| | | |
|---|---|---|
| agreement with antecedents | indefinite pronouns | possessive pronouns |
| case of pronouns | interrogative pronouns | reciprocal pronouns |
| demonstrative pronouns | numeral pronouns | reflexive pronouns |
| gender-neutral pronouns | personal pronouns | relative pronouns |

You may also want to refer to section 1.2, "Pronouns," in Component Chapter B, "Grammar and Usage Guide, with Exercises," in *Business Communication Today.*

## Lesson 4

## PARTS OF SPEECH:  VERBS

Verbs are a sentence's "action" or "being" words, that is, they tell what happens or what is.  Verbs may consist of one or several words—*wrote* and *would have written*, for example—and the form of a verb may change to indicate subtle meaning and to complement other words in the sentence.

Among the many action verbs used in business are *send, pay,* and *produce.*  The words underlined in the following sentences are action verbs as well:

They <u>bought</u> a $15 million company and <u>turned</u> it into an even bigger company.

I <u>have seen</u> the proposal, but I <u>cannot remember</u> some of its specific points.

<u>Will</u> you <u>stock</u> item 6-2993 next quarter?

Don <u>is eating</u> lunch in the cafeteria.

Notice that some of these verbs consist of a helping verb (such as *have*) and a main verb (such as *seen*).

Among being verbs, the most common is, logically enough, *be*:

|  | Present | Past | Other Tenses |
|---|---|---|---|
| I | am | was | will be (future), have |
| you | are | were | been (present perfect), |
| he, she, it | is | was | had been (past perfect), will have been (future |
| we | are | were | perfect) |
| they | are | were |  |

But other verbs—such as *feel, seem,* and *sound*—serve the same purpose and can substitute for *be*. All being verbs link the subject of a sentence with other qualities, like an equal sign; they indicate that the word on one side is linked with the word on the other side.  But they do not demonstrate any action.  For example, all of the following verbs describe a state of being:

Darla <u>was</u> happy about her promotion.

The figures <u>seem</u> accurate.

Your estimate <u>sounded</u> right.

I <u>will feel</u> better tomorrow.

In the following exercises, underline all being verbs:

1.  Andy feels ready to demonstrate the product.
2.  Chicago Fabricating sent holiday greetings to all its major customers.
3.  This procedure lasts only five minutes.
4.  We were reluctant to give a refund in this case.
5.  Will you be using my desk while I'm out of the office?

Verb tenses allow you to talk about things happening or existing in different time periods. For regular verbs, the present tense adds a final s to the main verb, but only when used with he, she, or it; the past tense adds ed to the main verb; and the future tense uses the main verb with the helping verb will. For example:

> Present: He <u>mails</u> the letters on Tuesday.
> Past: He <u>mailed</u> the letters on Tuesday.
> Future: He <u>will mail</u> the letters on Tuesday.

Although these are the three tenses most frequently used, you will also have occasion to use three "perfect" tenses, which use the helping verb have and usually the past tense of the main verb:

> Present perfect: He <u>has mailed</u> the letters on Tuesday.
> Past perfect: He <u>had mailed</u> the letters on Tuesday.
> Future perfect: He <u>will have mailed</u> the letters on Tuesday.

Write the verb tense called for in each of the following exercises:

6. repair (future perfect) _____

7. hire (past) _____

8. move (past perfect) _____

9. motivate (present perfect) _____

10. train (future) _____

Not all verbs are as regular as these; indeed, they are called irregular verbs because in one or more of the tenses they do not follow this pattern. The most irregular of the verbs is be, but many other common verbs are to some extent irregular. Here is a sample:

| PRESENT | <u>go</u> | <u>begin</u> | <u>drink</u> | <u>take</u> |
|---|---|---|---|---|
| PAST | went | began | drank | took |
| FUTURE | will go | will begin | will drink | will take |
| PRESENT PERFECT | have/has gone | have/has begun | have/has drunk | have/has taken |
| PAST PERFECT | had gone | had begun | had drunk | had taken |
| FUTURE PERFECT | will have gone | will have begun | will have drunk | will have taken |

Provide the irregular verb form called for in the following exercises:

11. I (present perfect, *became*) _____ the resident expert on repairing the copy machine.

12. She (past, *know*) _____ how to perform an audit when she came to work for us.

13. By the time you finish the analysis, he (future perfect, *take*) _____ his vacation.

14. Next week, call John to tell him what you (future, *do*) _____ for next month's sales meeting.

19. When Susan returned to our company, she (past perfect, *rise*) _____ in rank to analyst.

Another way to distinguish among verbs is to label them either transitive or intransitive. Transitive verbs—such as *give, lay, set,* and *raise*—transfer the action from the subject to the object. For example:

He <u>gave</u> a refund to Nissa Nelson.

In this sentence, the verb *gave* is what he (subject) did to or with the refund (object).

On the other hand, intransitive verbs—such as *feel, lie, sit,* and *rise*—do not transfer any action:

Profits <u>rose</u> in the first quarter.

The verb *rose* is what profits (subject) did, but profits did not act directly on anything in this sentence.

Some verbs may be transitive or intransitive. Consider the following:

He <u>feels</u> uncomfortable with the proposition.
She <u>feels</u> the texture of the cloth before deciding to buy.

In the first sentence, he (subject) feels (predicate), but nothing in the sentence receives the direct impact of his feeling. In the second sentence, however, she (subject) feels (predicate) texture (object); in other words, she performs an action that has a direct impact on something.

In the exercises below, underline the intransitive verbs and circle the transitive verbs:

16. Ms. Detweiler sent him a reminder.

17. What is the purpose of this memo?

18. When you have heard her story, call me about it.

19. They mentioned a name yesterday.

20. He stood next to my desk and described the whole thing.

The way you use verbs can have a great deal to do with the tone of your writing. For example, verbs may be either passive or active. An active sentence uses direct, subject-verb-object order:

We <u>will refund</u> your money.

Notice how much more indirect this passive sentence is:

Your money <u>will be refunded</u>.

It is not clear who is doing the refunding in this sentence.

Active sentences are more forceful than passive sentences, which is usually desirable. However, in business communication you may sometimes want to soften a statement or to avoid assigning responsibility for an action. Then you will find passive sentences useful.

Rewrite the sentences in the following exercises so that they use active verbs instead of passive verbs:

21. The report will be written by Leslie Cartwright. _____

_____

22. The failure to record the transaction was mine. _____

_____

23. Have you been notified by the claims department of your rights? _____

_____

24. We are dependent on their services for our operation. _____

_____

25. The damaged toaster had been returned by the customer. _____

_____

If you want to learn more about verbs, look in a grammar book for information on these topics:

| | | |
|---|---|---|
| auxiliary verbs | mood of verbs | verb tenses |
| irregular verbs | subjunctive mood | voice of verbs |
| linking verbs | transitive and intransitive verbs | |

You may also wish to consult sections 1.3, "Verbs," and 1.7.5, "Linking Verbs," in Component Chapter B, "Grammar and Usage Guide, with Exercises," in *Business Communication Today.*

## Lesson 5

## PARTS OF SPEECH: VERB AGREEMENT

To use verbs correctly, you must make decisions about verb forms based on the number represented by the subject. Take, for example, the present tense of the verb *vote*:

Singular: I vote                    Plural: we vote
       you vote                                you vote
       he/she/it votes                         they vote

In the present tense, a regular verb like *vote* takes a final *s* or *es* to agree with the singular pronouns *he, she,* and *it* or with any singular noun.

Other verbs are not so easy to deal with. Consider the present tense of these irregular verbs:

be:    I am, we are        have: I have, we have
       you are                  you have
       he/she/it is, they are       he/she/it has, they have

apply:  I apply, we apply     can:  I can, we can
       you apply                 you can
       he/she/it applies, they apply    he/she/it can, they can

In the following exercises, write in the present tense of each verb:

1. You (be) _____ eligible for a promotion already.

2. Dave (have) _____ another telephone line.

3. How (be) _____ I supposed to know when we've reached that point?

4. She (do) _____ her work quickly and accurately.

5. They (be) _____ sometimes difficult to deal with.

Getting the verb to agree with the subject in sentences like these is relatively simple. But problems arise when the sentence is complicated.

Each sentence is made up of at least one clause, a group of words with both a subject and a predicate. Sentences may also contain phrases, which do not have a subject-predicate set. Notice the difference here:

Clause:  he sent an invoice
Clause:  because he sent an invoice

Phrase:  with an invoice
Phrase:  after sending an invoice

The clauses have subjects and predicates; the phrases do not have subjects and predicates.

A simple sentence has only one clause like the first clause above, but many sentences combine clauses and phrases, like this:

He sent an invoice, and then he entered the amount in the books.
Because he sent an invoice, he decided not to call T&T Sales.

211

He presented the client with an invoice.
After sending an invoice, he began another project.

Notice that all the verbs in these examples are in the past tense; in other words, they agree.  Only if there were a good reason for the verbs to be in different tenses would they not agree.  For example:

Yesterday she prepared a sales report, today she is listing all her potential clients, and tomorrow she will call them.

In some sentences with two or more verbs, the helping verbs or the main verbs are sometimes identical.  In that case, the duplicated word or words can be dropped:

Consumers have been saving and (have been) spending.

But do not drop any part of a verb that is not an exact duplicate.  For example, this sentence is wrong:

They have not and will not be attending the workshops.

It becomes correct when part of the helping verb is restored:

They have not been and will not be attending the workshops.

Here is another type of agreement problem:

The building is attractive, economical, and has beautiful surroundings.

Because is and has are different and no verb is included with economical, this sentence is wrong.  It can be fixed by adding another verb:

The building is attractive, is economical, and has beautiful surroundings.

It can also be fixed by changing one of the items in the series so that it is the same type of word as the other two:

The building is attractive, economical, and beautifully situated.

In the following exercises, fill in the correct verb form:

6.  They identified the source of the problem, and then they (look) _____ for ways to solve it.

7.  When success (seem) _____ imminent, he panics.

8.  Jason Beaudry never has gone to Europe and probably never (go) _____.

9.  Why (do) _____ she ignore John when he talks?

10.  We (take) _____ that point into consideration before we decided what to do.

Another problem of verb agreement relates to the subject (noun or pronoun) of a sentence.  The verb should be in the plural form when the subject is plural.  Otherwise, the verb should be singular.  When a phrase separates the subject and the verb, the task of deciding whether to use a singular or plural verb becomes more complicated.  Look at this example:

The analysis of existing documents takes a full week.

Although documents is plural, the verb is in the singular form.  That's because the subject of the sentence is analysis, a singular noun.  The phrase of existing documents can be disregarded.  Here is another example:

Their <u>answers</u> to the question <u>are</u> in the minutes.

Take away the phrase *to the question*, and you are left with the plural subject *answers*. Therefore the verb takes the plural form.

Circle the correct verb form in the following exercises:

11. Each of the managers turn/turns in a monthly report.

12. The receptionist, not the clerks, take/takes all the calls.

13. Everyone upstairs receive/receives mail before we do.

14. The reasons for her decision sound/sounds logical.

15. All the products sell/sells well.

Verb agreement is also complicated when the subject is not a specific noun or pronoun and when the subject may be considered either singular or plural. In these cases, you have to analyze the surrounding sentence to determine which verb form to use. Observe carefully which of the following sentences contain *are* (plural form of *be*) and which contain *is* (singular form). The noun that controls the verb form is underlined in each sentence:

The <u>staff</u> is quartered in the warehouse.
The <u>staff</u> are at their desks in the warehouse.
The <u>computers</u> and the <u>staff</u> are in the warehouse.
Neither the staff nor the <u>computers</u> are in the warehouse.
<u>Every</u> computer is in the warehouse.
<u>Many a</u> computer is in the warehouse.

Did you notice that words like *every* use the singular verb form? In addition, when a *neither-nor* phrase combines singular and plural nouns, the verb takes the form that matches the noun closest to it.

Circle the correct form of the verb in the following exercises:

16. Brenda and Bill has/have responsibility for the project.

17. Neither the main office nor the branch offices is/are blameless.

18. Each programmer and analyst report/reports to Jennifer.

19. Your whole family enjoy/enjoys credit privileges at Mo's.

20. Either the secretaries or the office manager take/takes care of all inquiries about employee benefits.

In the business world, some types of subjects require extra attention. Company names, for example, are considered singular and therefore take a singular verb in most cases—even if they contain plural words.

But quantities are sometimes considered singular and sometimes plural. If a quantity refers to a total amount, it takes a singular verb; if a quantity refers to individual, countable units, it takes a plural verb. For example:

<u>Three hours</u> is a long time.

The <u>eight dollars</u> we collected for the fund are tacked on the bulletin board.

Fractions may also be singular or plural, depending on the noun that accompanies them:

One-third of the <u>warehouse</u> is devoted to this product line.

One-third of the <u>products</u> are defective.

Circle the correct verb form in the following exercises:

21. C & B Sales is/are listed in the directory.

22. When measuring shelves, 7 inches is/are significant.

23. About 90 percent of the employees plan/plans to come to the company picnic.

24. Carnegie Industries make/makes book-binding equipment.

25. Two weeks is/are all we need to complete our analysis.

To learn more about verb agreement, consult a grammar book on these topics:

| | | |
|---|---|---|
| agreement with *there* and *here* | compound subjects | verb agreement |
| collective nouns | indefinite pronouns | *who* clauses |
| complements | intervening elements | |

You may wish to refer to sections 1.3.2, "Irregular Verbs," and 1.7.2, "Longer Sentences," in Component Chapter B, "Grammar and Usage Guide, with Exercises," in *Business Communication Today.*

## Lesson 6

## PARTS OF SPEECH: ADJECTIVES AND ARTICLES

Adjectives modify (describe, explain, tell something about) nouns and pronouns. The adjectives in the following sentences do this job whether they come before or after the words they modify and whether they are truly adjectives or are nouns working as adjectives:

The Seattle office has received another payment from that customer.

A more attractive desk is earmarked for Ms. Brophy's fourth-floor office.

We are proud of your outstanding performance in many competitions.

These sentences would be much less descriptive without adjectives telling which, what kind of, and what. (Although possessive pronouns, such as your, seem to function as adjectives, they are classified as pronouns.)

Observe that the adjectives in these sentences fall into three categories: purely descriptive (such as *outstanding* and *more attractive*), limiting (such as *many*), and pointing (such as *that*). Descriptive adjectives are probably the easiest to identify in any sentence; they are words like *cold, impatient, useful, good.* Limiting adjectives are a little more difficult to pick out, but numbers and such words as *most, several,* and *no* are often used to specify quantity or amount. The pointing adjectives are *this, that, these,* and *those.* The sentences also contain articles: *a, an,* and *the.*

In the following exercises, underline all the adjectives and articles:

1. A pleasant surprise awaits you for taking advantage of our fantastic offer.
2. The newest accountant on our headquarters staff is a 1985 graduate of the most prestigious university in a neighboring state.
3. She slowly rose to speak to the assembled delegates.
4. Their approach is best described as a useful combination of grand design and careful execution.
5. The color photographs in that brochure were expensive.

Adjectives change form when they are used to compare items:

| One Item | Two Items | Three or More Items |
| --- | --- | --- |
| large | larger | largest |
| easy | easier | easiest |
| far | farther | farthest |
| good | better | best |
| bad | worse | worst |
| little | less | least |
| some | more | most |
| beautiful | more beautiful | most beautiful |

As you can see from this list, simple adjectives like *large* add the ending *er* when comparing two items and *est* when comparing three or more items. This is the normal pattern. Other words, such as *good*, are irregular. And words with three or more syllables use *more* and *most*, instead of the word endings, to make comparisons.

Some adjectives cannot be used to make comparisons because they themselves indicate the extreme. For example, if something is perfect, nothing can be more perfect. If something is unique or ultimate, nothing can be more unique or more ultimate. However, two or more things may be compared in their closeness to these extremes: more nearly perfect, most nearly unique.

In the following exercises, fill in the appropriate form of the adjectives that are supplied for you:

6. Of the two products, this one has the (great) _____ potential.

7. The (perfect) _____ solution is *d*.

8. Here is the (interesting) _____ of all the ideas I have heard so far.

9. Our service is (good) _____ than theirs.

10. The (hard) _____ part of my job is firing people.

Many adjectives used in the business world are actually combinations of words: *up-to-date* report, *last-minute* effort, *fifth-floor* suite, *well-built* engine. As you can see, they are hyphenated when they come before the noun they modify. However, when they come after the noun they modify, they are not hyphenated: the report is *up to date*, an effort made at the *last minute*, a suite on the *fifth floor*, the engine is *well built*.

Hyphens are not used when part of the combination is a word ending in *ly* (because the word ending in *ly* is usually not an adjective): a rapidly *shrinking* reserve, a highly *motivated* employee.

A hyphen is also omitted from combinations of words that are used frequently: *credit card* account, *data processing* department.

In the following exercises, insert hyphens wherever required:

11. A highly placed source revealed Dotson's last ditch efforts to cover up the mistake.

12. Please send a replacement that is large enough for me.

13. A top secret document was taken from the president's office last night.

14. A 30 year old person should know better.

15. If I write a large scale report, I want to know that it will be read by upper level management.

Adjectives often pile up in front of a noun, like this:

The <u>superficial,</u> <u>obvious</u> answer was the one she gave.

The most valuable animal on the ranch is a <u>small roan</u> horse.

The question is whether a comma should be used to separate the adjectives. The answer? Use a comma when the two adjectives independently modify the noun; do not use a comma when one of the adjectives is closely identified with the noun. In the first example above, the answer was both superficial and obvious. But in the second example, the roan horse is small.

Another way for you to think about this problem is to use a comma as a replacement for the word *and*. Here is another example for you to study:

We recommend a diet of <u>leafy green</u> vegetables.
We recommend a diet of <u>green,</u> <u>leafy</u> vegetables.

Because some green vegetables are not leafy (cucumbers and zucchini, for example), it is correct to leave out the comma in the first example so that you know which kind of green vegetables are being discussed. But because all leafy vegetables are also green (green and leafy), the comma must be included in the second example. Again:

> He is an <u>angry young</u> man.
> He is an <u>angry</u>, <u>dangerous</u> man.

There is a difference between a young man who is angry and a man who is angry and dangerous.

Another device for deciding whether to use a comma is to try switching the adjectives. If the order of the adjectives can be reversed without changing the meaning of the phrase, you should use a comma. If the order cannot be reversed, you should not use a comma. For example:

> Here's our <u>simplified credit</u> application.
> Here's our <u>simplified</u>, <u>easy-to-complete</u> application.
> Here's our <u>easy-to-complete</u>, <u>simplified</u> application.

A credit application may be simple or complex; at any rate, you cannot talk about a *credit, simplified application*. The application in the second and third examples, however, is both simplified and easy to complete, however you arrange the words.

In the following exercises, insert required commas between adjectives:

16. The two companies are engaged in an all-out no-holds-barred struggle for dominance.

17. A tiny metal shaving is responsible for the problem.

18. She came to the office with a bruised swollen knee.

19. A chipped cracked sheet of glass is useless to us.

20. You'll receive our usual cheerful prompt service.

In these last exercises, insert both hyphens and commas as necessary:

21. It was one of the first land grant colleges in the country.

22. Joan is the stern mother hen of a busy tightly run office.

23. Energy wasting unnecessary trips must be eliminated.

24. The new past due notices will go out with today's mail.

25. If a broken down unproductive guy like Carl can get a raise, why can't a take charge guy like me get one?

If you want to learn more about adjectives and articles, consult a grammar book on the following topics:

| | | |
|---|---|---|
| absolute adjectives | coordinate adjectives | limiting adjectives |
| comparative adjectives | descriptive adjectives | pointing adjectives |
| compound adjectives | independent adjectives | proper adjectives |

You may also wish to consult sections 1.4, "Adjectives," and 1.6.2, "Articles," in Component Chapter B, "Grammar and Usage Guide, with Exercises," in *Business Communication Today.*

**Lesson 7**

**PARTS OF SPEECH: ADVERBS**

Adverbs modify (describe, qualify, limit) verbs, adjectives, and other adverbs:

Verb:        He sent the specifications <u>promptly</u>. (How were they sent?  Promptly.)

Adjective:   Their <u>grievously</u> late report will not be accepted. (How late was the report?  Grievously late.)

Adverb:      He typed <u>very</u> quickly. (How quickly did he type?  Very quickly.)

Most adverbs are formed simply by adding *ly* to the end of an adjective (with the last letter of the adjective sometimes dropped or changed): *highly, quickly, truly, nicely, poorly,* and so on.  But some familiar adverbs—such as *quite, too, very, almost, often, soon, so,* and *many*—do not end in *ly*.

In the following exercises, underline the adverbs:

1. An unstable person is an obviously poor choice for this difficult job.
2. They are quite certain that the spaces will fill soon.
3. She often stays late to finish her rapidly accumulating paperwork.
4. Curly hair is yours with our newly developed perms.
5. A nicely organized report is soon read.
6. Too many of our customers have complained vigorously about her surly manner.
7. Trapped in a slowly shrinking market, the company is certainly doomed to fail eventually.
8. The market for anatomically correct dolls is too small.
9. Give the letter a quick review before you blithely send it.
10. A correctly operating bottom-of-the line model is much better than a malfunctioning top-of-the-line model.

Some adverbs are difficult to distinguish from adjectives.  For example, in the following sentences is the underlined word an adverb or an adjective?

They worked <u>well</u>.
The baby is <u>well</u>.

In the first sentence, *well* is an adverb modifying the verb *worked*.  In the second sentence, *well* is an adjective modifying the noun *baby*.

The secret to choosing correctly between adverbs and adjectives in this situation is to be able to identify such being verbs as *appear, be, become, feel, look, seem, smell, sound,* and *taste*.  Being verbs link a noun to an adjective describing the noun.  In contrast, an adverb is used if the verb that separates it from the noun is an action verb.  Here is another example:

Adjective:   This balance sheet looks <u>strange</u>. (The balance sheet does not itself use eyes to look; this sentence means that the balance sheet *is* strange.)

Adverb:      She looks at us <u>strangely</u>. (Here *looks* is an action verb, and *strangely* tells how she performs that action.)

If you can tell the difference between an adjective and an adverb in situations like these, you should have no trouble deciding when to use *good, real,* and *slow* (adjectives modifying nouns) as opposed to *well, really,* and *slowly* (adverbs modifying verbs, adjectives, and adverbs). For example:

Adjective

He is a <u>good</u> worker. (What kind of worker is he?)

It is a <u>real</u> computer. (What kind of computer is it?)

The traffic is <u>slow</u>. (What quality does the traffic have?)

Adverb

He works <u>well</u>. (How does he work?)

It <u>really</u> is a computer. (To what extent is it one?)

The traffic moves <u>slowly</u>. (How does the traffic move?)

In the following exercises, circle the correct choice:

11. Their performance has been good/well.

12. I sure/surely do not know how to help you.

13. He feels sick/sickly again today.

14. Customs dogs are chosen because they smell good/well.

15. The redecorated offices look good/well.

Like adjectives, adverbs can be used to compare items. Generally, the basic adverb is combined with *more* or *most,* just as long adjectives are—although some adverbs have one-word comparative forms:

| One Item | Two Items | Three Items |
|---|---|---|
| quickly | more quickly | most quickly |
| sincerely | less sincerely | least sincerely |
| fast | faster | fastest |
| well | better | best |

In these exercises, provide the correct form of the adverbs that are provided:

16. Which of the two programs computes (fast) _____?

17. Kate has 13 years of experience to draw on, but she was (recently)_____ employed by Graphicon.

18. Could they be (happily) _____ employed than they are now?

19. This is the (well) _____ designed model of the two we have in stock.

20. You are to be praised for presenting the (logically) _____ reasoned argument I have ever heard.

Negative adverbs—such as *neither, no, not, scarcely,* and *seldom*—are powerful words and therefore do not need any help in conveying a negative thought. In fact, using double negatives gives a strong impression of illiteracy, and so you would be well advised to avoid sentences like these:

I <u>don't</u> want <u>no</u> mistakes. (Correct: I don't want any mistakes. I want no mistakes.)

They <u>scarcely</u> noticed <u>neither</u> one. (Correct: They scarcely noticed either one. They noticed neither one.)

In the following exercises, correct the double negatives by crossing out unnecessary letters and words and writing in necessary letters and words:

21. He doesn't seem to have none.

22. That machine is scarcely never used.

23. They can't get no replacement parts until Thursday.

24. It wasn't no different from the first event we promoted.

25. We've looked for it, and it doesn't seem to be nowhere.

If you would like to learn more about adverbs, consult a grammar book on the following topics:

adverbs versus adjectives              double negatives
comparative adverbs                    redundant adverbs

You may also wish to refer to section 1.5, "Adverbs," in Component Chapter B, "Grammar and Usage Guide, with Examples," in *Business Communication Today.*

## Lesson 8

## PARTS OF SPEECH: VERBALS

Some forms of verbs take a special role in sentences. Verbals are verbs that are used as nouns, adjectives, and adverbs instead of as predicates. There are three basic types of verbals.

The first type of verbal, formed by adding *ing* to the end of a verb, is used as a noun:

Selling is an acquired skill.

*Selling* (a verbal) is the subject of this sentence, and *is* is the predicate.

Be careful not to mistake this form of verbal for predicates that use an *ing* ending. Compare these sentences:

Predicate: He is merchandising a new product.
Verbal: He has a knack for merchandising.

In the second sentence, *has* is the predicate, and *merchandising* is the object of a phrase.

The major problem that arises with verbals ending in *ing* is the use of a possessive noun or pronoun with them. The following sentence is incorrect:

We appreciate you calling about this matter.

Because *calling* takes the place of a noun in this sentence, *you* must be changed to a possessive pronoun, like this:

We appreciate your calling about this matter.

Only the second sentence below is correct:

Incorrect: Deborah delaying will jeopardize the whole thing.
Correct: Deborah's delaying will jeopardize the whole thing.

You can decide whether to use a possessive noun or pronoun with a verbal of this type by replacing the verbal with another noun. For example, if you replace the word *delaying* with the word *temper*, you will find that you must use a possessive noun in order to make sense:

Deborah's temper will jeopardize the whole program.

In the following exercises, circle the sentences that use this first type of verbal correctly:

1. Waiting for anything makes me impatient.
2. His handling of the irate customer was admirable.
3. You saw the result of George training.
4. Take the results to manufacturing.
5. You could attribute the difference to them cheating.

The second kind of verbal serves in sentences as an adjective. In the following sentences, observe how the verbals formed from the verb *finish* are used to modify nouns:

The typist put the <u>finishing</u> touches on the letter.

The <u>finished</u> assignment is in Ms. Boromisa's office.

In both of these sentences, a form of the verb *finish* is used to provide additional information about nouns: *touches* and *assigment*. Other verbs—*put* and *is*—work in these sentences as predicates.

In the following exercises, underline verbals functioning as adjectives:

6. The established procedures are rarely followed.

7. Use a roasting bag to avoid an overdone turkey.

8. Twice-audited Hodgkins & Company has become more careful with its record keeping.

9. The closed factory will be reopening in May.

10. During the editing process, most written reports are strengthened.

The third form of verbal is the infinitive, which you have probably heard of (as in "splitting infinitives"). An infinitive, such as *to be*, may function as a noun, an adjective, or an adverb. For example, in this sentence the infinitive works as a noun—in fact, as the subject of the sentence:

<u>To err</u> is human. (What is human?)

Here it is a noun too, but this time it's the object of the sentence:

We hope <u>to grow</u> this year. (We hope what?)

In the following sentence, the infinitive works as an adjective:

Their plan <u>to grow</u> was hampered by a weak economy. (What kind of plan?)

And here the infinitive works as an adverb:

It eventually grew <u>to be</u> a very large company. (How did it grow?)

Now, about splitting infinitives: in general, you should not put any word or phrase between *to* and the rest of the infinitive. But sometimes you must split an infinitive to protect your sentence's clarity or smoothness. For example, splitting the infinitive in this sentence is acceptable:

The best policy is <u>to</u> regularly <u>inspect</u> and <u>service</u> all the equipment.

But this one becomes awkward when the infinitive is split:

<u>To</u> predictably, promptly, and reliably <u>call</u> on customers is part of your job.

It would be better like this:

<u>To call</u> on customers predictably, promptly, and reliably is part of your job.

In the following exercises, circle the words that split an infinitive and draw an arrow to show where they would fit in more smoothly and logically:

11. Our goal is to, with your help, track down the error.

12. Did you tell her to promptly call me?

13. To cheerfully service these accounts, you need patience.

14. We have been trying to desperately avoid bankruptcy.

15. Ms. McMichaels tends to, with her great sense of timing, know just when she should sell.

In the next set of exercises, draw circles around the verbals and draw lines to the words they modify (if they indeed modify anything):

16. Handling explosives is our main business.

17. Your plan to analyze these trends is sound.

18. The trading experts recommend patience.

19. We planned to finish by Wednesday.

20. Streamlined DiTex has more flexibility than some of its competitors.

A glaring sign of carelessness in writing is the use of different types of verbals in situations that call for parallel structure. For instance, the following sentence is a mess:

> Your responsibilities include gathering sales figures, analysis of those figures, and to report them to management.

You could solve the problem by putting all the underlined verbals in the same form:

> gathering, analyzing, and reporting
> collection of, analysis of, and reporting of
> to gather, to analyze, and to report

Many other sentences can be improved by introducing parallelism:

Nonparallel:    He was an expert in writing and had learned well how to speak.
Parallel:       He was an expert in writing and speaking.
Parallel:       He had learned well how to write and to speak.

In the following exercises, cross out and add words to give the sentences a parallel structure:

21. These were my goals: finding suitable markets and to outline a plan for penetrating them.

22. Standing firm is more difficult than to allow an exception.

23. She has demonstrated an ability to plan and skill at organizing.

24. This remarkable new product will help you to keep your time organized and with writing your correspondence.

25. Retraining people already on the payroll is better than to hire new people.

If you would like to know more about verbals, consult a grammar book on these topics:

| | | |
|---|---|---|
| dangling modifiers | misplaced modifiers | verbal nouns |
| gerunds | parallelism | verbal phrases |
| infinitives | participles | |

You may also wish to refer to section 1.4, "Adjectives," in Component Chapter B, "Grammar and Usage Guide, with Exercises," in *Business Communication Today.*

## Lesson 9

## PARTS OF SPEECH: PREPOSITIONS

Prepositions are little words that can add a lot of meaning to sentences. These are some of the most frequently used prepositions:

| | | | |
|---|---|---|---|
| about | in | between | through |
| at | of | by | to |
| before | out | for | with |
| during | after | into | among |

Some prepositions consist of more than one word—like these:

| | |
|---|---|
| because of | in addition to |
| except for | out of |

Prepositions do not stand alone; they signal prepositional phrases that have a noun as an object:

| | |
|---|---|
| of the company | in other words |
| by taking part | into a bank |

Prepositional phrases always modify another part of a sentence:

Subject (she): Of all our technicians, she is the best trained.

Object (merit): They couldn't see the merit in my proposal.

Predicate (left): Someone left a folder on my desk.

In the following exercises, underline the prepositional phrases:

1. The knob on your radio broke after the expiration date.

2. A truckload of replacements has been sent to Dayton.

3. With her luck, she will soon be named head of the department.

4. He worked for our company about two years ago.

5. You will not be included in our benefits program during your training period.

When a pronoun is part of a prepositional phrase, it should always be in the object form—*me, you, him/her/it, us, them, whom:*

Give the documents to them.

They will choose between Harry and me.

In the following exercises, underline the correct pronoun:

6. Send the memo to Sandra and he/him.

7. The red sports car belongs to who/whom?

8. I hope they award the contract to us/we.

224

9. This information is just between you and I/me.

10. They asked for help from Don and her/she.

It was once considered totally unacceptable to put a preposition at the end of a sentence. Now you may:

I couldn't tell what they were interested <u>in</u>. (better than *I couldn't tell in what they were interested.*)

What did she attribute it <u>to</u>? (better than *To what did she attribute it?*)

Be careful, however, not to use the wrong form of a pronoun in sentences that end in a preposition. For example, is *who* or *whom* correct in this sentence?

(Who/Whom) did you speak <u>to</u>?

You can figure out the answer by moving the preposition and the pronoun back together:

<u>To whom</u> did you speak?

Be sure to use only the prepositions that are necessary. In the following sentences, the prepositions in parentheses should be omitted:

All (of) the staff members were present.

I almost fell off (of) my chair with surprise.

Where was Mr. Steuben going (to)?

They couldn't help (from) wondering.

The opposite problem is not including a preposition when you should. Consider the two sentences that follow:

Sales were over $100,000 <u>for</u> Linda and Bill.
Sales were over $100,000 <u>for</u> Linda and <u>for</u> Bill.

The first sentence indicates that Linda and Bill had combined sales over $100,000; the second, that Linda and Bill each had sales over $100,000, for a combined total in excess of $200,000. The extra *for* is crucial here.

Prepositions are also required in sentences like this one:

Which type <u>of</u> personal computer do you prefer?

Certain prepositions are used with certain words. When the same preposition can be used for two or more words in a sentence without affecting the meaning, only the last preposition is required:

We are familiar (<u>with</u>) and satisfied <u>with</u> your company's products.

But when different prepositions are normally used with the words, all the prepositions must be included:

We are familiar <u>with</u> and interested <u>in</u> your company's products.

In the following exercises, cross out unnecessary words and prepositions that are in the wrong place and add required prepositions:

11. Where was your argument leading to?

12. I wish he would get off of the phone.

13. This is a project into which you can sink your teeth.

14. U.S. Mercantile must become aware and sensitive to its customers' concerns.

15. We are responsible for aircraft safety in the air, the hangars, and the runways.

Here is an incomplete list of prepositions that are used in a particular way with particular words:

among/between: *among* used to refer to three or more  (Circulate the memo among the office staff); *between* used to refer to two (Put the copy machine between Judy and Dan)

as if/like: *as if* used before a clause (It seems as if we should be doing something); *like* used before a noun or pronoun alone (He seems like a nice guy)

have/of: *have*, a verb, used in verb phrases (They should have checked first); *of*, a preposition, never used in such cases

in/into: *in* used to refer to a static position (The file is in the cabinet); *into* used to refer to movement toward a position (Put the file into the cabinet)

And here is an incomplete list of some prepositions that have come to be used invariably with certain words:

| | |
|---|---|
| according to | independent of |
| agree to (a proposal) | inferior to |
| agree with (a person) | in search of |
| buy from | plan to |
| capable of | prefer to |
| comply with | prior to |
| conform to | reason with |
| different from | responsible for |
| differ from (things) | similar to |
| differ with (person) | talk to (without interaction) |
| get from (receive) | talk with (with interaction) |
| get off (dismount) | wait for (person or thing) |
| in accordance with | wait on (like a waiter) |

If in doubt about the preposition to use with a word, look up the word in the dictionary.
In the following exercises, insert the correct words:

16. Dr. Namaguchi will be talking_____ the marketing class on Tuesday, but she won't have time to answer students' questions.

17. Matters like this are decided after thorough discussion _____ all seven department managers.

18. Do you agree _____ this proposal?

19. We can't wait _____ their decision much longer.

20. CanCorp would _____ been in a good position if it had not diversified so soon.

21. Someone should try to reason _____ him.

22. Who is responsible _____ ordering sporting goods?

23. Their computer is similar _____ ours.

24. This model is different _____ the one we ordered.

25. She got her chair _____ the person who quit.

If you want to know more about prepositions, consult a grammar book on these topics:

idioms                      *like/as if*                    prepositional phrases

You may also wish to refer to section 1.6., "Prepositions," in Component Chapter B, "Grammar and Usage Guide, with Exercises," in *Business Communication Today.*

## Lesson 10

## PARTS OF SPEECH: CONJUNCTIONS

Conjunctions connect the parts of a sentence: words, phrases, and clauses. You are probably most familiar with the following conjunctions:

| | | | |
|---|---|---|---|
| and | or | for | nor |
| but | so | yet | |

In these sentences, the conjunctions are underlined:

That model is old <u>and</u> unpopular, <u>but</u> it should not be scrapped.

<u>Either</u> you <u>or</u> Gretchen should go.

<u>Because</u> she is out of town, she can't attend the meeting.

The report was late; <u>therefore</u>, we haven't made a decision yet.

Notice in the following examples that conjunctions may be used to connect clauses (which have both a subject and a predicate) with other clauses, to connect clauses with phrases (which do not have both a subject and a predicate), and to connect words with words:

Words with words:  We sell designer clothing <u>and</u> linens.

Clauses with phrases: Their products are expensive <u>but</u> still appeal to value-conscious consumers.

Clauses with clauses: I will call her on the phone today, <u>or</u> I will visit her office tomorrow.

In the following exercises, underline the conjunctions and write in each blank a code for the type of grammatical elements they join (*W-W* for word to word, *P-C* for phrase to clause, or *C-C* for clause to clause):

1. _____ She was not pleased, nor was she easy to reassure.

2. _____ The new model is sporty yet economical.

3. _____ We are proud of your accomplishments and of your reputation in the community.

4. _____ You promised but apparently forgot to send me the documents.

5. _____ We would cancel the order, for we have not yet sold the items already in stock.

Some conjunctions are used in pairs:

| | | |
|---|---|---|
| both . . . and | not only . . . but also | neither . . . nor |
| either . . . or | whether . . . or | |

In the following sentences, take special note of both the underlined conjunctions and the italicized words:

228

They <u>not only</u> *are* out of racquets <u>but also</u> *are* out of balls.
They *are* <u>not only</u> out of racquets <u>but also</u> out of balls.
They *are out of* <u>not only</u> racquets <u>but also</u> balls.

With paired conjunctions, you must be careful to construct each phrase in the same way. In other words, if you write *not only are out of racquets*, you cannot write *but also out of balls*; you must include the verb *are* after *but also*. But if you write *are not only out of racquets*, with the verb before the conjunction, you should not include the verb *are* after *but also*. The same need for parallelism exists when using conjunctions to join other parts of speech, as in these sentences:

He is listed in <u>either</u> *your* roster <u>or</u> *my* roster.

He is listed <u>neither</u> *in* your roster <u>nor</u> *on* the master list.

They <u>both</u> *gave* <u>and</u> *received* notice.

In the following exercises, cross out and insert words to make parallel the pairs of conjunctions and the other parts of speech that go with them:

6. She is active in not only a civic group but also in an athletic organization.

7. That is either a mistake or was an intentional omission.

8. The question is whether to set up a booth at the convention or be hosting a hospitality suite.

9. In both overall sales and in profits, we are doing better.

10. She had neither the preferred educational background, nor did she have suitable experience.

In all the previous examples of using conjunctions to join clauses, the clauses have been essentially equal. A different type of conjunction is used to join clauses that are unequal—that is, to join a main clause to one that is subordinate to or dependent on it. Here is a partial list of conjunctions used to introduce dependent clauses:

| | | | |
|---|---|---|---|
| although | once | before | unless |
| as soon as | so that | until | even though |
| because | that | if | when |

The dependent clause in each of the following examples is italicized, and the conjunction that links each one to the main clause is underlined:

Send your check now <u>*so that*</u> *you will not miss this offer.*

<u>*Until*</u> *we have seen the new personnel guidelines,* we cannot offer any raises.

We have stopped shipping that item, <u>*because*</u> *we have discovered problems with its safety mechanism.*

Can you see that the italicized part of each of these sentences is indeed subordinate to or dependent on the part that is not italicized?

Some of the conjunctions used to introduce dependent clauses, such as *before*, may also be used as prepositions. If a phrase follows such a word, the word is working in the sentence as a preposition; but if a clause follows it, the word is working in the sentence as a conjunction:

Preposition (phrase):   <u>Before</u> giving up, she tried calculating an acid-test ratio.
Conjunction (clause):   <u>Before</u> she gave up, she tried calculating an acid-test ratio.

In the following exercises, circle the conjunctions and underline the main clauses:

11. After making this phone call, I intend to leave.

12. He has already asked for a promotion, even though he started working here only a month ago.

13. Be sure to sign this document before you send it back.

14. If I show you how to use the spreadsheet program, will you show me how to use the word-processing program?

15. She'll jump at this once-in-a-lifetime opportunity when she finds out about it.

Some conjunctions function as adverbs. Here are some of them (and related transitional phrases):

| | | |
|---|---|---|
| also | meanwhile | indeed |
| as a result | nevertheless | that is |
| consequently | next | in fact |
| even so | on the other hand | therefore |
| furthermore | otherwise | instead |
| however | still | thus |

These words and phrases link clauses—and sometimes sentences—that are essentially equal. However, unlike other kinds of conjunctions, they may fall either at the beginning of a clause or somewhere within it. Observe the relationship of the conjunctions (underlined) to the verbs they modify in the following sentences:

They are, in fact, here today. (modifies *are*)

Therefore, we will send a replacement. (modifies *will send*)

The deadline has passed; however, we will accept your application. (modifies *will accept*)

Circle the conjunctions working as adverbs in the following exercises, and underline the verbs they modify:

16. The factory was shut down for two weeks; consequently, our stocks of Part C-118 are low.

17. It is indeed a fine example of cooperation.

18. Her experience is limited; on the other hand, her technical skills are excellent.

19. Ask him if he wants it; otherwise give it to me.

20. Meanwhile, they will be preparing the proposal.

In the final exercises for this lesson, underline all words working as conjunctions:

21. After your half-day presentation to management, you were undoubtedly tired but happy to have survived.

22. Send us a lightweight motor, two pulleys, and a winch.

23. Although you could perhaps find a substitute, you would have a hard time finding one.

24. We ask our credit customers to provide either a spotless credit record or substantial collateral.

25. The company nevertheless plans to distribute dividends equal to last year's.

You can learn more about conjunctions by looking up the following topics in a grammar book:

adverbial conjunctions
conjunctive adverbs
coordinating conjunctions
correlative conjunctions

dependent clauses
independent clauses
subordinating conjunctions

You may also wish to refer to sections 1.6.2, "Conjunctions, Articles, and Interjections," 1.7.2, "Longer Sentences," 1.7.3, "Sentence Fragments," 1.7.4, "Fused Sentences," and 4.4, "Transitional Words and Phrases," in Component Chapter B, "Grammar and Usage Guide, with Exercises," in *Business Communication Today.*

## Lesson 11

## PARTS OF SPEECH: MODIFYING ELEMENTS

You have already learned that adjectives and adverbs work in sentences as modifiers. Phrases and clauses may also work as modifiers. Often, however, they are misplaced or misused. To keep meaning clear, you should place these modifying elements (underlined in the following examples) as close as possible to the word or phrase that they modify (italicized):

The *engineer* with the microchip said nothing was wrong.
The engineer said nothing was *wrong* with the microchip.

The *secretary* who quit left a note for the staff accountant.
The secretary left a note for the staff *accountant* who quit.

During the meeting, they *learned* of the disturbance.
They learned of the *disturbance* during the meeting.

Some phrases and clauses modify, in effect, nothing. Therefore, they are called dangling modifiers:

Instead of introducing a new service, existing services were improved.

The modifying phrase in this sentence does not refer to anything; nothing in the sentence is capable of introducing a new service. Therefore, the sentence must be changed so that the modifier clearly refers to something that makes sense (italicized in the following sentence):

Instead of introducing a new service, *they* improved existing services.

In the revised sentence, *they* are capable of introducing a new service.
Here is another example that makes no sense:

Although a superb speaker, the organization did not invite her to make a presentation.

An organization cannot be a superb speaker. After a simple change, however, the sentence makes sense:

Although she was a superb speaker, the organization did not invite her to make a presentation.

In the following exercises, underline the modifying elements that are not in the right place and do not make sense:

1. Hampered by a slow economy, dropping the weakest product line seemed reasonable.

2. The typing went quickly, pausing only to get a cup of tea.

3. Because I was unable to make the figures add up, the senior accountant helped me complete the balance sheet.

4. Completely depleted, we must restock the warehouse.

5. While writing the proposal for them, my clients gave me all the information I needed.

6. Obviously a good worker, we should give him a raise.

7. The industry, pressured by imports, suffered losses.

8. Having <u>multiple product lines</u>, poor sales of one won't hurt them.

9. Joel wrote the report in two weeks <u>overwhelmed with other work</u>.

10. With a new batch of products in the warehouse, all orders can be filled next week.

11. <u>Grasping the tab firmly</u>, pull it toward you.

12. <u>Without a single hat in the store</u>, you cannot buy one.

13. Customers get <u>priority service</u> who have maintenance contracts.

14. Exhausted after a long day, sleep seemed the only cure.

15. <u>Despite careful preparation</u>, the proposal was not accepted.

Another sign of careful English is the proper use of *that* and *which*. To use them properly, you must understand the difference between restrictive and nonrestrictive modifiers. A restrictive modifier is essential to the sentence and cannot be omitted without changing its meaning; a nonrestrictive modifier, on the other hand, can be omitted without changing the sentence's essential meaning. Notice the difference:

Restrictive:       The proposal <u>that they submitted</u> will be accepted.
Nonrestrictive:   The proposal, <u>which they submitted far in advance</u>, will be accepted.

In the first sentence, the restrictive clause tells us an important fact about the proposal being discussed; without it, we would not know which proposal is meant. But in the second sentence, the essential meaning (*The proposal will be accepted*) is not affected by the nonrestrictive clause—only modified by it.

As you can see, *that* is used to introduce restrictive modifiers, with no commas separating such a modifier from the rest of the sentence. *Which* is used to introduce nonrestrictive modifiers, which are set off from the rest of the sentence with commas.

The difference between restrictive and nonrestrictive modifiers also applies to sentences that do not use *that* or *which*:

Restrictive:       The programmer <u>who designed the subroutine</u> will get a promotion. (identifies one of several programmers)

Nonrestrictive:   The programmer, <u>who designed the subroutine</u>, will get a promotion. (gives additional information about the only programmer)

In the following exercises, insert and delete words and commas so that restrictive and nonrestrictive modifiers are used correctly:

16. The one audit which I was working on is for Sparks, Ltd.

17. Anyone, who wants to advance, should develop job skills.

18. DeLora Johnson the director of planning is out of town.

19. Send your resume to the following address that is the address of our personnel office.

20. The carpeting, which you ordered, is not in stock.

21. We will offer the job to John Gates who has the most experience in our industry.

22. My desk that sits under the air conditioner needs to be moved.

23. Nobody wants to use the desk which sits under the air conditioner.

24. All employees, who carpool regularly, are entitled to half a day of paid vacation per year.

25. Tammy gathering her materials from the lectern added a few last words on third-quarter profits.

If you want to learn more about modifying elements, consult a grammar book on these topics:

| | | |
|---|---|---|
| appositives | nonrestrictive modifiers | relative pronouns |
| dangling modifiers | parallelism | restrictive modifiers |
| misplaced modifiers | | |

You may also wish to consult section 1.7.6, "Misplaced Modifiers," in Component Chapter B, "Grammar and Usage Guide, with Exercises" in *Business Communication Today*.

You can learn more about this subject by looking up the following topics in a grammar book:

exclamation points/marks                    periods                    question marks

You may also wish to refer to sections 2.1, "Periods," 2.2, "Question Marks," and 2.3, "Exclamation Points," in Component Chapter B, "Grammar and Usage Guide, with Exercises," in *Business Communication Today.*

## Lesson 13

## PUNCTUATION: COMMAS AND SEMICOLONS

Perhaps the most difficult punctuation mark to use correctly is the comma, which indicates a pause—not the full stop indicated by a period. The semicolon, the comma's cousin, indicates a pause greater than a comma but less than a period.

One use for commas is the linking of two independent clauses (sentence parts that contain both a subject and a predicate and can stand alone):

<u>We</u> <u>shipped</u> the ordered items on November 15, and <u>you</u> <u>confirmed</u> receipt on November 20.

The comma is necessary in this sentence because both parts have a subject and a predicate and are equal in importance. Independent clauses like these are joined by the conjunctions *and, but, for, nor, or, so,* and *yet.*

Sometimes independent clauses are linked by semicolons instead of commas (no conjunction necessary):

<u>We</u> <u>shipped</u> the ordered items on November 15; <u>you</u> <u>confirmed</u> receipt on November 20.

But do not use semicolons to link sentence elements that are not equal—such as clause to phrase or independent clause to dependent clause. The use of a semicolon in the following sentence is wrong:

We closed down the warehouse yesterday; because we needed to conduct an inventory.

The clause that begins with *because* cannot stand alone and is therefore dependent rather than independent.

Semicolons are also used when a transitional expression such as *however, for example,* or *therefore* is used between independent clauses:

We shipped the ordered items on November 15; <u>however,</u> you confirmed receipt on November 20.

Transitional expressions are followed by a comma when they introduce an independent clause—even when it stands alone as a sentence:

<u>In fact,</u> the first shift is understaffed at present.

Modifying elements (clauses and phrases) that introduce a sentence are also followed by a comma. For example:

<u>Because your application reached us after the deadline,</u> you will be considered for a position at a later time.

<u>Judging from your background,</u> I assume that you will be considered for a position at a later time.

<u>Yes,</u> you will be considered for a position at a later time.

However, commas may be left out if the introductory element is a short prepositional phrase (no subject and predicate) and cannot be misread:

<u>With your help</u> we will soon begin.

Be careful not to confuse readers by omitting necessary commas. Can you tell exactly what the following sentence means without backtracking or reading it twice?

Before leaving Ms. Danforth passed out some assignments.

The meaning becomes much clearer if a comma is added after the prepositional phrase:

Before leaving, Ms. Danforth passed out some assignments.

Within sentences, adjectives are sometimes used in combination to modify a single noun. When the order of the adjectives can be switched without affecting the meaning of the sentence, they are separated by commas (never semicolons):

A stale, metallic taste permeates the water.

But leave out the comma if the order of the two adjectives cannot be switched:

The last promising applicant has been interviewed.

Commas are also used to set off a variety of parenthetical words and phrases within sentences, including state names, dates, abbreviations, quotations, transitional expressions, and contrasted elements. Notice in the following examples that the commas are paired if the parenthetical element falls in the middle of the sentence:

Jerry noticed, before anyone else did, that the numbers don't add up.

They were, in fact, prepared to submit a bid.

Tall buildings, reaching for the sky, soon dominated the cityscape.

The best worker in the department is Ken, who joined the company just a month ago.

Habermacher, Inc., went public in 1979.

Our goal was increased profits, not increased market share.

Service, then, is our main concern.

"The Grant Avenue store," she said yesterday, "is next in line for renovation."

The new factory has been built in Chattanooga, Tennessee, to take advantage of the labor pool there.

Joanne Dubik, M.D., has applied for a loan from First Savings.

I started to work for this company on March 1, 1980, and soon received my first promotion.

Send the letter to Deborah Schneider, 1779 Church Street, Elmhurst, Illinois 60126.

Another common use for commas is to separate three or more items in a series. A comma follows every item except the last:

Send us the main unit, all available peripherals, and an operating manual.

Go to the personnel office, turn in your forms, and return here by 1:15.

Semicolons should be used to separate the items in a series when one or more of the items includes a comma:

The participants were Everett Johnston, Nagle Corporation; DeLynn Buckley, Restaurants Unlimited; and Connie Crichton, Tandem, Inc.

Insert required commas and semicolons in the following exercises, crossing out unnecessary words:

1. Send us four cases of filters two cases of wing nuts and a bale of rags.

2. Can you help teachers and office workers and sales representatives?

3. Mr. Pechman I hope to see you at our next meeting.

4. Your analysis however does not account for returns.

5. As a matter of fact she has seen the figures.

6. Before May 7 1982 they wouldn't have minded either.

7. You can reach me at this address: 717 Darby Place Scottsdale Arizona 85251.

8. Transfer the documents from Fargo North Dakota to Boise Idaho.

9. Sam O'Neill the designated representative is gone today.

10. An outstanding new product has just hit the market.

11. Beginning next week and continuing until January 3 our Austin offices will be closed.

12. She may hire two new representatives or she may postpone filling those territories until the spring.

13. After Martha has gone talk to me about promoting her.

14. Stoneridge Inc. will go public on September 9 1986.

15. We want the new copier not the old model.

16. "Talk to me" Sandra said "before you change a thing."

17. This letter looks good that one doesn't.

18. The Zurich airport has been snowed in therefore I won't be able to meet with you before Thursday January 27.

19. Because of a previous engagement Dr. Stoeve will not be able to attend.

20. Send a copy of the memo to Mary Kennedy Vice President of Marketing Robert Bache Comptroller and Dennis McMurphy Director of Sales.

21. She started attracting attention during the long hard recession of the mid-1970s.

22. We have observed your hard work and because of it we are promoting you to manager of your department.

23. After we see the outcome of the survey we will choose which product to introduce first.

24. Yes we will be able to supply you with all you need.

25. Tolbert & O'Toole is of course a leader in its industry.

To learn more, consult a grammar book on the following topics:

| | | |
|---|---|---|
| appositives | independent clauses | nonrestrictive modifiers |
| conjunctions | introductory clauses | parenthetical elements |
| contrasted elements | introductory phrases | series |

You may also wish to consult sections 1.7.4, "Fused Sentences," 2.4, "Semicolons," and 2.6, "Commas," in Component Chapter B, "Grammar and Usage Guide, with Exercises," in *Business Communication Today.*

## PUNCTUATION: ASIDES AND ADDITIONS

Some marks of punctuation—colons, parentheses, brackets, and dashes—are used to set off supplementary information from the main part of a sentence.

A colon, for example, calls attention to the words that follow—as if the colon meant "for example" or "that is." Therefore, colons are frequently used to introduce a word, phrase, or sentence of explanation:

> Only one word can describe your proposal: fantastic!
>
> This, then, is our goal for 1987: to increase sales 35 percent.
>
> Remember this rule: When in doubt, leave it out.

Colons are also used to introduce lists, although lists that are necessary to complete a thought are not set off by colons. Observe the difference between these two sentences:

> Next year we will have to hire a typist, a bookkeeper, and a receptionist.
> Next year we will have to hire three people: a typist, a bookkeeper, and a receptionist.

In the first example, the list actually serves as the object of the sentence (*What will we have to hire?*) and cannot be separated from the subject and predicate by a colon. But in the second example, the part before the colon could stand on its own as a sentence. It is a complete thought in itself and must be separated from the list.

Colons also introduce quotations of one long sentence or more:

> Chairman Dana Gerster said: "Over the past three years, our organization has made great progress in realizing its goals. But much remains to be done."

Finally, colons have a couple of specialized uses. In letters, of course, they are used with closed or mixed punctuation following the salutation (*Dear Ms. Norden:*); they are used with memo headings (*TO:*); and they are used to separate hours from minutes in time designations (*11:30 a.m.*).

Parentheses are also used to set off information from the main part of a sentence. Some sentences use commas to indicate a supplementary idea; parentheses do much the same thing, but they are used when the idea has little importance to the main part of the sentence. Compare these two examples:

> She drove her own car, an '85 Chrysler, last week.
> She drove her own car (an '85 Chrysler) last week.

The only difference between these two sentences is the degree of emphasis given to the type of car being discussed. Context and judgment should tell you whether to use commas or parentheses in a given situation.

Parentheses themselves are relatively easy to use; what is more difficult is to use other punctuation properly when you're using parentheses. For instance, what kind of punctuation do you use when a complete sentence is embedded in another sentence by means of parentheses? You should never use a period at the end of an embedded sentence, but you should use a question mark or an exclamation point:

When you hear from her (have you already heard?), call me.

Notice that the embedded sentence is not capitalized. Notice also that the comma that would normally be used at the end of the introductory clause is still included, although it follows the parenthetical statement. Semicolons and colons are also included after the closing parenthesis if necessary to the main part of the sentence.

If the material between the parentheses is a sentence by itself and is not embedded in another sentence, its punctuation is self-contained:

Our company's profit history is irregular. (See Table 2 for a complete rundown on company profits over the past ten years.)

Brackets, which look similar to parentheses, have a specialized use. In quoted material, they set off the writer's comments from the comments of the person being quoted:

"In the past seven years [during which Cass has dominated the market], we have exceeded our goals," Dr. Blevins noted.

"The closest airport of any size," said Carol Nichols, "is about 25 kilometers [15.5 miles] away."

One other way that you can insert parenthetical material into a sentence is to use dashes (which are typed as two hyphens with no extra spaces between or on either side). Dashes give inserted material more emphasis than either commas or parentheses and should be used sparingly.

Compare these sentences and note the weight given to the parenthetical thought by the three types of punctuation:

Model 7-103, the latest in our line of quality conveyors, will be introduced at the convention in Chicago.

Model 7-103 (the latest in our line of quality conveyors) will be introduced at the convention in Chicago.

Model 7-103—the latest in our line of quality conveyors—will be introduced at the convention in Chicago.

Abrupt interruptions to the main thought are also set off by dashes:

The file on Marian Gephardt—yes, we finally found it—reveals a history of late payments.

Dashes or parentheses, not commas, are used when the parenthetical statement itself contains commas:

Three qualities—speed, accuracy, and reliability—are desirable in any typist employed by our department.

Dashes are also used when a sentence begins with a list and then finishes with a summarizing statement:

Speed, accuracy, and reliability—these are the qualities we look for in any typist employed by our department.

In the following exercises, insert colons, parentheses, brackets, and dashes wherever necessary:

1. Only one thing increased productivity will save us.

2. Stealth, secrecy, and surprise those are the elements that will give us a competitive edge.

3. The clients were most interested in income statements, balance sheets, and payroll statements.

4. Her response see the attached memo is disturbing.

5. His motivation was obvious to get Meg fired.

6. Only two firms have responded to our survey J. J. Perkins and Tucker & Tucker.

7. Only two sites maybe three offer the things we need.

8. Sarah O'Roarke an appraiser will be here on Thursday.

9. The typist the one who just had a baby will have the document ready later today.

10. Kevin Langhans our top sales representative last year is at the bottom of the pile so far this year.

11. Your training kit consisting of a manual, supplementary reading, and product samples has already been shipped.

12. Please be sure to interview these employees next week Harry Golden, Doris Hatch, and George Iosupovich.

13. The new offices will be spacious, well-lit, and inviting.

14. The convention kit includes the following response cards, giveaways, brochures, and a display rack with samples.

15. Glenda she's the union representative has been helpful.

16. Professor Pettit had this to say "We cannot assume a larger market, even with an increase in population. Demographic patterns have changed radically."

17. Send the memo to all the sales reps, the sales managers, and the Director of Marketing.

18. Ron Franklin do you remember him? will be in town Monday.

19. I want to make one thing perfectly clear neither of you will be promoted if the sales figures do not improve.

20. Four items ladders, workbench kits, fluorescent light fixtures, and pegboard supplies will go on sale March 1.

21. Service and value those are Krasner's watchwords.

22. We will operate with a skeleton staff during the holiday break December 21 through January 2.

23. Refinements in robotics may prove profitable. More information about this technology appears in Appendix B.

24. Please return it before the deadline January 31, so we may send all the documents to you by the end of February.

25. Lucy has a math background an enormous advantage.

To learn more about these types of punctuation, consult a grammar book on the following topics:

| | | |
|---|---|---|
| brackets | dashes | parentheses |
| colons | embedded sentences | parenthetical elements |

You may also wish to refer to sections 2.5, "Colons," 2.7, "Dashes," and 2.11, "Parentheses," in Component Chapter B, "Grammar and Usage Guide, with Exercises," in *Business Communication Today*.

## Lesson 15

## PUNCTUATION: QUOTATIONS

You may often want to use someone else's words in your business writing, especially in reports and persuasive sales letters. Quotation marks are indispensable for reporting what someone else has said:

Dan Hurtig said, "Only five companies will remain after the coming shakeout in our industry."

According to Inez Castro, the hospital supply department is "coping heroically under difficult circumstances."

"Where there's a will, there's a way," she remarked.

Notice that the first word of a quotation is capitalized only when the quotation begins a sentence (as in the third example) or is itself a sentence and is preceded by a word like *said* (as in the first example). When the quotation is only part of a sentence and serves as the object of the sentence, the first word is not capitalized (as in the second example).

Direct quotations, whether spoken or written, should always be put between quotation marks and attributed to the person who originated them. Indirect quotations, however—paraphrased statements—do not require quotation marks. In the following sentence, the introductory word *that* is a clue that the quotation is indirect:

Alice Montero said that few of the new employees have opted for day-care benefits.

Quotation marks are also used to set off words and phrases that are being treated with irony or are being used in a special context.

The "benefits" of working for him include frequent criticism and scant praise.

A "request for proposal" is a government notice that proposals will be accepted.

When you are defining a word, put the definition in quotation marks:

The word *etc.* means "and so forth."

Quotation marks are also used in reference notes to set off the titles of articles, book chapters, and other small works or parts of larger works:

Did he find "Seeking Profits in the Eighties" in *Business Today*?

Periods and commas always fall within the last set of quotation marks, but semicolons, colons, and dashes always fall after the last set:

"Given their recent performance," she said, "we probably should not risk a large investment."

They note "a marked lack of respect"; however, Drake was not working directly for them at that point.

Two things affect "demand curves": price and quantity.

Harry DeLuca—our plant's "labor analyst"—should undertake that project.

In using quotation marks with question marks and exclamation points, however, you must use your judgment. If the quoted passage is itself a question or an exclamation, the punctuation should be placed inside the last set of quotation marks:

"Can you find the source of the problem?" she asked.

He spoke in frustration: "These developers! I wish they would just accept the zoning plan!"

Notice in the first example that no comma is used to set the quoted passage apart from the rest of the sentence. Do not use a comma in combination with a question mark or an exclamation point.

Question marks and exclamation points are set outside the quotation marks when the quoted material is merely part of a sentence that is itself a question or an exclamation:

They themselves drew our attention to these "irregularities"!

Do you know who asked for "bilateral decisions"?

When quoting a long passage (more than three lines), you should set off the material by indenting it on both sides and single-spacing. This treatment makes quotation marks unnecessary.

Sometimes you will find that material you want to quote contains more than you need. In that case, use points of ellipsis to indicate that you have left out words:

"It is in our nature . . . to look for advantage."

Ellipses (omissions) are always indicated with only three dots, although a fourth dot—a period—is included when necessary:

"It is in our nature to look for advantage. . . ."

Underlining and italics are often used in connection with quotations, for citing a printed source. If possible, use italics for the titles of books, magazines, newspapers, movies, and other inclusive reference materials; otherwise, underline the titles:

Our ad will appear in *The Wall Street Journal*.

The Wealth of Nations proposed an early version of this notion.

Underlining and italics are also used to mark words used as words and to emphasize (sparingly) words and phrases:

The word *profit* has a variety of meanings.

The result of this campaign did not justify the expense.

In the following exercises, insert all necessary punctuation in the right places:

1. Be sure to read How to Sell by Listening in this month's issue of Fortune.

2. Contact is an overused word.

3. I don't care why you didn't fill my order; I want to know when you'll fill it.

4. We all make mistakes sometimes, the letter said.

5. Where did you put the Hartnet file? he asked.

6. Do you remember who said And away we go?

7. I can't believe that she doesn't know how to find, as Dr. Frankel puts it, sufficient resources.

8. Whom do you think Time magazine will select as its Man of the Year?

9. Bah! Humbug! said Scrooge.

10. The term up in the air means undecided.

11. As the report that I read concluded, Crown Products' best avenue for growth is the consumer market; I believe we should follow up on this analysis.

12. Susan said that she could not find the source of the error.

13. A computer nerd would have no trouble with it.

14. Professional bookkeepers use the double-entry method.

15. Business is the lifeblood of our country! she exclaimed.

16. Can you see the difference between debits and credits?

17. Only two were listed in the manager's little black book: Cathy Navasitis and Jeff Stamper.

18. Stephen Roussin made this point: The element of surprise would be of little use to us in this case; therefore, we should seek information wherever we can find it.

19. Then she asked, Do you have any disabilities that would prevent you from taking this job?

20. Can you believe that he would say something like We're only here to serve larger corporations?

21. Do you know anything about read-only memory?

22. The SBP's next conference, the bulletin noted, will be held in Minneapolis.

23. Patrick Henry is supposed to have challenged them with Give me liberty, or give me death!

24. Let's subscribe to Advertising Age.

25. What about taxes? we asked.

If you want to learn more about quotations, consult a grammar book on these topics:

| | | |
|---|---|---|
| direct quotations | italics | reference notes |
| ellipses | quotation marks | underscoring |
| indirect quotations | | |

You may also wish to consult sections 2.10, "Quotation Marks," 2.12, "Ellipses," and 2.13, "Underscores and Italics," in Component Chapter B, "Grammar and Usage Guide, with Exercises," in *Business Communication Today.*

## Lesson 16

## PUNCTUATION: WITHIN WORDS

The main marks of punctuation used within words are apostrophes and hyphens.  Apostrophes are used to indicate left-out letters; hyphens are used to link words or parts of a word into one.

One use for apostrophes is within contractions like the following:

| | | | |
|---|---|---|---|
| don't | do not | it's | it is |
| we'll | we will | '86 | 1986 |

In the most formal writing, contractions should be avoided.  They are acceptable, however, in speech and in informal writing.

Be careful that you do not confuse contractions with possessive pronouns. *It's* and *its* are often confused, as are *there's* and *theirs* and *they're* and *their*.  If you have trouble deciding which one to use, take a moment to remember what words the contraction stands for.  If the sentence still makes sense when you substitute those words, you can use the contraction.  Otherwise, use the possessive pronoun.

What makes the distinction between contractions and possessive pronouns so confusing to some people is the fact that apostrophes are also used to make words possessive:

Robert's pen  report's cover  employees' wages

Be careful to use the possessive form only when "ownership" is indicated; change the words around and add *of* as a test:

| | |
|---|---|
| Robert's pen | pen of Robert |
| report's cover | cover of the report |
| employees' wages | wages of the employees |

It is sometimes hard to figure out where to put the apostrophe when showing ownership.  As a rule, you simply add *'s* to the end of any word that does not already end in *s*, whether the word is singular or plural:

| | |
|---|---|
| Sarah Boswell's letter | children's books |
| Grady Inc.'s main office | people's needs |

If the word is plural and does end in *s* or an *s* sound, you usually add just an apostrophe at the end.

| | |
|---|---|
| consultants' recommendations | twenty dollars' worth |
| Morrises' home | companies' plans |

You add *'s* to singular words that end in *s* or an *s* sound except when the word is a proper noun with three or more syllables:

boss's chair  Ms. Hernandez' application

Groups of words add the apostrophe to the last word:

someone else's idea  attorney general's opinion

When two or more individuals each own something separately, you should use the apostrophe for both names. But when they own something together, use the apostrophe with only the second name:

Paul's and Sam's offices                    Paul and Sam's office

The use of apostrophes in business can become complicated. For example, some organizations use the apostrophe and some don't:

Harrison's Hardware, Inc.                    United States Post Office

There is no hard and fast rule for using apostrophes with the names of organizations. Check the organization's letterhead or a directory.

Nor is there a rule you can consult to decide whether to use an apostrophe in phrases like these:

employee handbook            employees' handbook            employee's handbook

Consult other company documents for guidance in these cases—or use your judgment to figure out the real meaning behind the words you are using.

With most abbreviations, the apostrophe is used just as it would be with any other word—although you must be careful to put the apostrophe after the period, if there is one:

CBS's report                              R.N.'s schedule

You should not use an apostrophe to indicate plural numbers (for example, *1980s* is correct), but you should use apostrophes with letters used as letters (*A's* and *B's*).

Test your ability to use apostrophes properly by adding them wherever necessary in the following exercises:

1. Collect every employees timecard on Friday.
2. Is that Tracys or Nicks?
3. The outcome of the test is anyones guess.
4. All the attorneys offices are cleaned every night.
5. Well discuss the mens coat department tomorrow.
6. Mr. Dunne completed the course in the 1960s with all *A*s.
7. Its hard to see how their situation could improve.
8. We might buy a thousand dollars worth.
9. Where did you get IBMs annual report?
10. The electronics industry gives its best wages to Ph.D.s.

The other type of punctuation mark commonly used within words is the hyphen. Hyphens are always used to separate the main part of a word from the prefixes *all, ex,* and *self*; the main part from the suffix *elect*; a prefix from a capitalized word; and a prefix or suffix from numbers or letters:

all-inclusive              ex-athlete              self-controlled
chairperson-elect          non-European            mid-1980s

Other words that combine parts may or may not use a hyphen. In fact, they may or may not be two separate words:

half hour                    half-baked                    halfway

The best way to find out whether to use a hyphen in words like these is to look them up in a dictionary. (However, remember that dictionaries take different approaches to hyphenating words.) If the combined word does not appear in the dictionary, it should be written as two separate words.

Hyphens are used to combine whole words too. For example, the following nouns use a hyphen:

programmer-analyst                    sister-in-law

Hyphens are more often used in adjectives that combine two or more words—but only when they come before a noun:

| | |
|---|---|
| often-used formula | formula that is used often |
| high-level manager | manager at a high level |
| fact-finding mission | mission for finding facts |
| how-to manual | manual describing how to . . . |
| all-inclusive set | set that includes all |
| well-organized report | report that is well organized |
| up-to-date styles | styles that are up to date |
| blue-green paint | paint combining blue and green |

But do not hyphenate combinations of an adjective and a modifier ending in *ly*—because a modifier that ends in *ly* is actually an adverb: *poorly marketed product, newly hired employee.*

When a sentence contains a series of hyphenated words that are similar, you may shorten it by dropping the repeated word:

We need to order some three- and four-compartment servers.

Hyphens may also be used to prevent misreading. Notice how the meaning of the first sentence changes with the addition of a hyphen:

We plan to start a <u>small business</u> publication. (a business publication that is small)
We plan to start a <u>small-business</u> publication. (a publication for small businesses)

Here is another example:

Ask the intern to prepare a <u>short term</u> paper. (a term paper that is short)
Ask the intern to prepare a <u>short-term</u> paper. (a paper dealing with the short term)

Insert hyphens only where necessary in the following exercises:

11. A highly placed source explained the negotiations.

12. They're selling a well designed machine.

13. A bottle green sports jacket is hard to find.

14. How many owner operators are in this industry?

15. Your ever faithful dog deserves Meaty Mix.

16. The table is well placed in the text.

17. Myrna Talefiero is the organization's president elect.

18. I need a small business loan of $10,000 so I can expand my boutique.

19. How can we possibly please all the higher ups?

20. Try to eliminate your self consciousness.

21. We must carefully limit aid to truly needy residents.

22. High living bureaucrats receive extra scrutiny.

23. Your devil may care attitude affects us all.

24. His new office is well decorated.

25. What decision making processes will the group use?

To learn more about punctuation within words, you may wish to consult a grammar book on the following topics:

apostrophes                          prefixes
compound words                       suffixes
hyphens

You may also wish to consult sections 2.8, "Hyphens," and 2.9, "Apostrophes," in Component Chapter B, "Grammar and Usage Guide, with Exercises," in *Business Communication Today*.

## Lesson 17

## MECHANICS: NUMBERS

In general, numbers from one to ten are spelled out, and numbers over ten are written in figures. (If your organization has adopted its own style for dealing with numbers, use it.) But when a number begins a sentence, it should always be spelled. You can avoid writing an awkwardly large number (more than two words) at the beginning of a sentence by rewriting the sentence. For example:

Awkward:  Five hundred thirty-seven people have signed up.
Better:    Sign-ups number 537.
Better:    About 540 people have signed up.

Approximate numbers that can be expressed in one or two words are also spelled out (notice the use of hyphens with some numbers):

About twenty-five people have applied for the job.

Over one hundred software titles are in stock.

We're looking for something in the seventy-five-dollar range.

In dealing with numbers over 999, remember to use a comma to separate thousands from hundreds: *2,384.* Numbers in the millions and billions combine words and figures: *7.3 million, 2 billion.*

Usually, however, words and figures should not be combined. In a series of related numbers, spell all (if all are ten or under) or write all in figures:

Please send 12 copies of <u>Bridge for Beginners</u>, 6 copies of <u>Bridge Strategies</u>, and 3 copies of <u>Secrets of the Life Masters</u>.

The general rule about using words and figures may also be ignored when two numbers fall next to each other in a sentence. Regardless of the size of the numbers, use figures for the number that is largest, most difficult to spell, or part of a physical measurement; use words for the other:

I have learned to manage a classroom of 30 twelve-year-olds.

She's won a bonus for selling 24 thirty-volume sets.

You'll need twenty 3-inch bolts.

In money expressions, approximate dollar amounts may be expressed in words: *five dollars.* But specific dollar amounts are written in figures with a dollar sign: *$5.95, $27, $3 million.*

For amounts less than one dollar, use figures and the word *cents: 5 cents.* But if you are writing a series of money expressions and at least one has a dollar sign, all the rest should too. Remember also to include cents with all the numbers if one of them is not an even dollar amount:

The skins retail for $12.00 each; the hole punches, $3.59 each; and the grommets, $0.19 each.

In dates, the month is always spelled out, and the date and year are written in figures: *August 29, 1986.* In foreign, military, and some government correspondence, however, the order of the date and month is reversed: *29 August 1986*. Observe how dates are written when the year is not specified:

29th of August                                    August 29

the 29th

References to centuries or decades may be in words or in figures:

twentieth century                                20th century

sixties                                                  1960s

Time expressions that use *a.m.* or *p.m.* should be written in figures, but time expressions that use *o'clock* should be written in words. Compare:

The meeting starts at 9:30 a.m.

The meeting starts at eleven o'clock.

Most other time expressions are spelled out for the numbers ten and under and written in figures for the numbers over ten. The only exception is that figures are sometimes used for emphasis in detailing the terms of doing business:

Your account will be credited within 5 working days.

In addresses, all street numbers except *One* are in figures. So are suite and room numbers and ZIP codes. But what about street names that are numbered? Because practice varies so widely, you should use the form specified on an organization's letterhead or in a reliable directory. All of the following are correct:

One Fifth Avenue                                297 Ninth Street

1839 44th Street                                11026 West 78 Place

Telephone numbers are always expressed in figures. Usually, parentheses separate the area code from the rest of the number, but a slash or dash may be used instead if the entire phone number is enclosed in parentheses:

(602) 382-8329                    (602/382-8329)                    (602-382-8329)

Figures are also used for extension numbers: *(602) 382-8329, extension 71.*

Percentages are another type of number that is always expressed in figures. The word *percent* is used in most situations (for example, *27 percent*), but % may be used in tables, forms, and statistical writing.

Physical measurements—distance, weight, and volume—are also expressed in figures (*9 kilometers*). Notice that no comma is used in expressions like the following: *5 feet 3 inches, 7 pounds 10 ounces.*

Ages are usually expressed in words—except when a parenthetical reference to age follows someone's name:

Mrs. Margaret Sanderson is seventy-two.

Mrs. Margaret Sanderson, 72, swims daily.

And ages expressed in years and months are treated like physical measurements that combine two units of measure: *5 years 6 months.*

Figures are used to designate a great many other things as well, such as parts, forms, pages, and accounts. Even if these numbers have four or more digits, they do not use commas:

When you need to indicate numbered order, use numbers that end with *st, nd, rd,* and *th*—in words or figures as required by the situation:

fifth grade                                    April 5th

19th floor                                     nineteenth (or 19th) century

Decimal numbers are always written in figures. Add a zero to the left of the decimal point if the number is less than one and does not already start with a zero:

1.38                              .07                              0.2

In a series of related decimal numbers with at least one number greater than one, make sure that all numbers smaller than one have a zero to the left of the decimal point: *1.20, 0.21, 0.09.* And express all decimal numbers in a series to the same number of places by adding zeroes at the end:

The responses were Yes, 37.2 percent; No, 51.0; Not Sure, 11.8.

Simple fractions are written in words, but more complicated fractions are expressed in figures or, if easier to read, in figures and words:

two-thirds                        9/32                        2 hundredths

A combination of a whole number and a fraction should always be written in figures. Note in the following examples that a hyphen is used to separate the fraction from the whole number when a slash is used for the fraction:

$9\frac{5}{8}$                              $7\frac{1}{2}$                              2-11/16

In the following exercises, correct numbers wherever necessary:

1. Let's invite about 20 outstanding college students.

2. Fifty-two typewriters were purchased.

3. We need to hire one office manager, four bookkeepers, and twelve clerk-typists.

4. They want to spend about $300.

5. The population of Guatemala is almost six million.

6. The agency's report totaled 1835 pages.

7. The 1st person who makes a purchase wins a prize.

8. Our offices are open between 9 o'clock and 5 o'clock.

9. Can you make it on the 7th?

10. We have enclosed checks for $45 and $37.50.

11. Deliver the couch to 1 South Thirty-eighth Avenue.

12. 95 percent of our customers are men.

13. Your measurement appears to be off by .7 centimeter.

14. Over 1/2 the U.S. population is female.

15. Our building is three miles past the intersection.

16. Hanna Hilgersen just turned thirty.

17. You'll find a definition of coverages on page five.

18. Of the fifteen applicants, seven are qualified.

19. Last year I wrote twenty-one fifteen-page reports.

20. Set up enough chairs for an audience of at least 100.

21. 50,000,000 Americans can't be wrong.

22. This is the thirty-fifth request for confirmation.

23. Plan to be here for interviews from 1:00 to 4:30 p.m.

24. We need a set of shelves ten feet, eight inches long.

25. Check the following specifications: A, 2.39; B, .5; C, .09.

To learn more about this subject, consult a grammar book on the following topics:

| | |
|---|---|
| decimals | hyphenated numbers |
| fractions | ordinals |

You may also wish to consult section 3.3, "Numbers," in Component Chapter B, "Grammar and Usage Guide, with Exercises," in *Business Communication Today*.

## MECHANICS: ABBREVIATIONS AND SYMBOLS

Abbreviations and symbols provide a short, convenient way to express yourself, but some readers may not know what they stand for. Even if you think that readers will recognize them, you should generally limit their use to tables, graphs, lists, forms, technical documents, and informal memos. In any case, approach the abbreviation decision with this rule in mind: When in doubt, spell it out.

One way to handle an abbreviation that you want to use throughout a document is to spell it out the first time you use it, follow it with the abbreviation in parentheses, and then use the abbreviation in the remainder of the document.

The commonly used abbreviations for most organizations are capitalized and lack periods:

AT&T  UNICEF  NFL  WETA-TV

Some abbreviations of organizations' names are more than just initials; instead, they are shortened versions of the full name:

Bell Labs  Georgia Tech  the States

You may use these shortened names only in informal writing.

Abbreviations are also commonly used in addresses. Company names, for instance, often end with *Inc., Ltd., Co.,* or *Corp.* If the company uses any of these abbreviations in its letterhead or in references to itself, you should use them too. For repeated reference to the same company, however, you may drop such abbreviations and use only the main part of the name.

Compass points (north, south, east, west) are usually not abbreviated when they come before a street name; however, the compass points that sometimes follow a street name (NW, NE, SW, SE) are usually abbreviated. Do not abbreviate other parts of the street name (such as *Street* and *Avenue*) unless you have very little space.

Most place names are not abbreviated: Fort Lauderdale, Port Arthur, Mount Pleasant, South Milwaukee. The exception is place names that include the word *Saint:* St. Louis.

Within addresses, use the two-letter postal abbreviations for state names, such as *KY* and *CO.* If you must abbreviate state names elsewhere but are not using ZIP codes, you may use such abbreviations as *Ky.* and *Colo.*

The names of countries are usually spelled out, both in addresses and in the body of letters, memos, and reports. The two most common exceptions are *USSR* and *U.S.*

What about the names of people? Do not abbreviate unless a person wants to be known by first and middle initials or by an abbreviated first name (B. J. Brooks, Geo. F. Carlisle). Notice that the initials are separated by a space.

Titles are another matter. The abbreviations *Mr., Ms., Mrs.,* and *Dr.* should always be used when they appear before a person's name. (Do not use *Mr., Ms., Mrs., Dr.,* or *Esq.* (Esquire) with any other title.) Other titles that come before a person's name may or may not be abbreviated if they are used with the person's full name but should never be abbreviated if they are used with the last name alone:

| | |
|---|---|
| Sen. Elizabeth Clarke | Senator Clarke |
| Capt. Robert Leinert | Captain Leinert |
| Prof. Patricia Stone | Professor Stone |

Another sort of abbreviation comes after a person's full name:

Nathaniel Grob, Jr.                              Artis Remer, M.B.A. (or MBA)

Richard Taylor, Esq.                             Peggy Klein, D.V.M. (or DVM)

In statistical or technical writing and in tables and charts, you may use abbreviations for units of measurement.  For example:

gal.        ft.        mpg        m        wpm        kg        cu. yd.

Notice that metric measures (m, kg) have no period; nor do the abbreviations for miles per gallon and words per minute.

Some references to time are typically abbreviated:

a.m.                          A.D.                          CST (Central Standard Time)

The following list shows one way of using periods and capital letters in abbreviations of some business terms; your source may recommend another:

| | | | |
|---|---|---|---|
| acct. | account | LIFO | last in, first out |
| A/P | accounts payable | mdse. | merchandise |
| ASAP | as soon as possible | mfg. | manufacturing |
| bal. | balance | mgr. | manager |
| b/l | bill of lading | MIS | management information system |
| cc | carbon copy | mtg. | meeting |
| CEO | chief executive officer | N/30 | net due in 30 days |
| c/o | care of | no. | number |
| C.O.D. | cash on delivery | p., pp. | page, pages |
| CPS | Certified Professional Secretary | pd. | paid |
| cr. | credit | PR | public relations |
| CRT | cathode ray tube | P.S. | postscript |
| cwt | hundredweight | R&D | research and development |
| dept. | department | rm. | room |
| div. | division | R.R. | railroad, rural route |
| doz. | dozen | RSVP | please respond (from French) |
| DP | data processing | std. | standard |
| ea. | each | ste. | suite |
| e.g. | for example | VIP | very important person |
| e.o.m. | end of month | WP | word processing |
| et al. | and others | / | per |
| etc. | and so forth | # | number, pound |
| ext. | extension | % | percent |
| FIFO | first in, first out | @ | at |
| fig. | figure | $ | U.S. dollar |
| F.O.B. | free on board | Can$ | Canadian dollar |
| FYI | for your information | ™ | trademark |
| GDP | gross domestic product | ¶ | paragraph |
| GNP | gross national product | ® | registered |
| i.e. | that is | © | copyright |

For the following exercises, assume that the reader is an "insider," and substitute abbreviations wherever possible:

1. Paul Hansen, Registered Nurse, is joining our staff.

2. The Young Men's Christian Association has a center here.

3. Send it to Mister H. K. Danforth, Rural Route 1, Warrensburg, New York 12885.

4. She is a candidate for the master of business administration degree at the University of Michigan.

5. Call me at 8 in the morning, Pacific Standard Time.

6. The data processing department will work on it as soon as possible.

7. The core sample weighs 1.7 kilograms.

8. The Securities and Exchange Commission sent notice to them.

9. General George Armstrong Custer fought in the West.

10. We are sending it cash on delivery, net due in 15 days.

For the remaining exercises, assume that the reader is an "outsider," and spell out abbreviated words wherever possible:

11. The FBI is based near Washington, D.C.
*The Federal Bureau of Investigation is based near Washington District of Columbia.*

12. Nashville, Tenn., is their headquarters.
*Tennessee*

13. Mr. Geoffrey Finley is the CEO of TrendWell, Inc.
*Chief executive officer    Company,*

14. Call me at 818-3948, ext. 72, between 10 a.m. and 3 p.m.
*extension*

15. Send the package to Mrs. C. W. Crane, 9382 W. Florida Ave., Ft. Bragg, Calif. 95437.
*West    Avenue    California*

16. FYI, the Bilbray accts. are past due.
*For your Information    the Bilbray accounts*

17. I have an M.S. degree from MIT.
*Master of Science ;    Massachusetts Institute of Technology.*

18. It's 3 km from our office to the nearest restaurant.
*kilometer*

19. Over 50% of our engineering staff have Ph.D.s.
*Percent*

20. Christine Jarvis, CPS, is joining the mfg. div.
*Certified Professional Secretary ,    manufacturing division*

21. The UN is headquartered in NYC.
*United Nations    New York City*

22. The Hon. Donna Stroeb-Atkins will speak at our meeting.
*Honorary*

23. Send your std. #10 envelopes, @ $9.95/box.
*Standard Number    at $9.95 per box*

24. RSVP ASAP.
*Please Responde as soon as possible*

25. Capt. Macek et al. participated in setting up the MIS.
*Captain    and others    management information system.*

If you would like to study more about this subject, consult a grammar book under the following headings:

| | |
|---|---|
| acronyms | names |
| addresses | periods |
| capitalization | scientific/technical terms |
| dates | titles and degrees |
| measurements | trade names |

You may also wish to consult section 3.2, "Abbreviations," in "Grammar and Usage Guide, with Exercises," in *Business Communication Today.*

**Lesson 19**

**MECHANICS: CAPITALS**

Capital letters are used, of course, at the beginning of sentences. But they are also used at the beginning of other word groups:

> *Formal statement following colon*: She has a favorite motto: Where there's a will, there's a way.

> *Phrase used as sentence*: Absolutely not!

> *Quoted sentence embedded in another sentence*: Scott said, "Nobody was here during the lunch hour except me."

> *Set-off list of items*: Three preliminary steps are involved:
> 1. Design review
> 2. Budgeting
> 3. Scheduling

Capital letters are also used with proper nouns and proper adjectives, such as the following:

> Darrell Greene                    Victorian mansion

A proper noun is separated from a prefix with a hyphen:

> ex-President                    anti-American

People's titles are capitalized when they are used in addressing a person, especially in a formal context. They are not usually capitalized, however, when they are used merely to identify the person. Observe the difference here:

> Address the letter to <u>Chairperson</u> Anna Palmer.
> I wish to thank <u>Chairperson</u> Anna Palmer for her assistance.
> Please deliver these documents to board <u>chairperson</u> Anna Palmer.
> Anna Palmer, <u>chairperson</u> of the board, took the podium.

Titles should also be capitalized if they are used by themselves in addressing a person:

> Thank you, <u>Doctor</u>, for your donation.

Titles used to identify a person of very high rank are capitalized regardless of where they fall or how much of the name is included:

> the <u>President</u> of the United States

> the <u>Prime Minister</u> of Canada

> the <u>Pope</u>

In addresses, salutations, signature blocks, and some formal writing (such as acknowledgments), all titles are capitalized whether they come before or after the name.

258

The names of organizations are capitalized, of course; so are the official names of their departments and divisions:

> Route this memo to <u>Personnel</u>.
>
> Larry Tien was transferred to the <u>Microchip Division</u>.
>
> Will you be enrolled in the <u>Psychology Department</u>?

However, when referring in general terms to a department or division, especially one in another organization, do not capitalize:

> Someone from the <u>engineering department</u> at EnerTech stopped by the booth.
>
> Our <u>production department</u> has reorganized for efficiency.
>
> Send a copy to their <u>school of business administration</u>.

Capitalization is also unnecessary when using a word like *company, corporation,* or *university* alone:

> The <u>corporation</u> plans to issue 50,000 shares of common stock.

The names of specific products should be capitalized, although the names of general product types should not be:

> Praxis typewriter                    Tide laundry detergent

Many writers have trouble with the capitalization of compass directions. For instance, should you use *south Florida* or *South Florida, north county* or *North County*? Capitalize when the compass direction is part of a place's name, whether in official or in common use; do not capitalize when referring to a direction or general location. Here are some examples:

> the West                    the western half of Canada
> the South                    southern Minnesota
> the Northeast                    northeasterners

Another problem that often arises in writing about places is the treatment of two or more proper nouns of the same type. When the common word comes before the specific names, it is capitalized; when it comes after the specific names, it is not. Observe the capitalization here:

> Lakes Ontario and Huron
>
> Allegheny and Monongahela rivers

The names of languages, races, and ethnic groups are also capitalized: *Japanese, Negro, Hispanic.* But racial terms that denote only skin color are not capitalized: *black, white.*

In referring to the titles of books, articles, magazines, newspapers, reports, movies, and so on, you should capitalize the first and last words and all nouns, pronouns, adjectives, verbs, adverbs, and prepositions and conjunctions with five letters or more. Except for the first and last words, do not capitalize articles, and do not capitalize conjunctions and prepositions with fewer than five letters. For example:

> *Economics During the Great War*
>
> "An Investigation into the Market for Long-Distance Services"
>
> "What Successes Are Made Of"

When *the* is part of the official name of a newspaper or magazine, it should be treated this way too: *The Wall Street Journal.*

References to specific pages, paragraphs, lines, and the like are not capitalized: *page 72, line 3.* However, in most other numbered or lettered references, the identifying term is capitalized:

Chapter 4                    Serial No. 382-2203                    Item B-11

Words for specific markings or instructions on documents are also capitalized:

Stamp this letter "Confidential" before it goes out.

Finally, the names of academic degrees are capitalized when they follow a person's name but are not capitalized when used in a general sense:

I received a <u>bachelor of science</u> degree.

Thomas Whitelaw, <u>Doctor of Philosophy</u>, will attend.

Similarly, general courses of study are not capitalized, but the names of specific classes are:

She studied <u>accounting</u> as an undergraduate.

She is enrolled in <u>Accounting 201</u>.

Remember that the principles described here are well accepted but that your organization may have its own rules for capitalization.

In the following exercises, capitalize wherever appropriate:

1.  Yates & co. is in suite 303 of park towers.

2.  The luxury of chinese silk is yours.

3.  Pat swink said, "my research shows something else."

4.  The president of the company has adopted this motto:  look before you leap.

5.  I'm taking two psychology courses.

6.  Let's invite dr. lynne jamison, the director of personnel.

7.  See page 143 in chapter 5.

8.  We plan to establish a sales office on the west coast.

9.  The personnel department has submitted its budget.

10. Do you know how to fix the xerox machine?

11. Check in the *dictionary of occupational titles.*

12. We're at the corner of madison and center streets.

13. Did you see the file labeled "overdue accounts"?

14. The staff at university hospital deserves praise.

15. Address it to art bowers, chief of production.

16. Our new tractor, the sodbuster, has been developed to solve the special problems of midwestern grain farmers.

17. See if you can find "in search of a stable economy."

18. We're forming a partnership with a south american corporation.

19. You could reserve the regency and embassy rooms.

20. New caressa skin cream smooths wrinkles.

21. I have a graduate degree in business administration.

22. She characterized the movie as "an orwellian fantasy."

23. Tell me, professor, do you plan to come?

24. The company is forming a new policies group.

25. Maybe we should consider a location in the deep south.

To learn more about this subject, consult a grammar book on the following topics:

| | |
|---|---|
| abbreviations | proper nouns |
| addresses | quotations |
| bibliographies | titles and degress |
| personification | trademarks |
| place names | |

You may also wish to consult section 3.1, "Capitals," in Component Chapter B, "Grammar and Usage Guide, with Exercises," in *Business Communication Today*.

## Lesson 20

## WORDS

One of the greatest sources of trouble for business writers are groups of words that look alike, sound alike, or have special connotations. Note carefully the differences in meaning among the following:

| | | | |
|---|---|---|---|
| accept | to take, to agree | biannual | twice a year |
| except | excluding | biennial | once every two years |
| access | entry, means of approaching | bloc | group of people |
| excess | too much | block | solid mass, to put up an obstacle |
| adapt | to adjust | born | brought forth by birth |
| adept | skilled | borne | carried |
| adopt | to take on | breath | air inhaled and exhaled |
| adverse | unfavorable | breathe | to inhale and exhale |
| averse | against | capital | money, seat of government |
| advice | recommendation | capitol | building occupied by a legislature |
| advise | to counsel, to recommend | casual | informal |
| affect | to change, to have an impact | causal | related to a cause |
| effect | result of action | cite | to refer to |
| aggravate | to make a problem worse | sight | vision, to see |
| annoy | to bother | site | location |
| irritate | to cause anger or impatience | clothes | garments |
| allusion | reference to | cloths | fabrics |
| illusion | appearance of | coarse | rough |
| among | referring to three or more | course | direction, route |
| between | referring to two | command | order, to order |
| anxious | nervously anticipating | commend | to praise |
| eager | enthusiastically anticipating | complement | something that completes or makes perfect, to make whole |
| appraise | to estimate a value | compliment | expression of praise, to praise, to congratulate |
| apprise | to inform | | |
| apt | naturally inclined or able | compose | to formulate |
| likely | probable, appropriate | comprise | to include, to contain |
| assistance | help | confidant | person who hears secrets |
| assistants | helpers | confident | self-assured |
| assure | to personally promise | conscience | sense of right and wrong |
| ensure | to guarantee | conscious | aware |
| insure | to issue an insurance policy | constant | recurring in the same way |
| beside | next to | continual | recurring at frequent intervals |
| besides | other than | continuous | ongoing |

| | | | |
|---|---|---|---|
| core | center | incidence | rate of occurrence |
| corps | group | incidents | occurrences |
| council | committee | ingenious | clever |
| counsel | adviser, to advise | ingenuous | naive and innocent |
| deference | submission | instance | case |
| difference | dissimilarity | instants | moments |
| dependence | reliance | intense | heightened |
| dependents | those who rely on someone | intents | purposes |
| deprecate | to protest, to belittle | interstate | between states |
| depreciate | to lessen value | intrastate | within a state |
| detract | to take away from | its | of it |
| distract | to divert | it's | it is |
| device | mechanism | later | more advanced in time |
| devise | to construct | latter | item closest to the end |
| disapprove | to condemn | lead | metal, to show the way |
| disprove | to prove wrong | led | showed the way |
| disburse | to pay out | lend | to give the use of |
| dispense | to distribute | loan | something lent |
| disperse | to scatter | liable | legally responsible |
| discreet | prudent | libel | written defamation |
| discrete | separate | local | of the surrounding area |
| elicit | to draw out | locale | place |
| illicit | unlawful | loose | unrestrained |
| eminent | notable | lose | to misplace, to fail to win |
| imminent | impending | moral | honest, lesson |
| envelop | to surround | morale | mental condition |
| envelope | paper covering for a letter | passed | went by |
| explicit | clearly stated | past | bygone |
| implicit | unstated, hidden | pedal | foot lever, to move with the feet |
| farther | more distant | peddle | to sell |
| further | more, additional, to advance | perquisite | benefit |
| feasible | desirable and possible | prerequisite | qualification |
| possible | able or likely to happen | persecute | to harass |
| practicable | possible given existing conditions | prosecute | to start legal proceedings |
| formally | in a formal manner | personal | of the person |
| formerly | previously | personnel | staff, employees |
| human | relating to people | perspective | view |
| humane | compassionate | prospective | potential, forthcoming |
| imitate | to copy | populace | inhabitants |
| intimate | personal | populous | having many people |
| imply | to hint | | |
| infer | to interpret | | |

| | | | |
|---|---|---|---|
| practicable | able to be done | straight | not curved |
| practical | workable (things), sensible (people) | strait | narrow waterway, difficult position |
| pragmatic | hard-headed, realistic | | |
| precede | to go before | than | compared with |
| proceed | to continue | then | time past |
| preposition | a part of speech | their | of them |
| proposition | scheme | there | in that place |
| | | they're | they are |
| presence | attendance | | |
| presents | gifts | to | opposite of from |
| | | too | overly, also |
| principal | main, head, capital (money) | two | 2 |
| principle | rule | | |
| | | vice | immorality |
| raise | to lift | vise | instrument for gripping |
| rise | to get up, to go up | | |
| | | waiver | abandonment of a right |
| role | part | waver | to flicker, to hesitate |
| roll | bread, to throw, to turn over | | |
| | | who's | who is |
| set | to put down | whose | of whom |
| sit | to take a seat | | |
| | | your | of you |
| stationary | in one place | you're | you are |
| stationery | paper | | |

Underline the correct word in each of the following exercises:

1. Everyone accept/except Barbara King has registered.

2. The whole debt was born/borne by his parents.

3. We need to find a new security device/devise.

4. They decided to sue for liable/libel.

5. The passed/past few days have been hectic.

6. How much farther/further is the convention center?

7. Just set/sit it on the credenza.

8. Enter the number of dependence/dependents in this box.

9. Were you able to determine their intense/intents?

10. You will be asked to sign a waiver/waver.

11. I assure/ensure/insure you that all will be ready.

12. From my perspective/prospective, this is a bad move.

13. The moral/morale is this: Expect the worst.

14. We have styles to complement/compliment every face.

15. I'd like a later/latter appointment.

16. Scientists have established a direct casual/causal relationship between sunburn and skin disorders.

17. He didn't mention it outright, but his need for a decision was explicit/implicit.

18. This month's balance is greater than/then last month's.

19. Can you appraise/apprise us of her qualifications?

20. Look up their/there/they're address.

21. We can't let outside events detract/distract us now.

22. The study group will compose/comprise all the analysts.

23. I'd like to precede/proceed my remarks with a question.

24. An ambitious person will raise/rise above challenges.

25. Dr. Khoury is an eminent/imminent chemist.

If you need help in using words correctly, you may wish to consult a grammar book on the following topics:

| | |
|---|---|
| diction | usage |
| homonyms | vocabulary |
| idioms | |

You may also wish to consult sections 4.1, "Frequently Switched Words," 4.2, "Frequently Misused Words," and 4.3, "Frequently Misspelled Words," in Component Chapter B, "Grammar and Usage Guide, with Exercises," in *Business Communication Today.*